I0810284

IMAGES
of America

LaGrange

On the cover: The Moore's Mills school was constructed about 1907 on Oswego Road. It was in District 4, which also served part of Union Vale. Previously, students living in the area attended a school on Skidmore Road. The class pictured is probably from 1908. (Courtesy of Robert DeCarlo.)

IMAGES
of America

LaGrange

Lynn Owen

ARCADIA
PUBLISHING

ISBN 978-0-7385-6452-4

Published by Arcadia Publishing
Charleston SC, Chicago IL, Portsmouth NH, San Francisco CA

Printed in the United States of America

Library of Congress Control Number: 2008938753

For all general information contact Arcadia Publishing at:
Telephone 843-853-2070
Fax 843-853-0044
E-mail sales@arcadiapublishing.com
For customer service and orders:
Toll-Free 1-888-313-2665

Visit us on the Internet at www.arcadiapublishing.com

In loving memory of my mother, Inez Masterson, and to Rod and my supportive family, who gave their constant encouragement.

Contents

ACKNOWLEDGMENTS

I would like to express my appreciation to the following individuals and organizations for their invaluable help in making this book possible: George and Nancy Wade, Irving Miller, Mildred (Alley) Doughty, former town historian Emily Johnson and her family, Art Church, Sandra Jobson and the department of transportation, Bob DeCarlo, William Hubbard, Prof. Lucille Johnson, Long Island Collection of the East Hampton Library, Jay Webber, the Freedom Plains Presbyterian Church, the Trinity United Methodist Church and church historian Barbara Sinclair, Steve Mann of the Dutchess County Historical Society, Thomas K. and Sally Cross, LaGrange town historian Georgia Herring-Trott, Andy Arensen and the Arlington Central School District, LaGrange town clerk Christine Reilly-Rao, Kenneth Lutters and the New York State Office of Parks, Recreation, and Historic Preservation–Taconic Region, and last but not least, Arcadia Publishing editor Rebekah Collinsworth for her continuous support.

Unless otherwise noted, all images appear courtesy of the LaGrange Historical Society. Other images appear courtesy of George Wade (GW), Irving Miller (IM), Mildred Doughty (MD), Art Church (AC), the department of transportation (DOT), William Hubbard (WH), Prof. Lucille Johnson (LJ), Long Island Collection of the East Hampton Library (LIC), Jay Webber (JW), the Freedom Plains Presbyterian Church (FPPC), the LaGrange Town Hall (LTH), Trinity United Methodist Church (TUMC), the Freedom Plains Grange (FPG), Thomas Cross (TC), Arlington Central School District (ACSD), LaGrange town historian Georgia Herring-Trott (GHT), Jane Geisler (JG), Kenneth Lutters and the New York State Office of Parks, Recreation, and Historic Preservation–Taconic Region (OPRHP), and Steve Mann of the Dutchess County Historical Society (SM).

INTRODUCTION

LaGrange, the name sounds rather elegant, especially when pronounced as the French do, *la grawnge*. However, it translates to "the barn," an appropriate name when first bestowed on this town in its rural beginnings. Much has changed since that earlier time—the first families who settled here would not recognize it, the farms and meadows having been turned into scores of homes and businesses. But look closely, and you can still discern traces of LaGrange's past, in old apple trees and tumbling stone walls.

Long before Colonial times, the Wappinger Indians made their home along the shores of the Muhheakunnuck, meaning "river that flows both ways," what we now call the Hudson. For hundreds of years, they were the only inhabitants, existing by hunting, farming, and fishing. They were respectful guardians of the fertile land and clean water, leaving little imprint of their long tenure, other than the occasional arrowhead found in a field.

Recorded history of the area begins with the arrival of the first Dutch explorers in the early 17th century, who originally made their living in the fur trade. Then, in 1664, England's Duke of York took control and began the issuing of "patents"—deeds to land that could be purchased through bargaining with the natives. The Crown offered the ownership of these parcels in order to promote settlement; the earliest of these, in 1685, was the Rombout patent, followed by the Beekman patent a few years later. These two areas encompassed land that eventually became several towns, including LaGrange, originally called Freedom.

The early settlers wasted no time, working hard to clear fields, build their homes, and establish farms. Sheep and beef cattle were raised; dairy cows dotted the pastures. A town government was established, and the offices of town clerk, path master (in charge of roads), poor master, and others were filled. Voting for elections took place in homes, then later at Wolven Hall. Circuit preachers traveling through the area helped to organize the first Methodist Church.

The population would have increased dramatically, with parents often having 10 or more offspring, but town death records show that many died young. Ailments easily cured now were frequently fatal then. It was also common for men to have a second wife, as many women died in childbirth. Farm and mill accidents are also noted in many cases of premature deaths. Still, the number of residents gradually grew, and more areas were cultivated for the growing of wheat, corn, and even hops for beer.

In the years leading up to the Revolution, the town saw heated arguments between those desiring a continued allegiance to England and those in favor of liberty. Even families were sometimes divided in their loyalties, as was the case with the Livingston clan. When the war finally came, local citizens were spared from actual battle, but captured soldiers did march through the southern end of town on the Old Upper Road, on their way to the prison camp in Fishkill. There was also an encampment of Tory soldiers within the town at one point, at the farm owned by the Clapps. Known afterward as the camp lot, it was the home base for Tories who attacked Washington Hollow.

The early 1800s was a time of growth throughout the county. More families settled in LaGrange, contributing their various skills and trades; however, agriculture continued to be the focus. On some of the larger farms, the need for extra laborers led to the purchase of slaves. Modern-day citizens might be surprised to know that slavery existed in New York, including Dutchess County. Although nowhere near as prevalent here as it was in the South, documents from the era attest to the fact that slaves were often present in the households of some of the wealthier individuals. The practice was deplored by many on principle; therefore, beginning in the early 1800s, LaGrange residents joined in the outcry to end it. Certain local families, if the stories are true, even participated in helping some slaves escape to freedom in Canada.

The Industrial Revolution led to what was perhaps the most important of modern inventions—the railroad. When the first train came whistling through, it set the stage for LaGrange's gradual transformation. Once a rather isolated farming community, it now was accessible from all areas, and a new mode of travel was available to its inhabitants as well. Hamlets quickly sprouted around each station stop, to take advantage of this new source of prosperity.

In LaGrange, still a farming community for the most part, groups such as the Grange and the 4-H continued to be popular through the 1980s. Many local residents and their children continued to show animals at the Dutchess County Fair each year and participate in producing the agricultural displays that the Grange is known for. But as farming became less profitable, and land taxes rose, the landscape of the town began the shift to a more suburban layout. This trend would grow dramatically as IBM employees found LaGrange to be an appealing home for their families.

Momentous changes were taking place here, as everywhere, at the dawn of the new century. Society's rapid development in every field left those who had now lived in both eras wondering what could be next. In spite of the push toward modernity, LaGrange was able to maintain some of its rustic charm even as it headed into the new millennium. Town leaders, with the overwhelming approval of residents, are now planning how best to control the growth of LaGrange, while protecting its history and remaining open spaces.

It has now been 400 years since Henry Hudson first viewed the lovely landscape of the valley that would be named after him. As Dutchess County celebrates its quadricentennial, LaGrange citizens can ponder the town's long history and be amazed at the progress. But let them also spare a moment to think of those first brave settlers, who paved the way for those to follow. Like them, today's residents are fortunate to be able to make their home in LaGrange.

One

Settlement through the Civil War

The area around the present intersection of Route 82 and East Noxon Road was the earliest settlement within Freedom. Called Morey's Corners, it utilized the Jackson Creek as power for its milling operations. It was followed closely by Moore's Mills, a hamlet that sprang up around the gristmills and sawmills run by the Moore family on Oswego Road.

Before long, farms began to appear, and the first roads were established. Strong stone walls, remains of which are still visible in some spots, were put up, both to mark boundaries and to keep cattle from straying. Settlement continued at a slow but steady pace over the next 50 years.

In the early 1800s, many towns were named Freedom due to the recent battle for independence. To lessen confusion in those early days of the postal system, the adoption of a new name was considered. Gen. Marquis de Lafayette, a great ally during the Revolution, had recently toured the area and was very popular with local citizens. The lovely landscape, he mentioned, reminded him of his estate, LaGrange, back in France. The town leaders, no doubt flattered by this comparison, suggested adopting the title as the new name for Freedom, and the residents agreed. LaGrange it has been ever since.

From the town's earliest days, the Quakers were a respected presence in the community, known for their ongoing efforts to abolish slavery. Several homes in LaGrange were said to have been used as hiding places for fugitive slaves being transported along the Underground Railroad. Later the group would become divided over doctrinal issues, splitting into the Hicksite and Orthodox factions.

More settlers, mostly from New England, continued to arrive. Mills and farms were the two most common livelihoods as the nation felt the first rumblings of the approaching Civil War. Dutchess County's infantry regiment, the 150th, included many LaGrange lads. The regiment lost more than twice as many soldiers to disease as to actual battle with over 130 casualties.

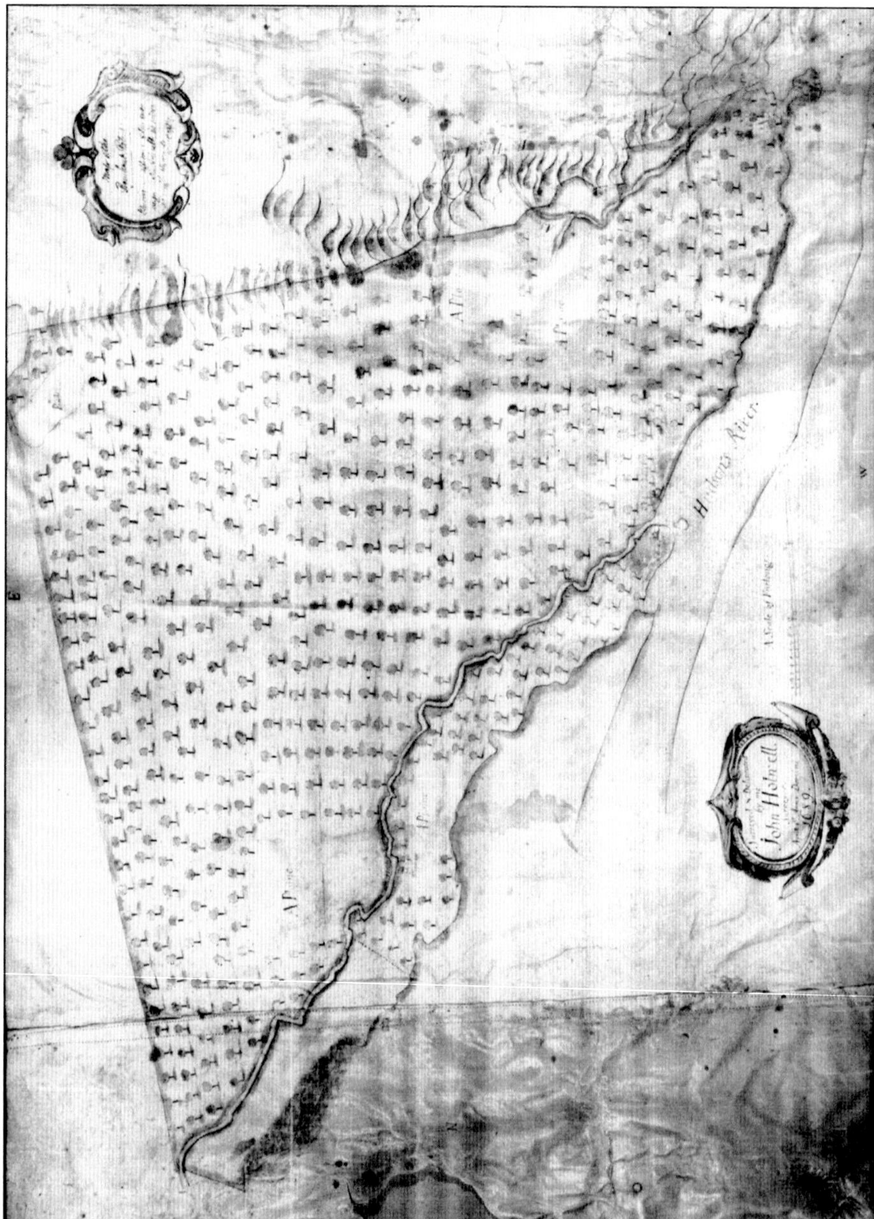

The first Dutchess County patent, the Rombout patent, was granted in 1685 to business partners Francois Rombout, Gulian Verplanck, and Stephanus Van Cortlandt and covered an area of approximately 85,000 acres. The Beekman patent, to the east, followed in 1697. This map conveys how untamed the Hudson River valley was in those early days. Vast areas were heavily wooded, as the local natives were partly nomadic and had no need of lumber for dwellings. Settlement by whites took place very slowly in the first part of the 18th century. Then gradually the population increased, with Dutch immigrants tending to settle along the Wappingers Creek; the English often came over from New England, and made their homes just over the eastern border. In 1821, the borders of the hamlet of Freedom were established, when land was annexed from the towns of Fishkill and Beekman (both of which extended much farther north at the time).

These arrowheads are some of the assortment collected by the Skidmore family, found in their farm fields. The oldest date from more than 6,000 years ago. The various sizes and shapes show the modification of designs used by the Wappingers over generations. The Wappingers were in the Mahican family; their totem, or symbol, was the wolf. (LJ.)

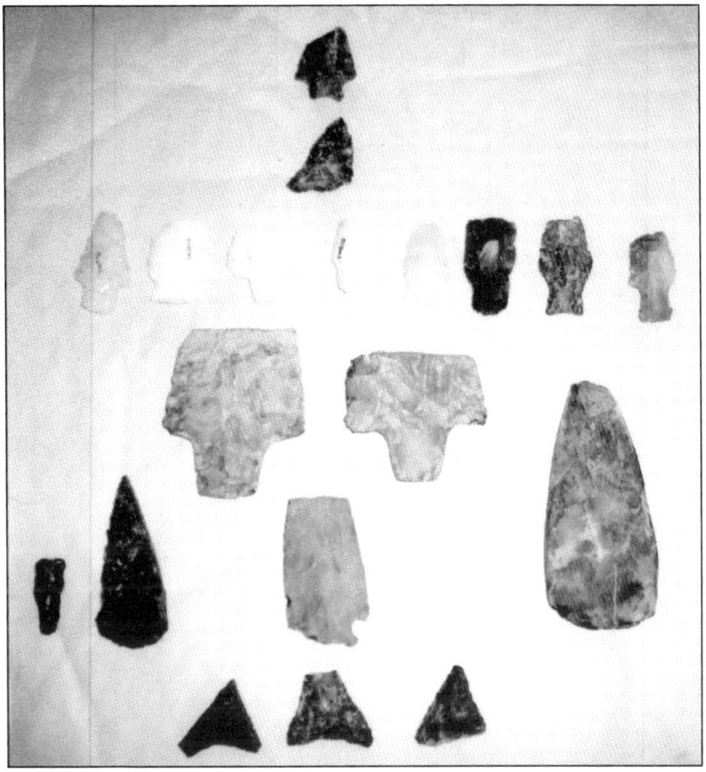

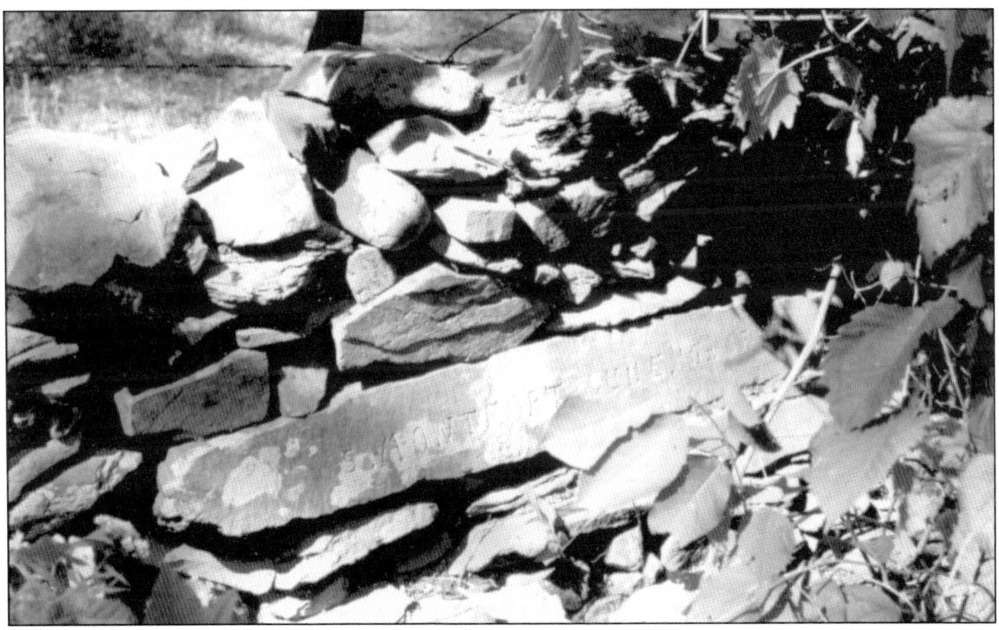

Stone walls were erected by the earliest settlers to define the boundaries of the original patents. Some traces of these walls are still in existence, although difficult to locate. Pictured is the marker on Stringham Road, erected in 1985 to commemorate the 300th anniversary of the issuing of the Rombout patent. Sadly, most of the stones themselves have tumbled down long ago or been removed by newer tenants. (IM.)

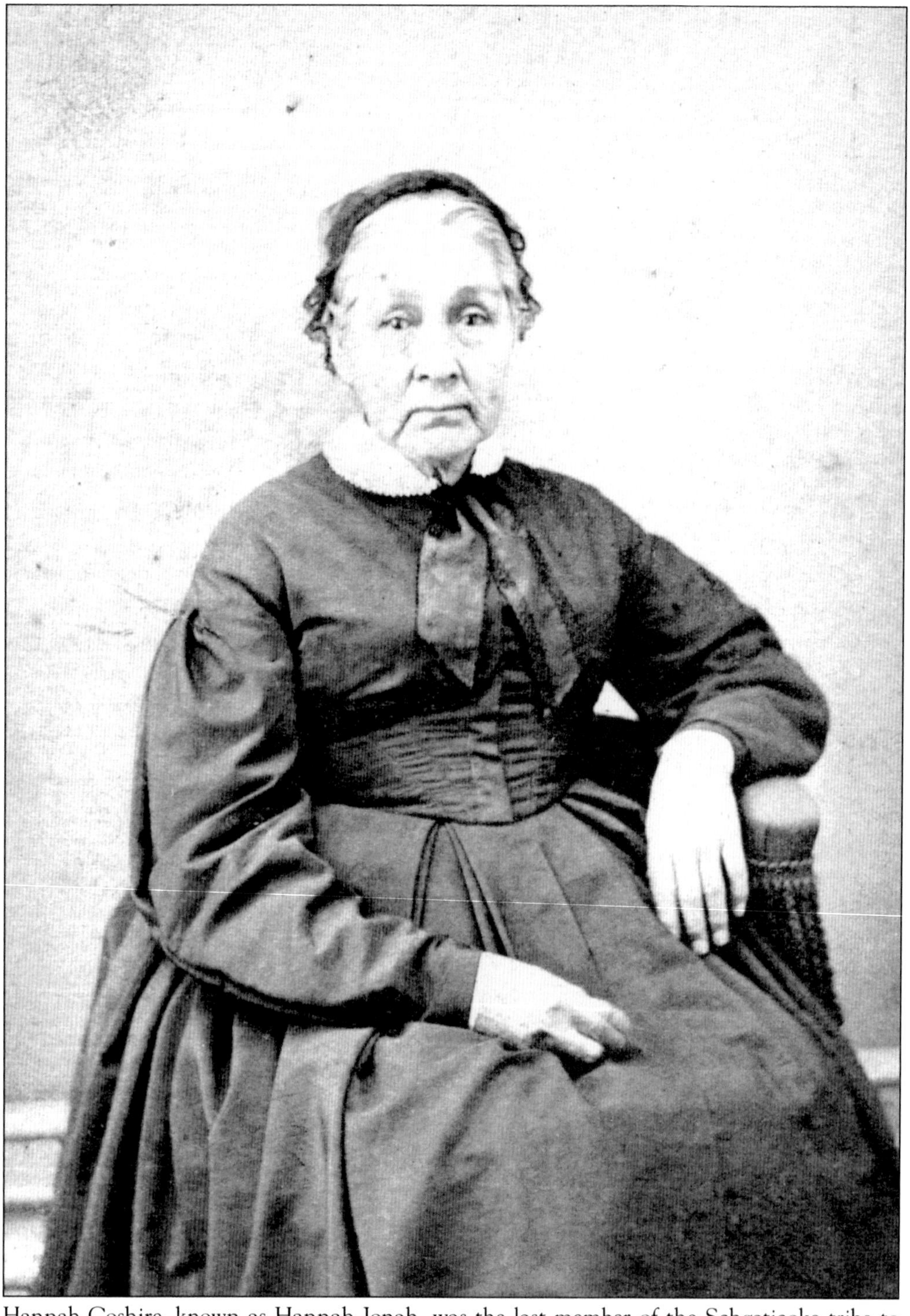

Hannah Coshire, known as Hannah Jonah, was the last member of the Schgaticoke tribe to live in the area. She resided with the Skidmore family in her last years, passing away in 1877. Hannah Coshire adopted the Quaker faith, regularly attending meetings, but retained much of her ancestors' ways, including the use of herbal remedies for healing. (EP.)

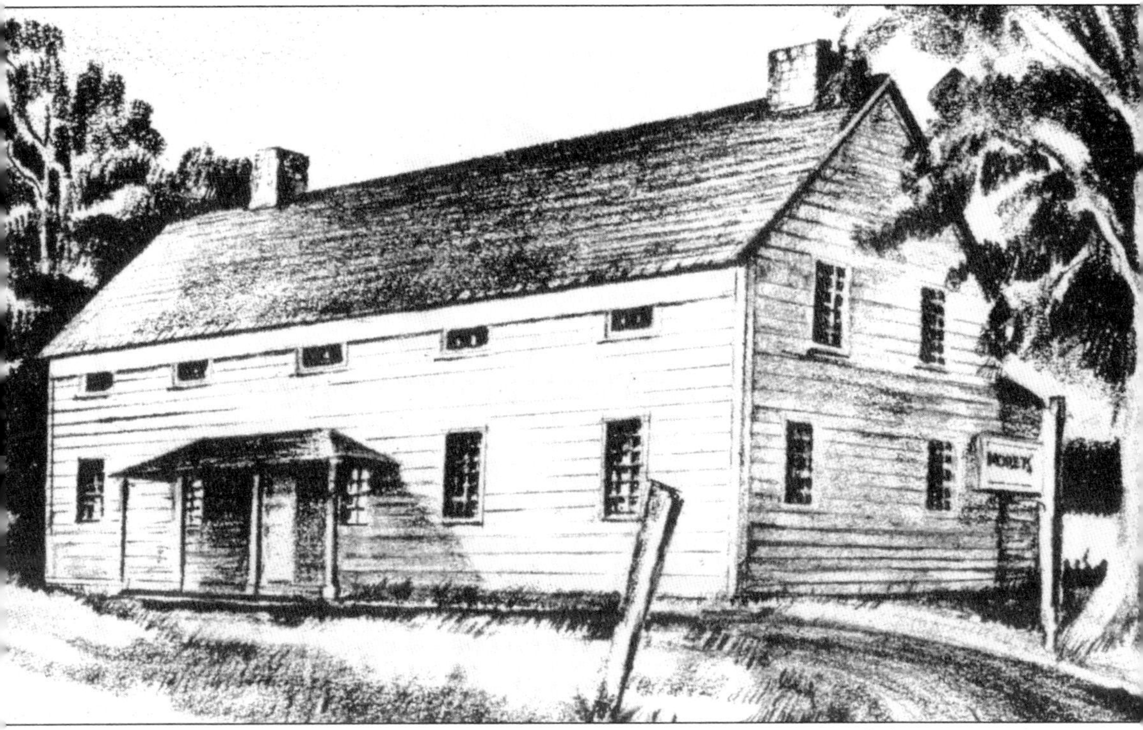

One of the earliest stopping places in LaGrange, Morey's tavern can still be seen at the intersection of Noxon Road and Upton Road. This was a stop on the Old Upper Road, used by Revolutionary War soldiers. The owner, Jacob Morey, worked as a blacksmith while also running the tavern. It later served as the parsonage for the Methodist church.

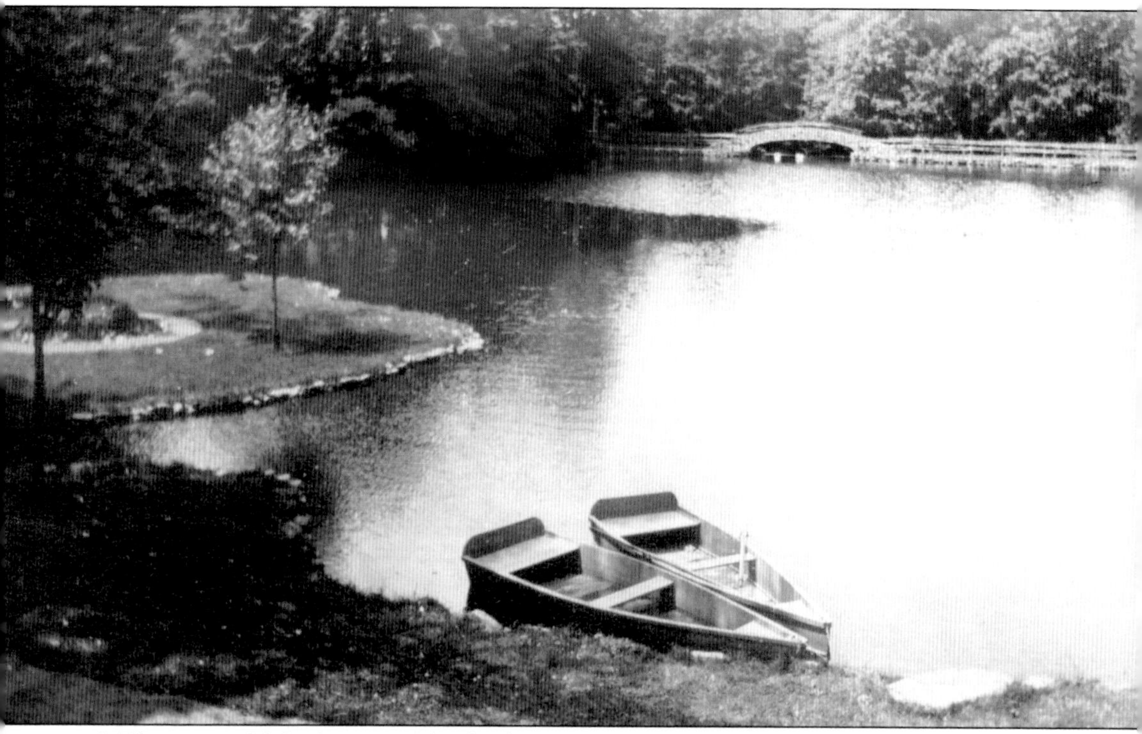

Mills were established as one of the first businesses and were necessary for all types of production. The gristmills and sawmills established by the Moore family started in 1765 and operated until 1903, when they were torn down. The pond supplied the water for the mills to operate and later served as a relaxing spot for the family and guests to gather. Local resident Gertrude Sammis recalled swimming in the pond when she was a youngster.

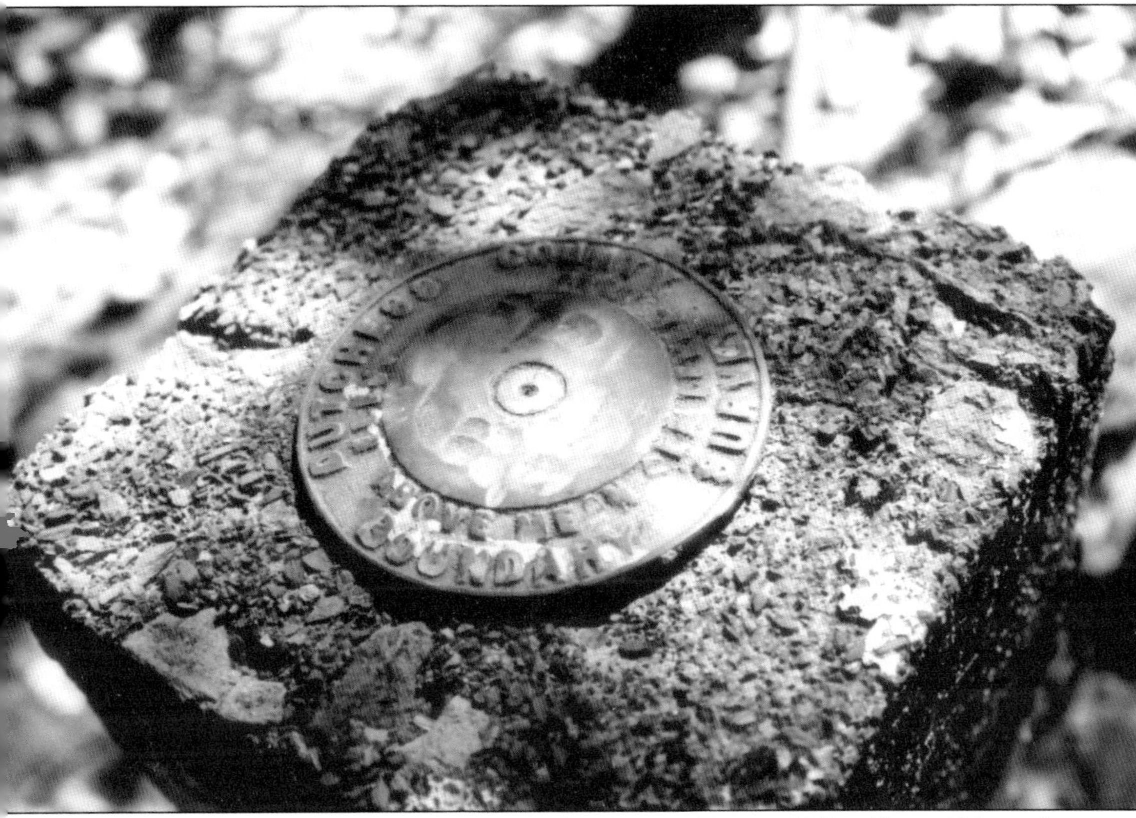

This post marks the spot of the intersection of LaGrange, Pleasant Valley, Union Vale, and Washington, which lies within the 110 Rod and Gun Club property. The nearby Pond Gut area is the site where Tory sympathizers supposedly hid stolen horses, in order to supply British troops. A group of Patriots hoped to round up the thieves one night, but they got away through the woods and avoided capture. (JG.)

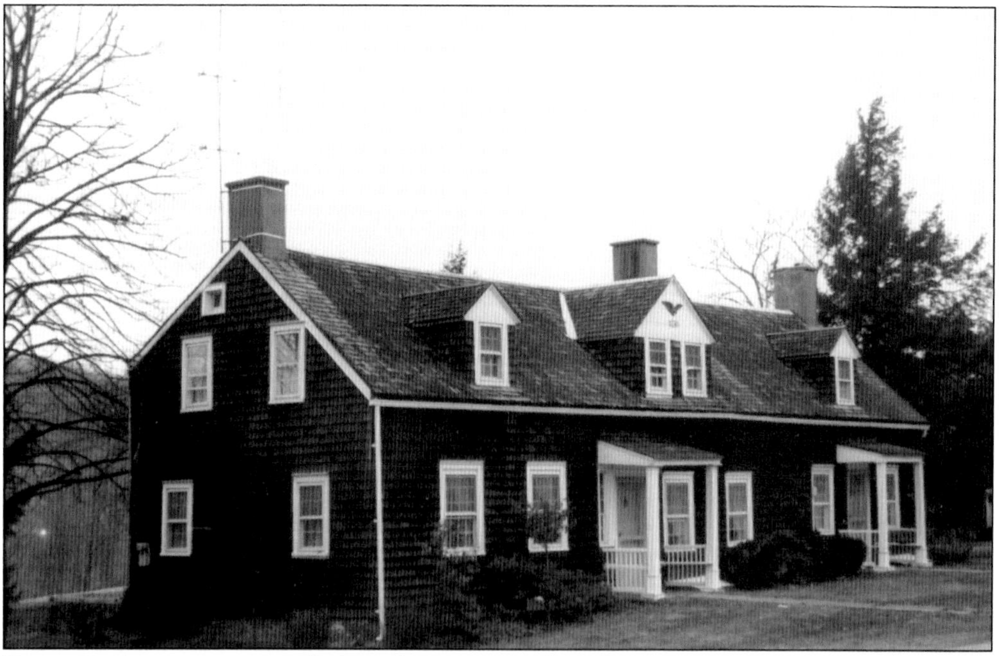

Known as Crossways in its early days, this structure along Route 82 near Barmore Road probably dates from the 1730s. It was formerly owned by John Taylor, an elder of the Presbyterian Church, and previous to that, by Samuel Hake, an officer in the Revolutionary War. It is believed to have served as an inn as well.

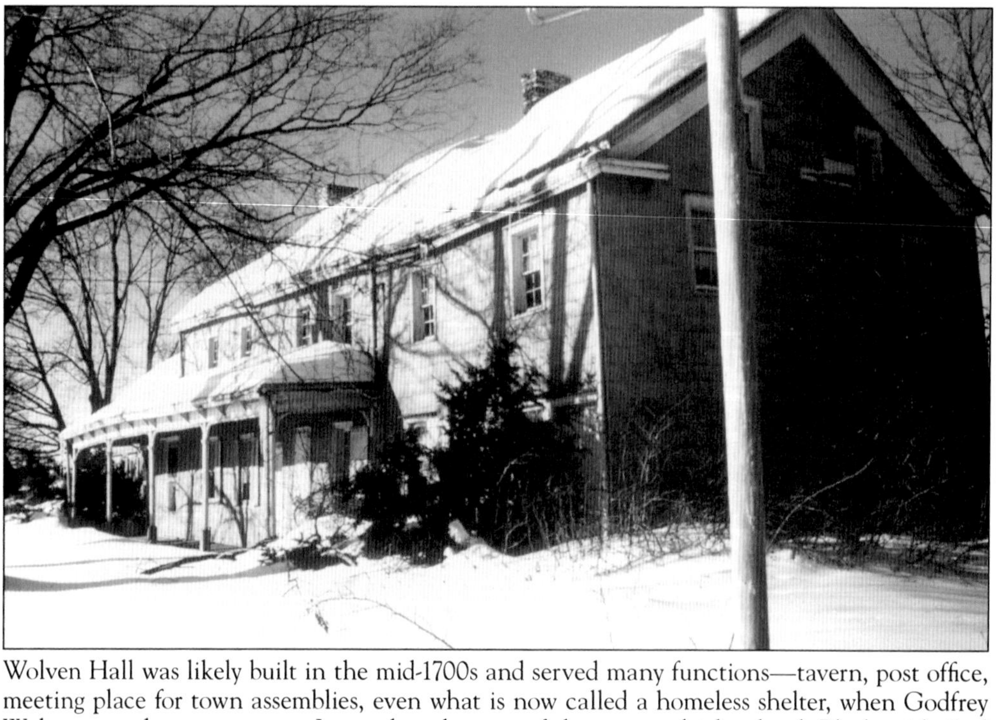

Wolven Hall was likely built in the mid-1700s and served many functions—tavern, post office, meeting place for town assemblies, even what is now called a homeless shelter, when Godfrey Wolven was the poor master. It stood to the east of the present high school. Blacksmith Paul Berger, Wolven's son-in-law, ran his shop next to it.

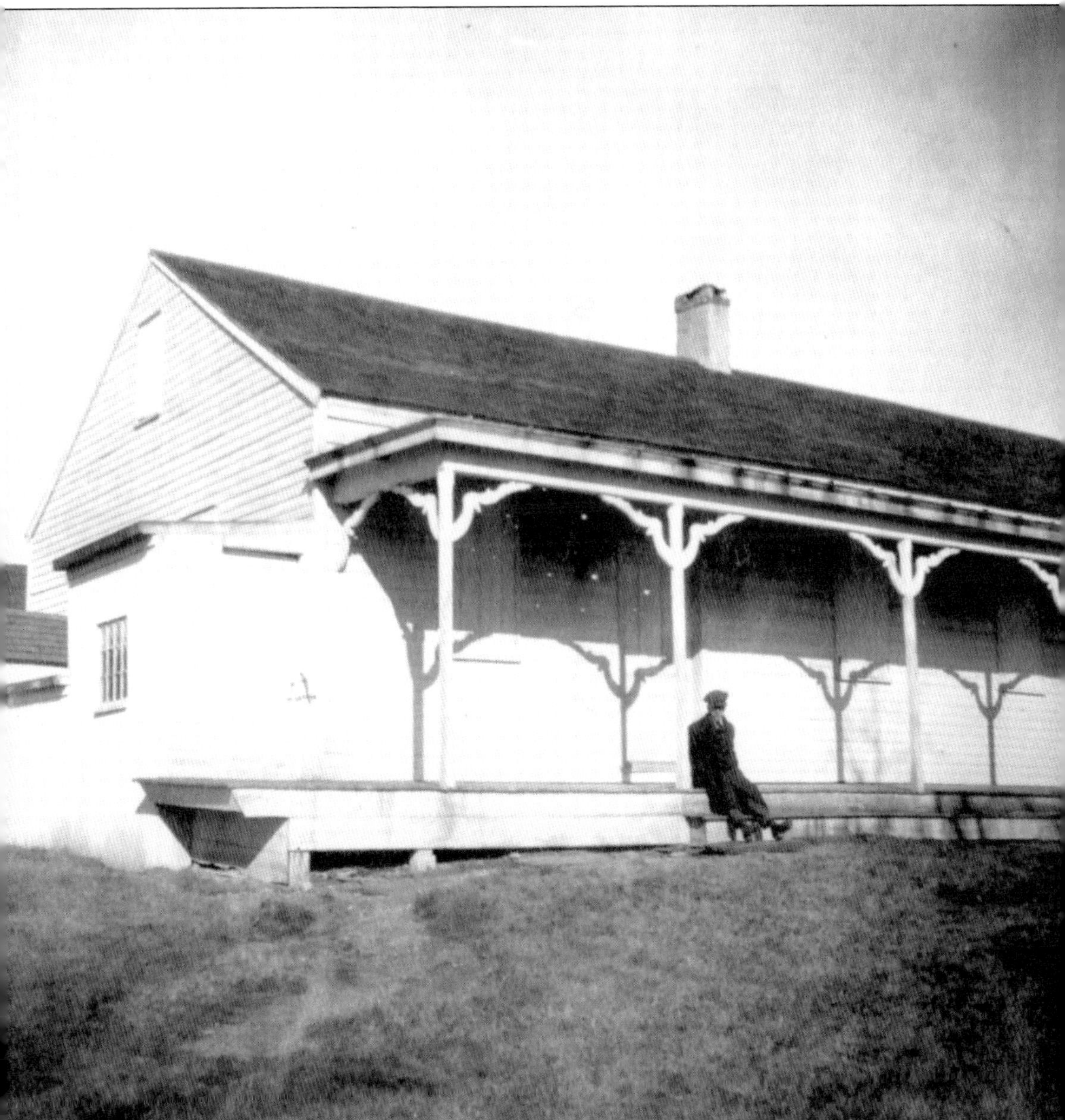

The Oswego meetinghouse, still standing at the corner of Smith and Oswego Roads, was built around 1760. In 1827, land along LaGrange's eastern side, including Smith Road, was taken to form the new town of Union Vale. Many of the original Quaker family members (Yeomans, Moores, Irish) are buried in the graveyard in front. At one time, the group operated a school for Quaker children near the meetinghouse.

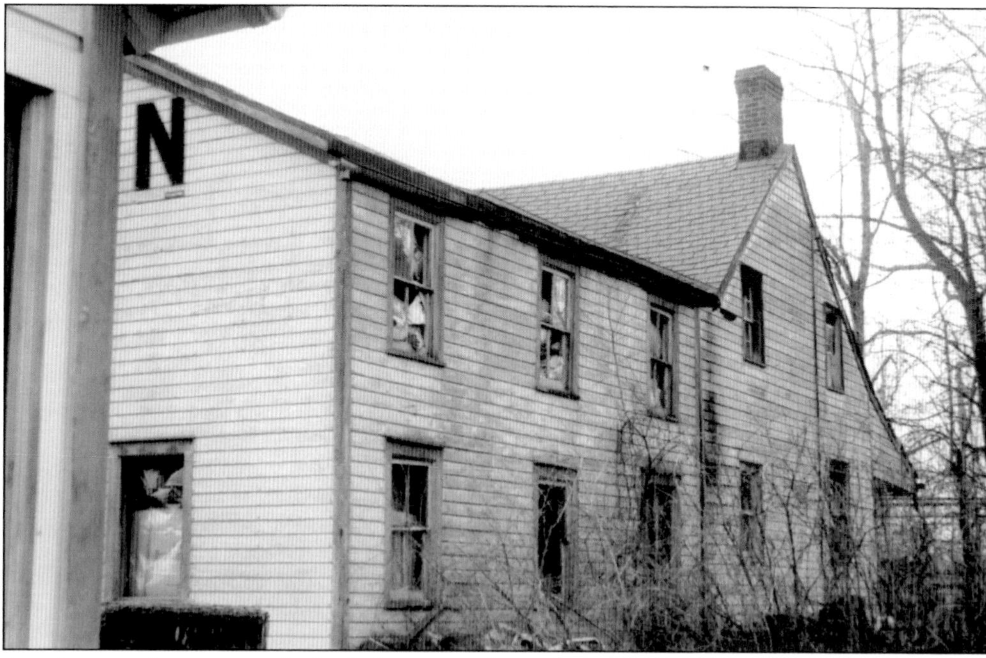

Another popular rest stop for both farmers and travelers was the DeGroff tavern, located near the Manchester Bridge area. Probably dating from around 1760, it operated as a store in the late 1880s. By the 1970s, it was dilapidated and was soon after torn down, leaving no trace of its long history.

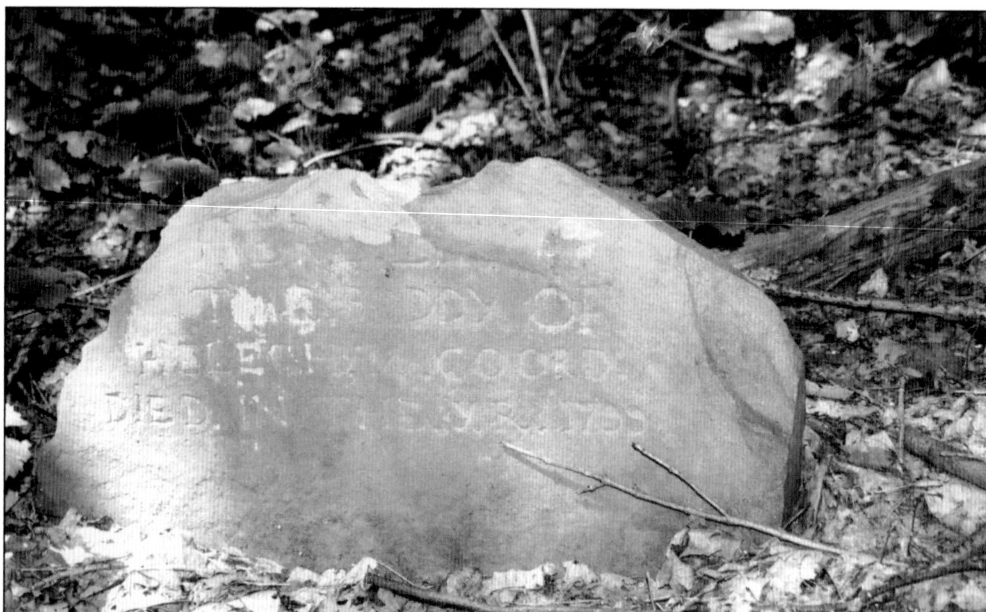

This headstone for Helecy McCord is one of a group of some of the oldest gravestones in LaGrange in the West Branch cemetery off Mountain Road. There was a Quaker meetinghouse on the property until 1865. The writing on the other stones is no longer legible, but older residents used to say that some of the graves were those of the Coshires, the last Native Americans in the area. (GHT.)

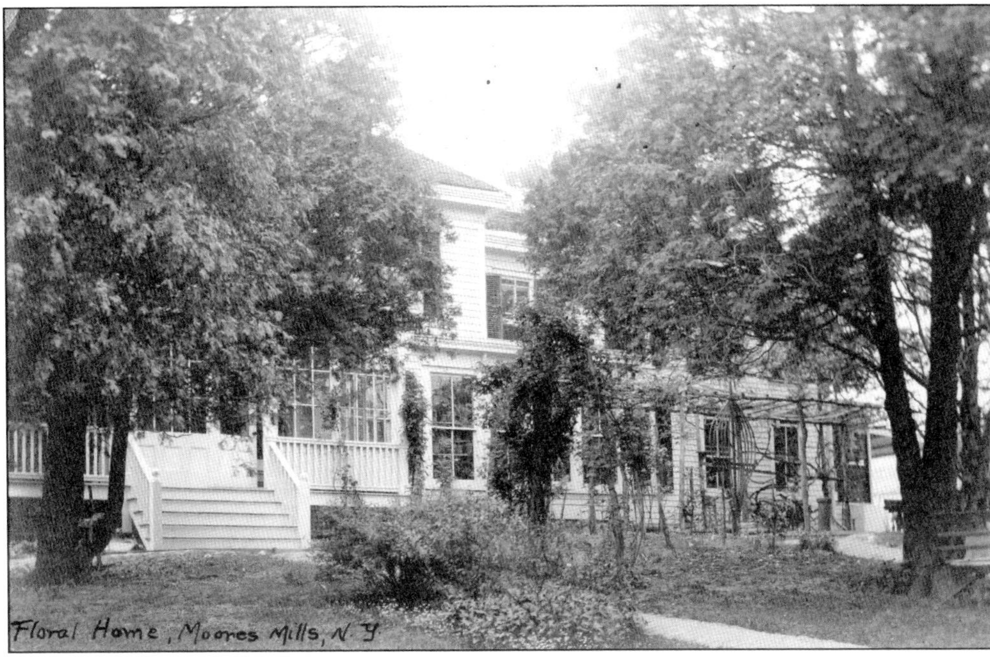

Several generations of the Moore family, all Quakers, resided in this home that dates from the mid-1700s. A passageway found in the 1970s is believed to have been used to hide runaway slaves. The house would later become the Floral Home, run by Susan Moore, and can still be seen at the junction of Route 82 and Oswego Road.

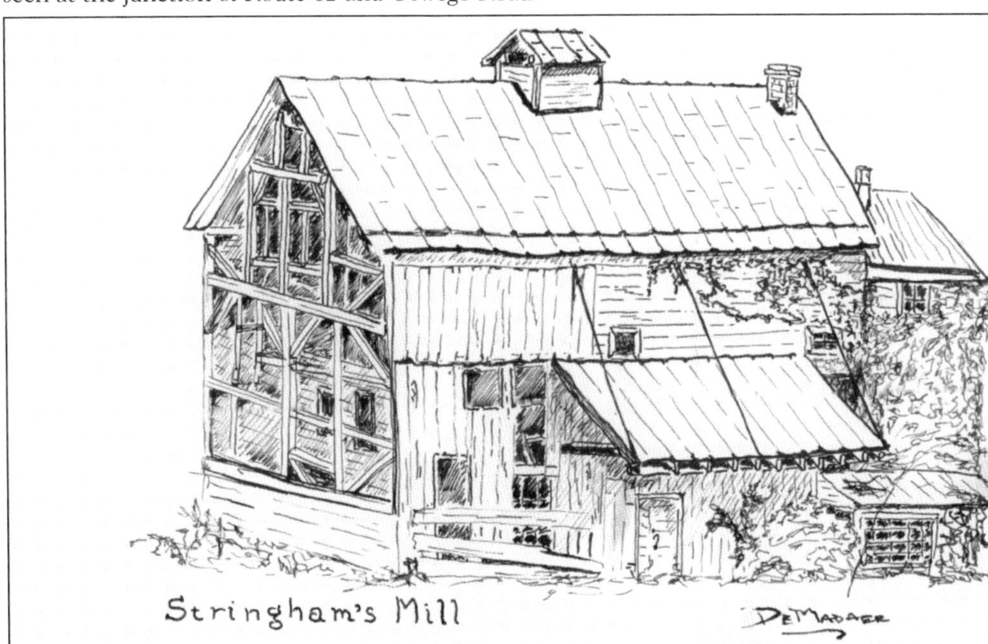

This line drawing by John DeMadaler shows the mill operated by Edward Barnes Stringham, in the area that is now Red Oaks Mill. The mill was previously run by A. Bloodgood Van Wyck, Edward's father-in-law. Edward's father was James Alley Stringham, for whom Stringham Road was named. (DCHS.)

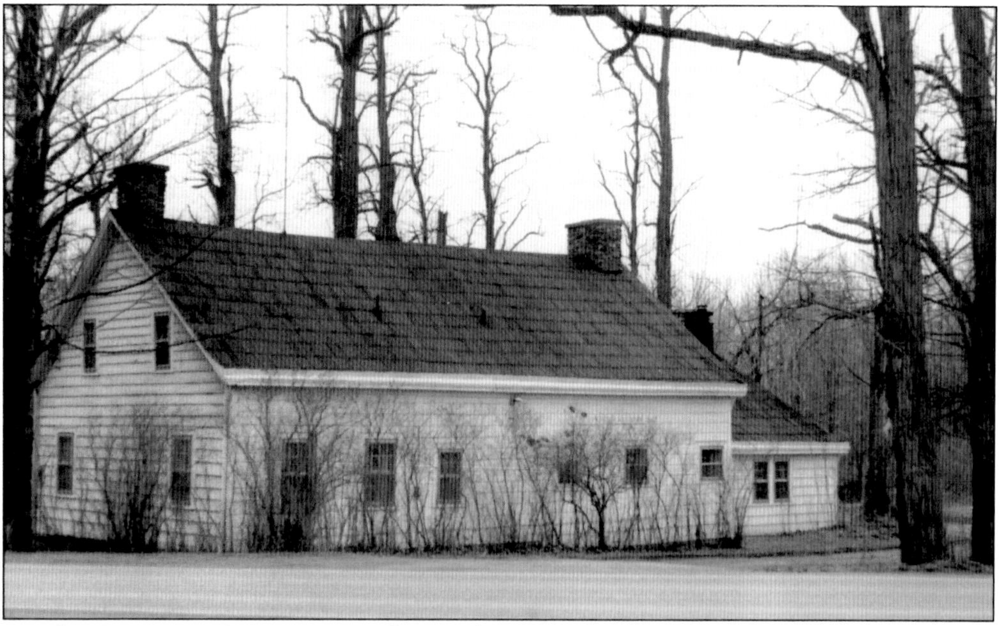

Monfort Tavern in the Sprout Creek area dates from pre–Revolutionary War times. It was a well-known stop for drovers and other travelers for many years, as well as soldiers. It still stands at the corner of Noxon Road and Robinson Lane. In the 1970s, it was the home of artist Emile Walters.

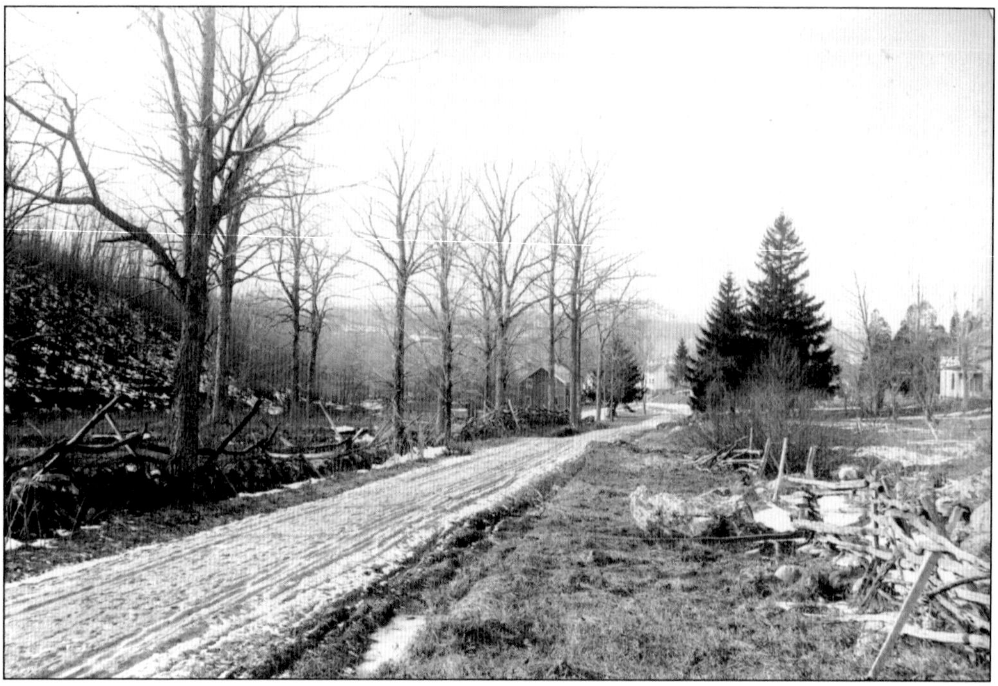

This country lane was typical of many of the roads in LaGrange until the 1930s. The town retained its rural character longer than many surrounding areas where farming was not done on the same scale. The dirt roads, which seem charmingly rustic now, could be trying to travelers then, with dust, mud, and potholes.

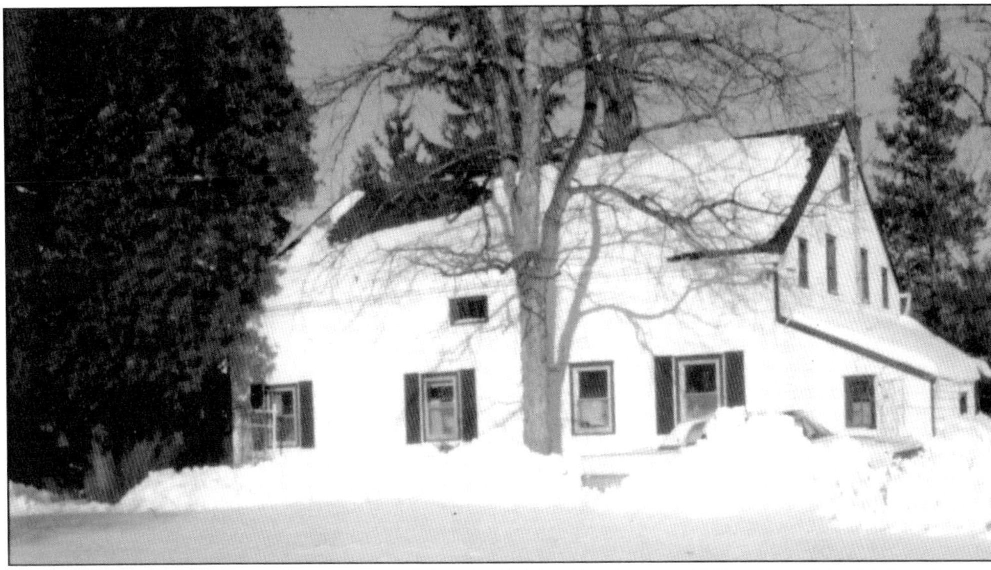

This home on Alley Road was owned by the Hulst family in 1900, when Mr. Hulst planted the hickory tree that now towers over the west end. Helen Hulst, born in the house that year, shared many memories of the family farm she grew up on. The home is believed to have been built around 1783 and was once the farmhouse for a large piece of property that bordered the Alley farm.

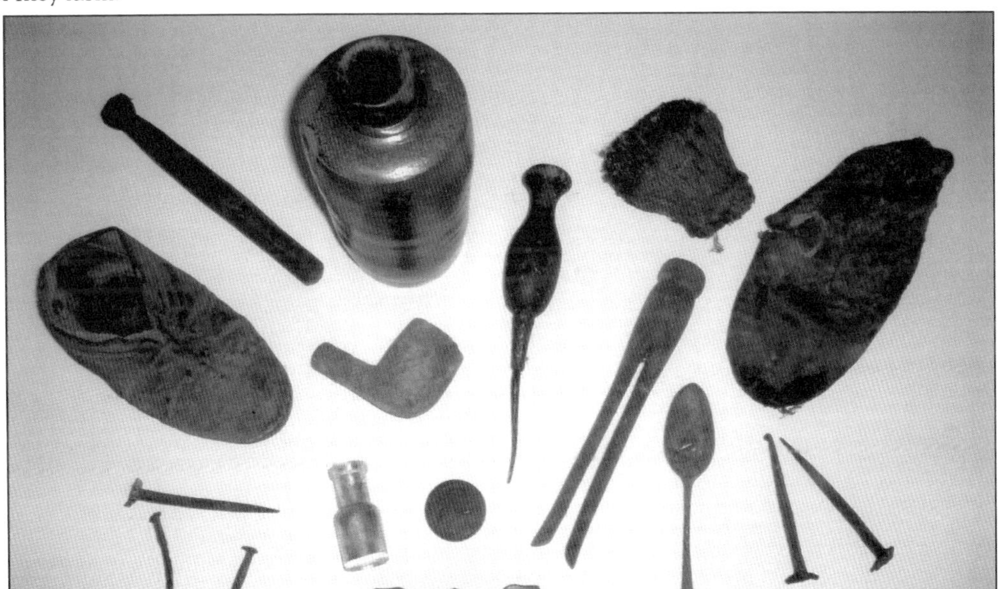

Items found in the walls of the Hulst home include clay pipes, awls for punching leather, bottles, and button shoes. Hand-cut nails are typical of the Colonial period and may have been made either by a local blacksmith or the owner himself. The coin, a 1¢ piece, is dated 1821.

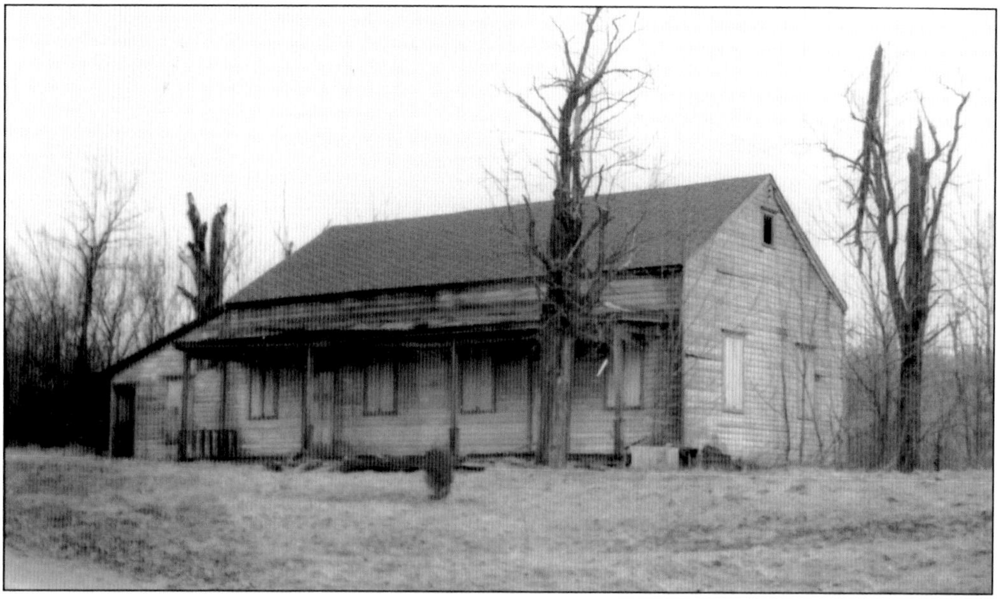

The Arthursburg meetinghouse on East Emans Road was constructed in 1823, after the Oblong (Pawling) group granted permission, but the Quaker yearly meetings had been held in the hamlet since at least 1790. Throughout the next century, Quakers were one of the largest religious denominations in LaGrange. The building was later used as a Grange hall for a time.

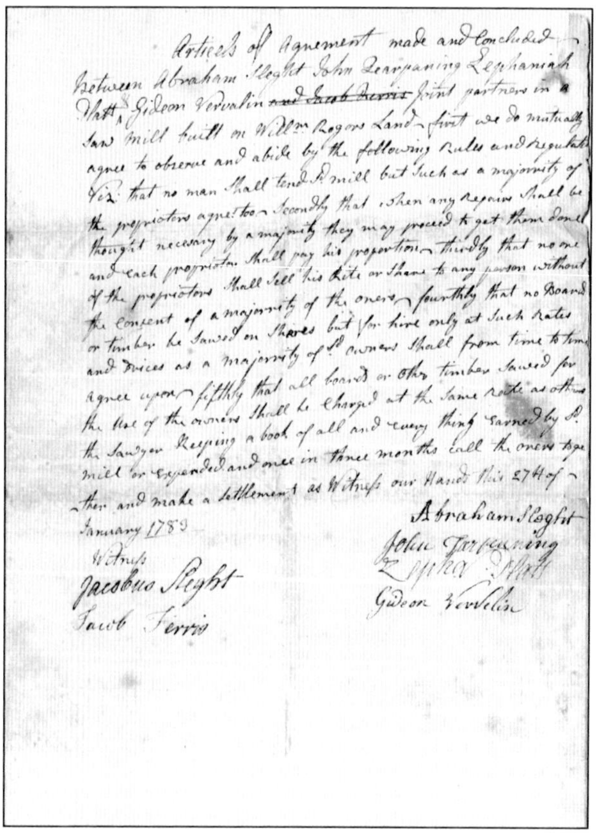

Articles of Agreement made and Concluded
between Abraham Sleght John Tarpaning Zephaniah
Platt Gideon Vervalin ~~and Jacob Ferris~~ Joint partners in a
Saw mill built on Willm Rogers Land first we do mutually
agree to observe and abide by the following rules and regulations
Viz: that no man Shall tend sd mill but Such as a majority of
the proprietors agree too Secondly that when any repairs Shall be
thought necessary by a majority they may proceed to get them Done
and each proprietor Shall pay his proportion thirdly that no one
of the proprietors Shall Sell his Rite or Share to any person without
the consent of a majority of the oners fourthly that no Board
or timber be Sawed on Shares but for hire only at Such Rates
and Prices as a majority of sd owners Shall from time to time
agree upon fifthly that all board or other timber Sawed for
the Use of the owners Shall be Charged at the Same Rate as others
the Sawyer keeping a book of all and every thing Earned by sd
mill or Expended and once in three months call the oners toge-
ther and make a Settlement as Witness our Hands this 27th of
January 1783

Abraham Sleght
John Tarpaning
Zepha Platt
Gideon Vervelin

Witness
Jacobus Sleght
Jacob Ferris

Jacobus Sleight, a captain in the Revolutionary War, survived the burning of Kingston by the British and relocated his family to LaGrange. In 1783, he signed as a witness to this document, a contract between his son Abraham and his business partners in a sawmill. The family home, a sturdy stone structure, was built in 1798; it sits at the corner of Sleight Plass Road.

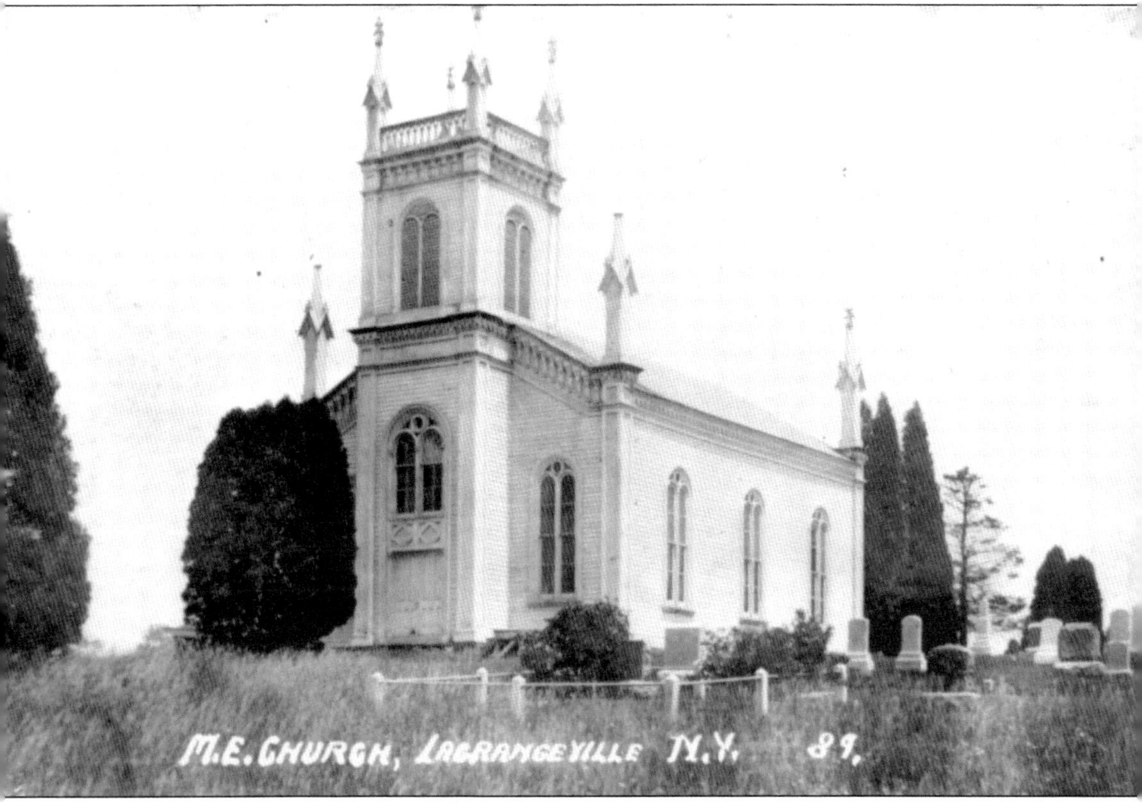

Organized in 1821, the Trinity Methodist Church, which is now on Cross Road, used to stand next to the Potter's Corners cemetery at the intersection of Route 55 and County Route 21. The gravestone of one of the first ministers of the church, Rev. Cornelius Cook, can still be seen there. The church was moved to its current location in 1863.

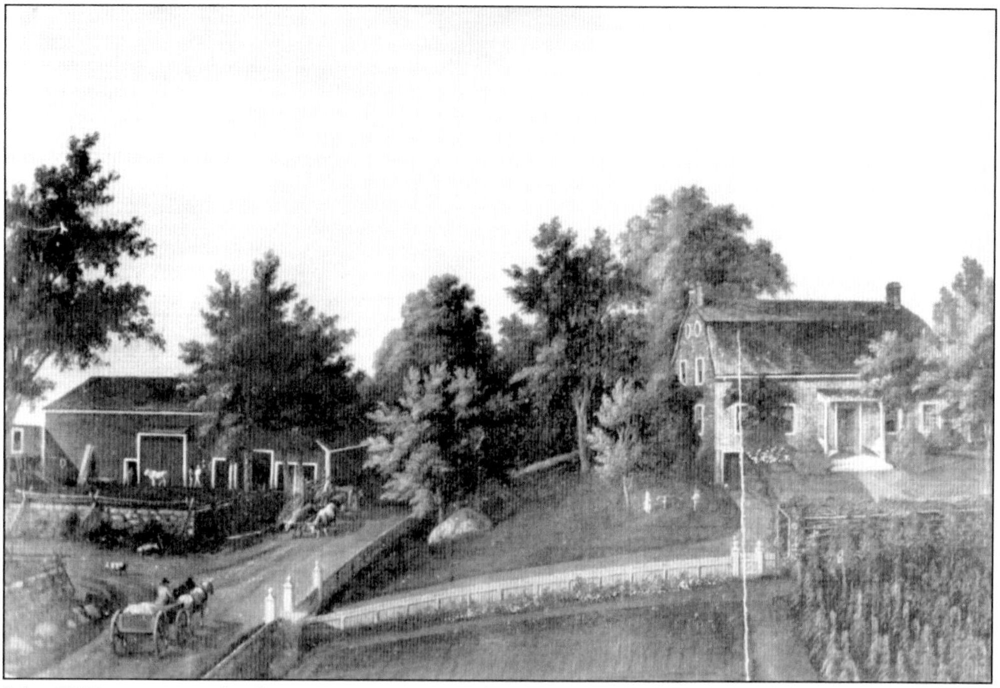

John Wilkinson was the first town supervisor of LaGrange, elected when the town was formed in 1821. This sketch is of his home, a Dutch Revival house on East Barmore Road. Wilkinson also served as town supervisor for Union Vale and Beekman.

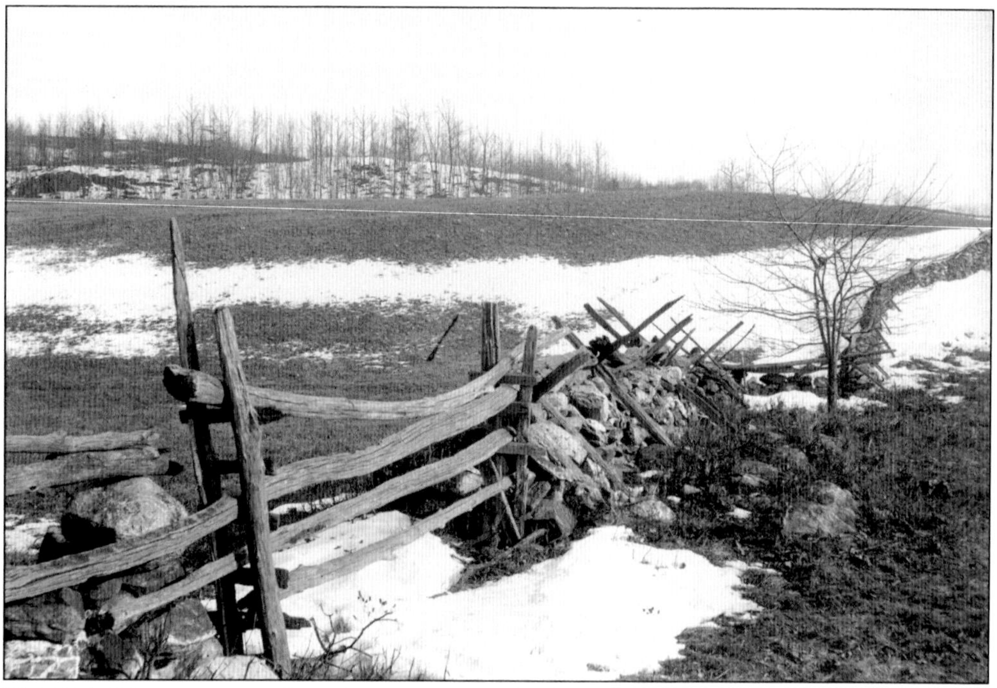

This "rider" fence, commonly used to contain cattle, formed the border of one of the local farms. Building stone walls was a skill passed down from father to son in those days; great care was taken in the construction so that they would not collapse. Many have lasted for generations.

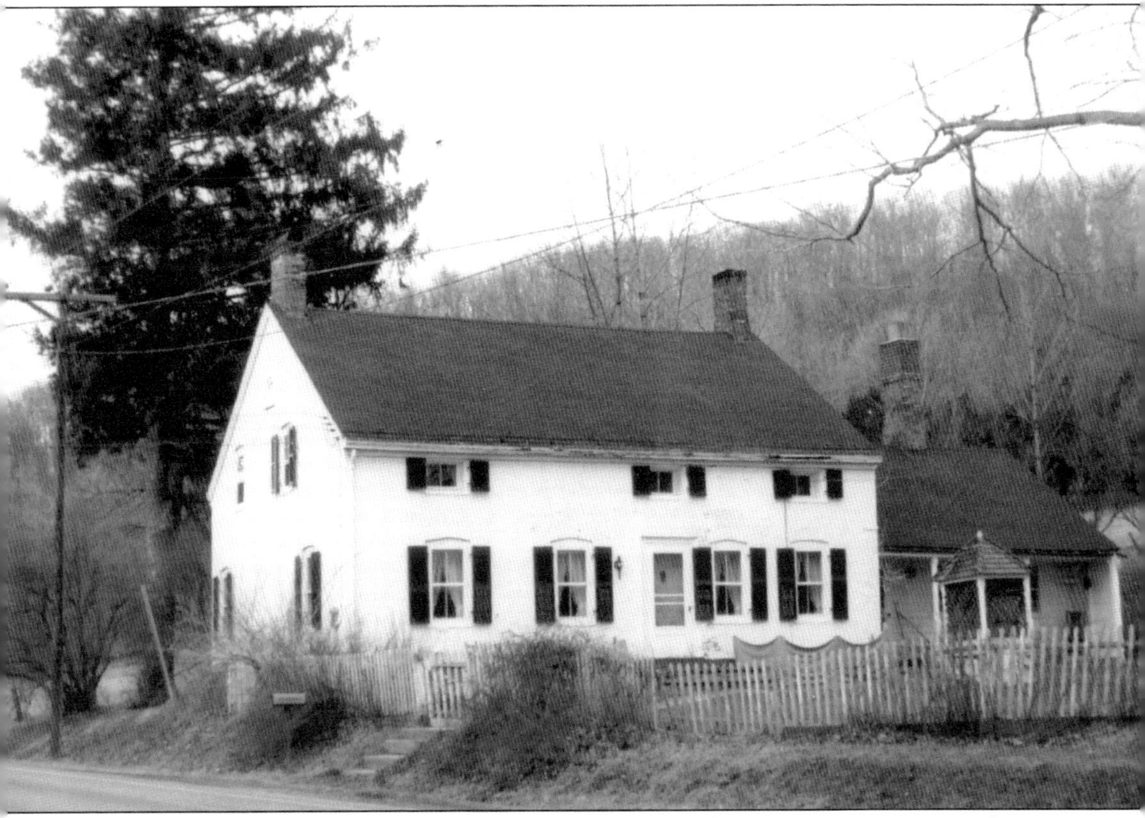

The Mark Wheeler homestead dates from 1806. It is fairly unique in LaGrange, being constructed of brick. The Carlo's Furniture business across the street is housed in what were once barns belonging to the farm. Wheeler was the benefactor of the chapel of the Freedom Plains Presbyterian Church, leaving the funds in his will in 1908. The chapel was opened and dedicated in 1914.

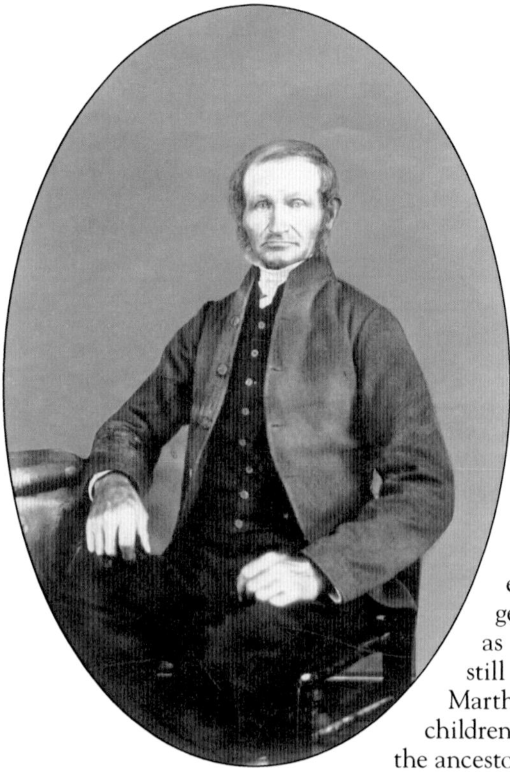

James C. Alley came to LaGrange in the early 1800s, probably from Canada. Several generations later, the Alley family continues as one of the well-known names in the town, still running the local Agway store. James's wife, Martha, was a Washburn. She and James had three children, including daughter Mattie and son Henry, the ancestor of the present store owners. (MD.)

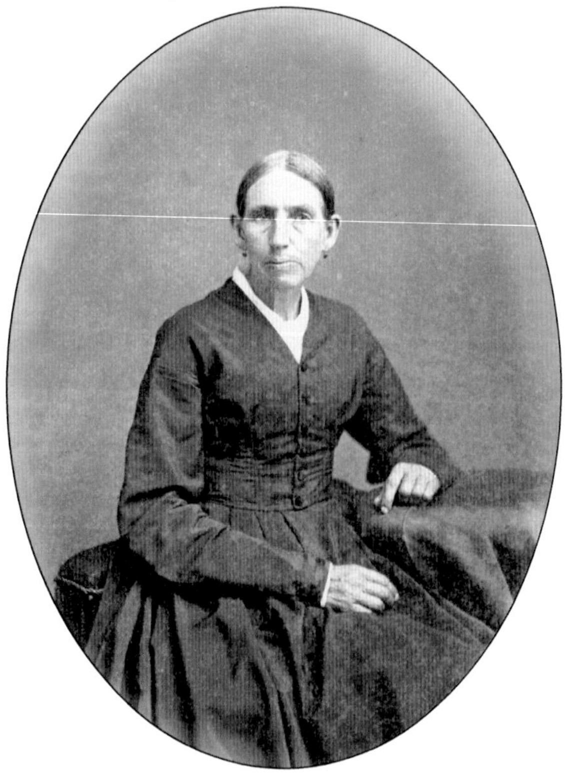

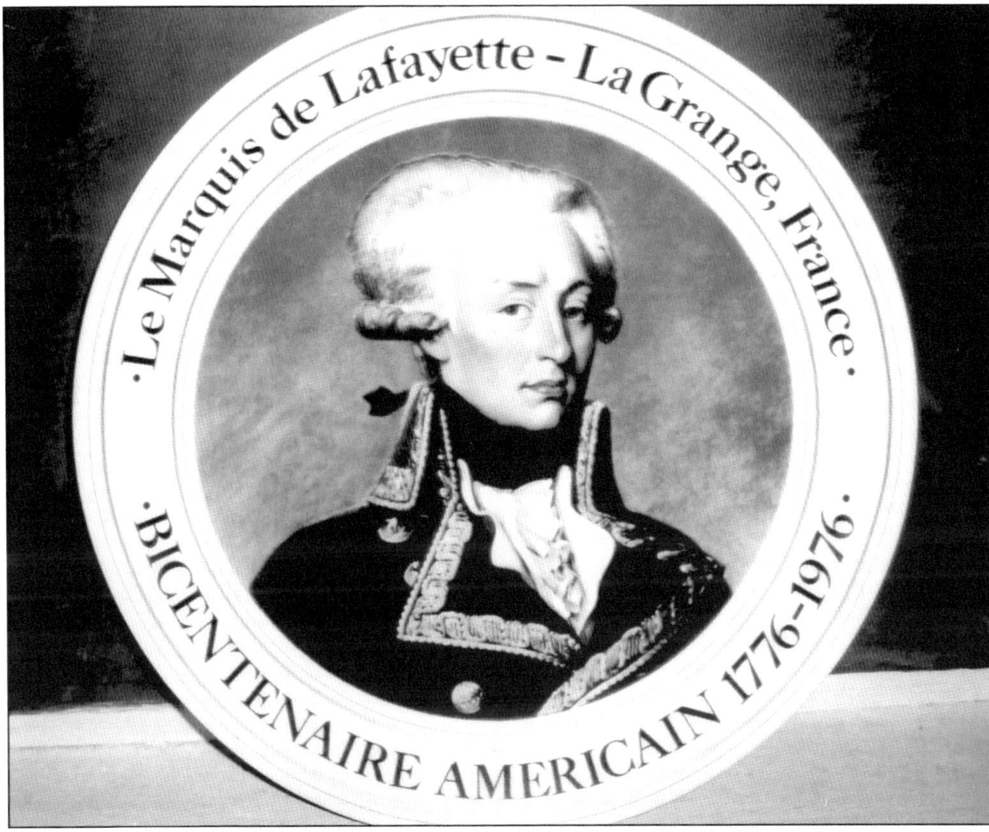

This commemorative plate portrays the Maquis de Lafayette, friend of the colonists and ally in the Revolutionary War. At the urging of resident Enoch Dorland, the town was rechristened LaGrange in 1829 in honor of Lafayette's French estate of the same name. The plate was issued during the American bicentennial in 1976.

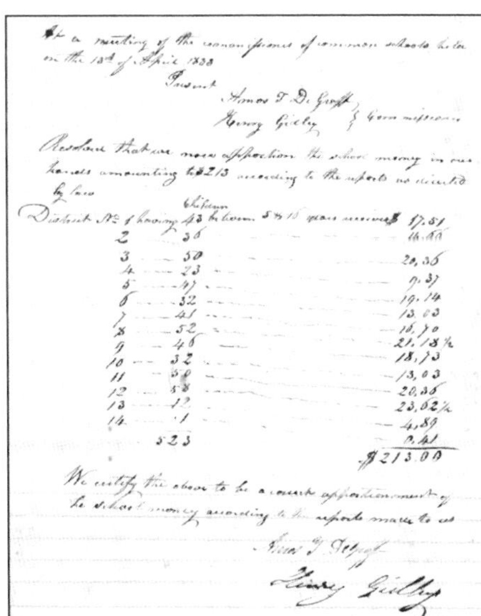

At a meeting of the commissioners of common schools held on the 13th of April 1833

Present

Amos T. DeGroff
Henry Gidley } Commissioners

Resolved that we now apportion the school money in our hands amounting to $213 according to the reports as directed by law

District No.	Children between 5 & 16 years	Received
1	43	$17.51
2	36	[illegible]
3	50	20,36
4	23	9.37
5	47	19.14
6	32	13.03
7	41	16,70
8	52	21.18½
9	46	18,73
10	32	13,03
11	50	20,36
12	58	23,62½
13	12	4,89
14	1	0.41
	523	$213.00

We certify the above to be a correct apportionment of the school money according to the reports made to us

Amos T. DeGroff
Henry Gidley

In 1833, Amos DeGroff and Henry Gidley noted the funds available for local schools—a total of $213. Acting as commissioners of common schools, they apportioned the money according to the number of students in each establishment. Several of the schoolhouses listed are still standing within the town, most having been converted into homes.

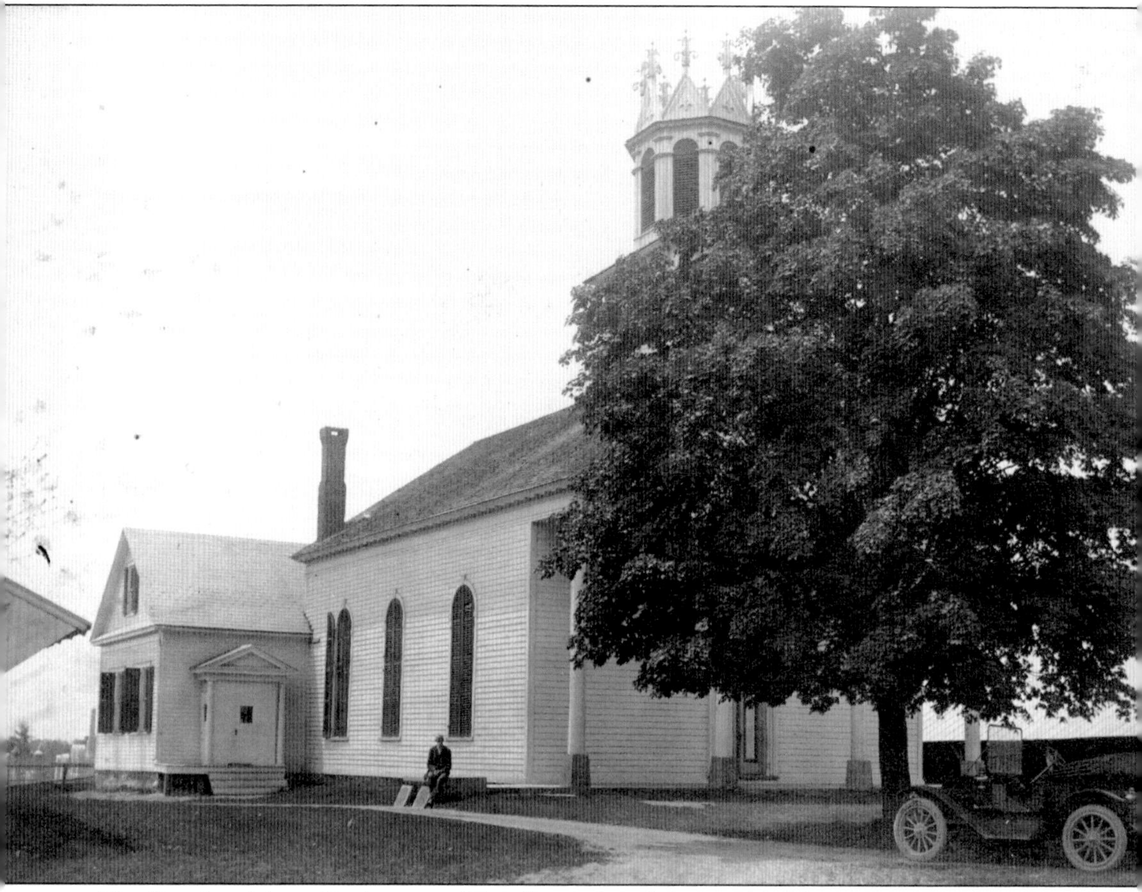

The Freedom Plains Presbyterian Church was founded in 1828. The site was purchased from William Wolven, whose residence was opposite it, for $75. The chapel was added in 1914, and in 1956, the fellowship hall was constructed. It has been the site of many potluck suppers and other community gatherings over the years. (GW.)

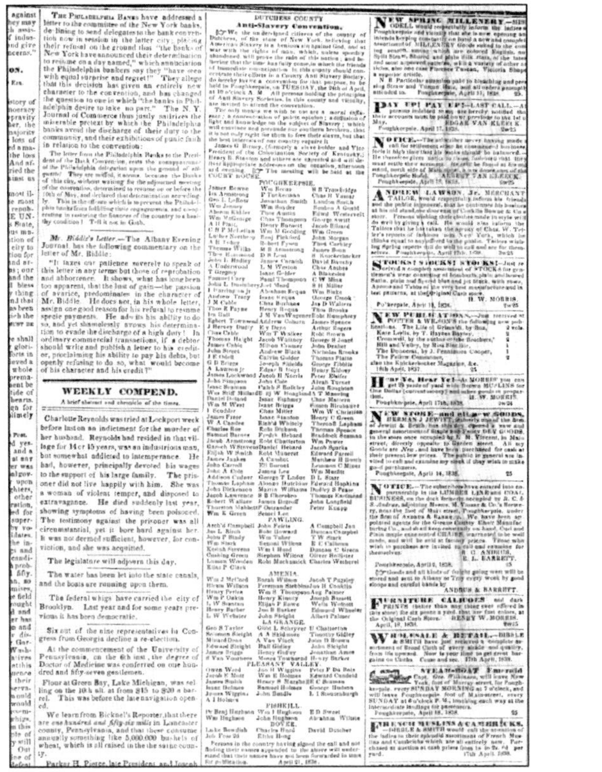

Antislavery sentiment ran strong in many communities in Dutchess County. The Quakers especially were early supporters of abolition. This page is from the *Poughkeepsie Telegraph* of 1838, announcing the antislavery convention to be held the following week. In the listing of abolitionist citizens, the small town of LaGrange is well represented.

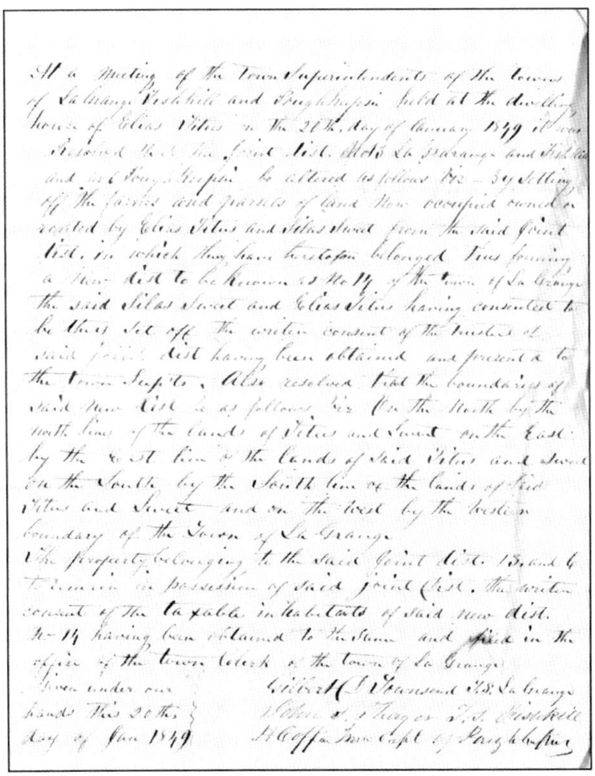

At a meeting of the Town Superintendents of the towns of LaGrange Fishkill and Poughkeepsie held at the dwelling house of Elias Titus on the 20th day of January 1849 it was Resolved that the joint dist. No 13 La Grange and Fishkill and no 6 Poughkeepsie be altered as follows viz — by setting off the farms and parcels of land now occupied owned or rented by Elias Titus and Silas Sweet from the said joint dist. in which they have heretofore belonged thus forming a new dist to be known as No 14 of the town of La Grange the said Silas Sweet and Elias Titus having consented to be thus set off the written consent of the trustees of said joint dist having been obtained and present to the Town Supts. Also resolved that the boundaries of said new dist is as follows viz On the North by the north line of the lands of Titus and Sweet on the East by the east line of the lands of said Titus and Sweet on the South by the South line of the lands of said Titus and Sweet and on the West by the western boundary of the Town of La Grange.
The property belonging to the said joint dist. 13 and 6 to remain in possession of said joint dist. the written consent of the taxable inhabitants of said new dist. No 14 having been obtained to the same and filed in the office of the town clerk of the town of La Grange.

Given under our hands this 20th day of Jan 1849

Gilbert … Townsend T.S. La Grange
… Thayer T.S. Fishkill
… Coffin Town Supt of Poughkeepsie

Titusville got its name from the family that established mills there in 1828. The woolen mill, which burned around the dawn of the 20th century, made blankets for the Civil War soldiers. In 1849, Elias Titus and his brother-in-law, Silas Sweet, agreed per this document to the formation of a new school district encompassing some of their land near Manchester Road.

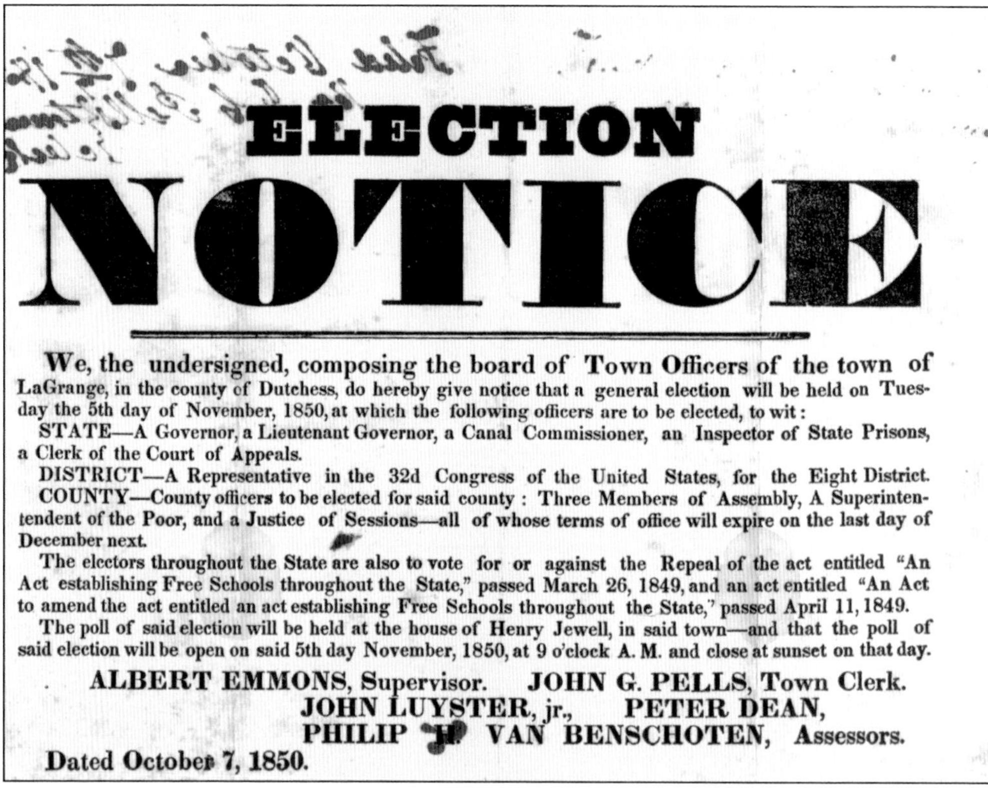

ELECTION NOTICE

We, the undersigned, composing the board of Town Officers of the town of LaGrange, in the county of Dutchess, do hereby give notice that a general election will be held on Tuesday the 5th day of November, 1850, at which the following officers are to be elected, to wit:

STATE—A Governor, a Lieutenant Governor, a Canal Commissioner, an Inspector of State Prisons, a Clerk of the Court of Appeals.

DISTRICT—A Representative in the 32d Congress of the United States, for the Eight District.

COUNTY—County officers to be elected for said county : Three Members of Assembly, A Superintendent of the Poor, and a Justice of Sessions—all of whose terms of office will expire on the last day of December next.

The electors throughout the State are also to vote for or against the Repeal of the act entitled "An Act establishing Free Schools throughout the State," passed March 26, 1849, and an act entitled "An Act to amend the act entitled an act establishing Free Schools throughout the State," passed April 11, 1849.

The poll of said election will be held at the house of Henry Jewell, in said town—and that the poll of said election will be open on said 5th day November, 1850, at 9 o'clock A. M. and close at sunset on that day.

ALBERT EMMONS, Supervisor. JOHN G. PELLS, Town Clerk.
JOHN LUYSTER, jr., PETER DEAN,
PHILIP H. VAN BENSCHOTEN, Assessors.

Dated October 7, 1850.

This announcement was distributed in 1850 to alert LaGrange citizens to the upcoming election of officers, including a superintendent of the poor for Dutchess County and a canal commissioner for the state. Local citizen Henry Jewell volunteered his home for polling purposes, since an official town hall did not yet exist.

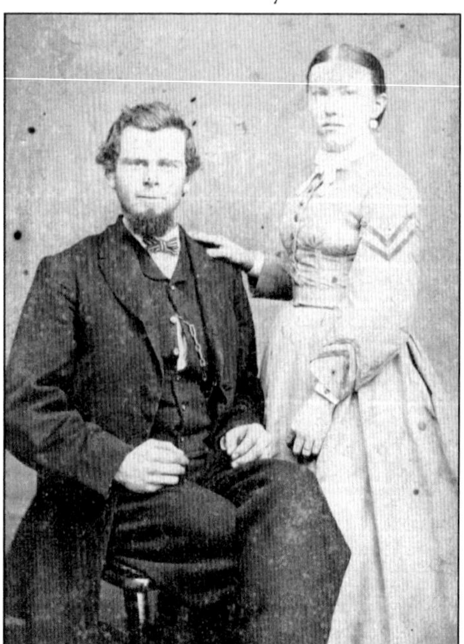

George Wade I married Mary Van Kleeck and inherited her father Monfort's meat delivery business. The couple later set up a market on Cramer Road. Their son, another Monfort, would continue in the family profession throughout his life and in turn pass it on to his son and grandson. (GW.)

Edward Flagler wrote this acceptance letter in 1853 after being elected overseer of highways. Oliver P. Monfort was the town clerk to whom it is addressed. Flagler would no doubt be shocked to see today's local roads, highways indeed compared to the country lanes that he was in charge of then.

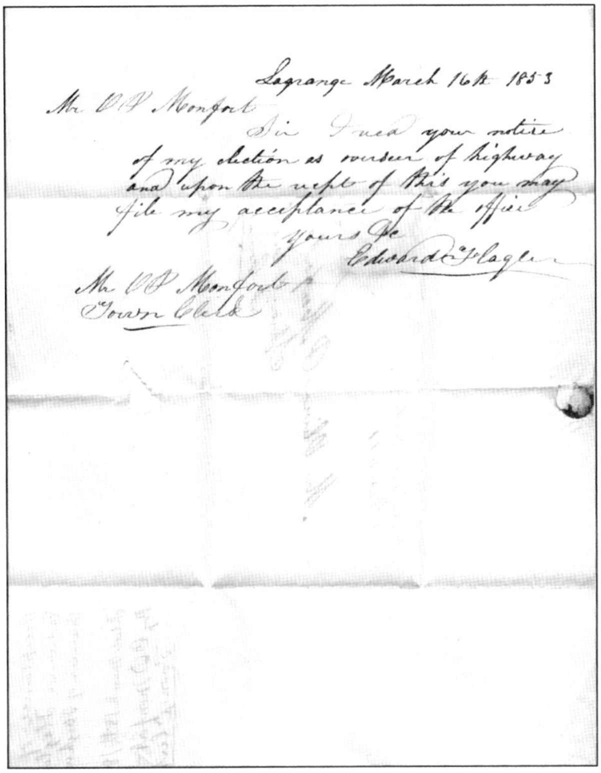

Lagrange March 16th 1853

Mr. O P Monfort

Sir I rec'd your notice of my election as overseer of highway and upon the receipt of this you may file my acceptance of the office

Yours &c

Edward Flagler

Mr O P Monfort

Town Clerk

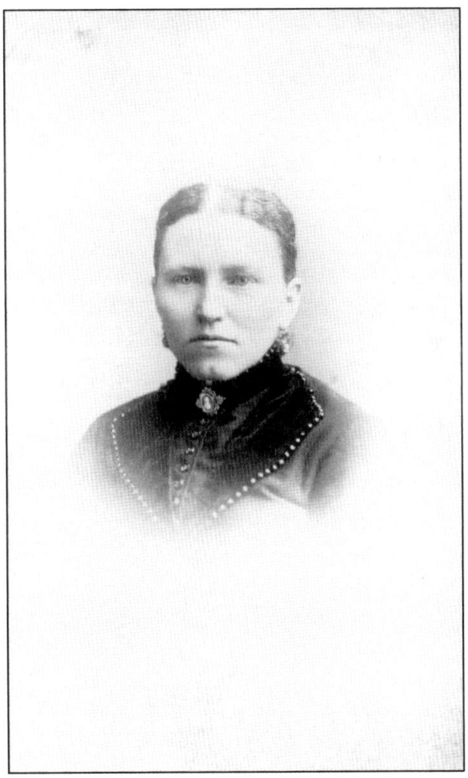

Mary Elizabeth was one of seven daughters born to Monfort Van Kleeck. They all assisted him in the butchering business, which was started in 1840, as well as tending to the many duties of running their farm. Their father had no cause to regret the lack of sons, with such hardworking female offspring. The Van Kleeck homestead was on Noxon Road. (GW.)

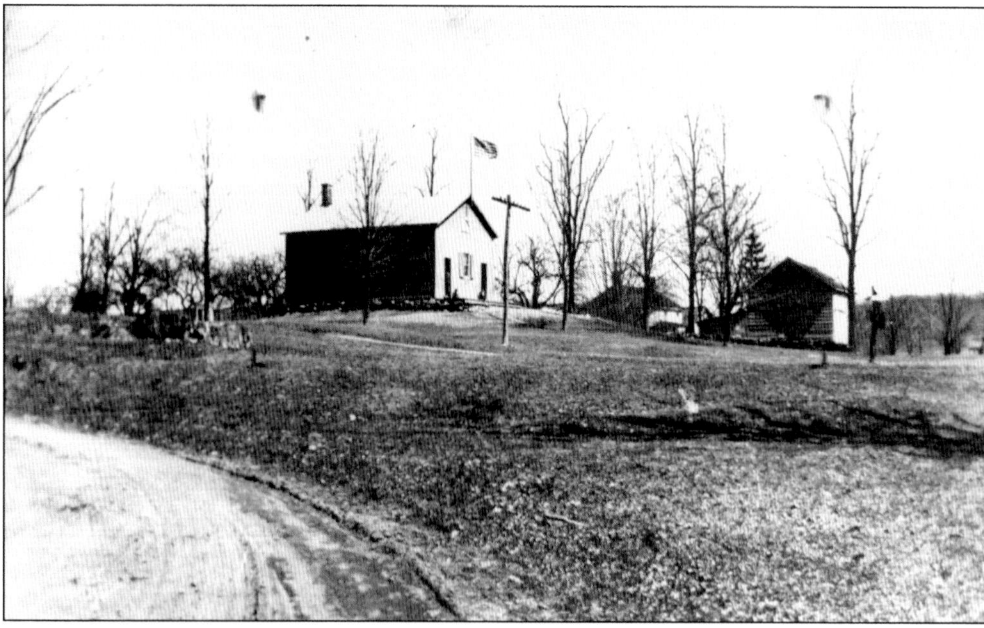

The schoolhouse at the corner of Dr. Fink and Freedom Roads was built around 1860 and was used until the 1940s. Owned by the LaGrange Historical Society since 1962, it houses a collection of desks and other school-related items. This photograph shows the spot as it looked in 1917, with Lauer Road in the foreground.

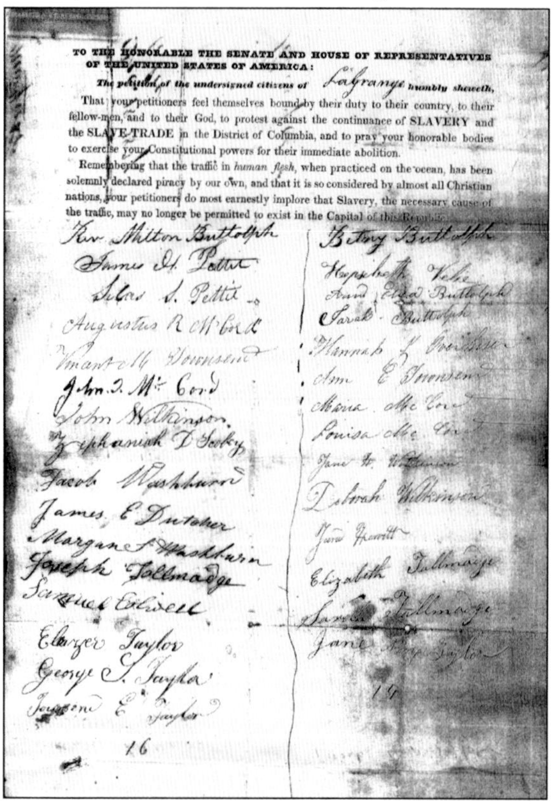

TO THE HONORABLE THE SENATE AND HOUSE OF REPRESENTATIVES OF THE UNITED STATES OF AMERICA:

The petition of the undersigned citizens of LaGrange *humbly sheweth,*

That your petitioners feel themselves bound by their duty to their country, to their fellow-men, and to their God, to protest against the continuance of SLAVERY and the SLAVE-TRADE in the District of Columbia, and to pray your honorable bodies to exercise your Constitutional powers for their immediate abolition.

Remembering that the traffic in *human flesh,* when practiced on the ocean, has been solemnly declared piracy by our own, and that it is so considered by almost all Christian nations, your petitioners do most earnestly implore that Slavery, the necessary cause of the traffic, may no longer be permitted to exist in the Capital of this Republic.

This 1860s document shows the signatures of LaGrange residents who considered it their moral duty to attempt to end the slave trade. The petition was sent to Washington, D.C., in the hope that Congress would take action. Many of the signers were well-known local businesspeople and town leaders.

This ledger of military enrollment shows the names of the local men, aged 18–45, who were required to report to duty if needed. The most common occupations listed are farmer and laborer. Some of the entries under "remarks" are poignant, "two fingers off," "defective eyes," and some wry, "claims to be 46."

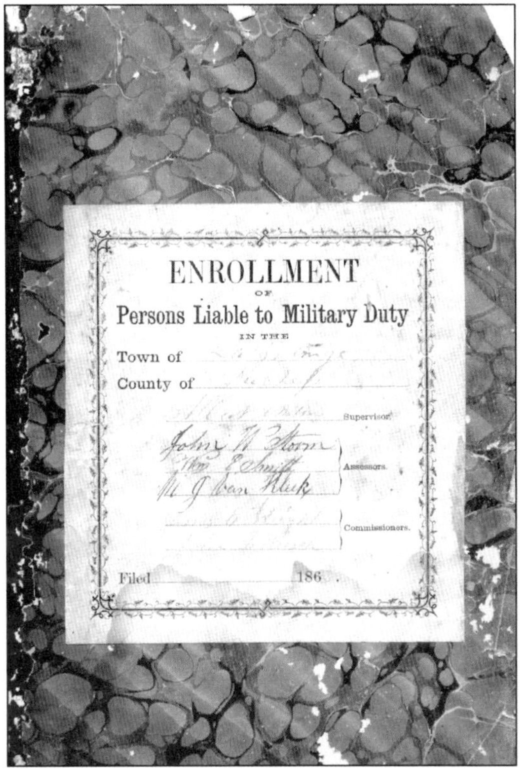

ENROLLMENT

OF

Persons Liable to Military Duty

IN THE

Town of

County of

Supervisor.

John W. Storm

Wm. E. Smith

M. J. Van Fleck

Assessors.

Commissioners.

Filed 186 .

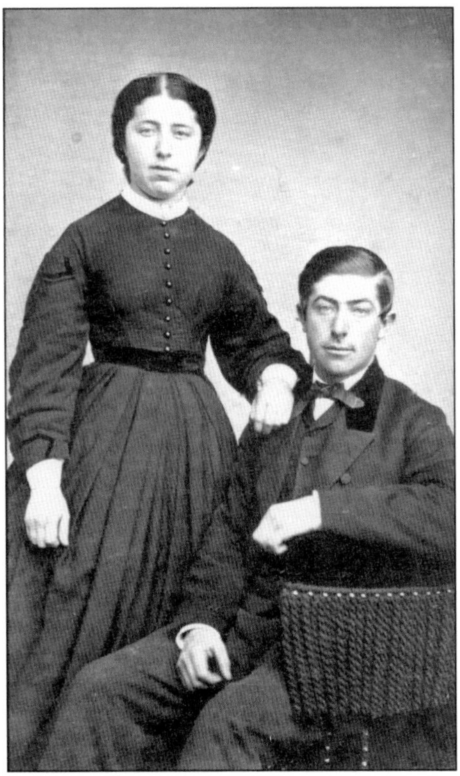

Alfred Moore and his first wife, Phoebe (Willets), pose for this photograph in the Civil War era. After Phoebe's death a few years later, he married Mattie Alley. Alfred was a notary public, in addition to running the family mills for most of his life. He also helped to establish the Quaker school on Oswego Road.

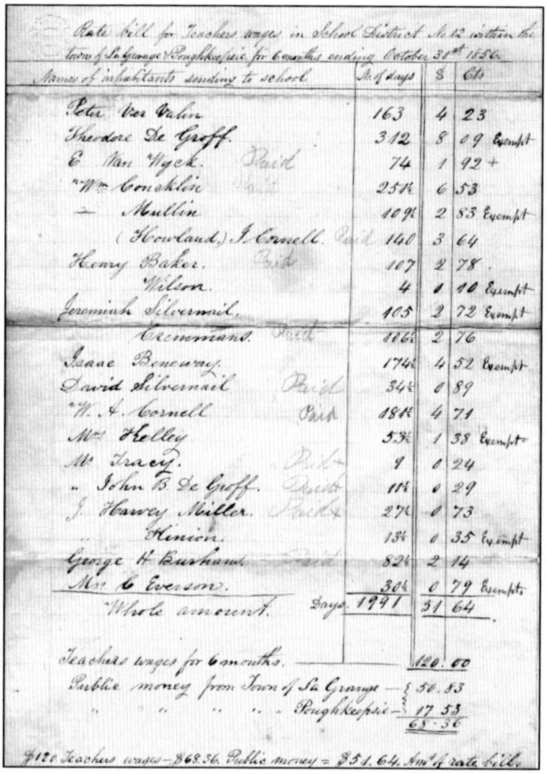

Rate bill for Teachers wages in School District No 12 within the town of La Grange & Poughkeepsie for 6 months ending October 31st 1856.

Names of inhabitants sending to school	No of days	$	Cts	
Peter Van Valin	163	4	23	
Theodore De Groff.	312	8	09	Exempt
E. Van Wyck. Paid	74	1	92 +	
" Wm Concklin Paid	251½	6	53	
— Mullin	109½	2	83	Exempt
(Howland) J. Cornell. Paid	140	3	64	
Henry Baker. Paid	107	2	78	
Wilson.	4	0	10	Exempt
Jeremiah Silvernail.	105	2	72	Exempt
Cremmans. Paid	106½	2	76	
Isaac Beneway.	174½	4	52	Exempt
David Silvernail Paid	34½	0	89	
" W. A. Cornell Paid	181½	4	71	
Mrs Kelley	53½	1	38	Exempt
Mr Tracy. Paid	9	0	24	
" John B. De Groff. Paid	11½	0	29	
J. Harvey Miller. Paid	27½	0	73	
" Hinion.	13½	0	35	Exempt
George H. Burham. Paid	82½	2	14	
Mr. C Everson.	30½	0	79	Exempt
Whole amount. Days	1991	51	64	

Teachers wages for 6 months. 120.00
Public money from Town of La Grange — 50.83
" " " " Poughkeepsie — 17.53
68.36

$120 Teachers wages — $68.36 Public money = $51.64 Amt of rate bill.

A rate bill, dated 1856, shows the amounts collected from residents for the Manchester Bridge teacher's wages. It appears that the town governments of Poughkeepsie and LaGrange each contributed a percentage also, to make up the total: $120 for 6 months. The collector is instructed to note those who refuse to pay, so that the seizure of their property ("goods and chattels") may be enacted.

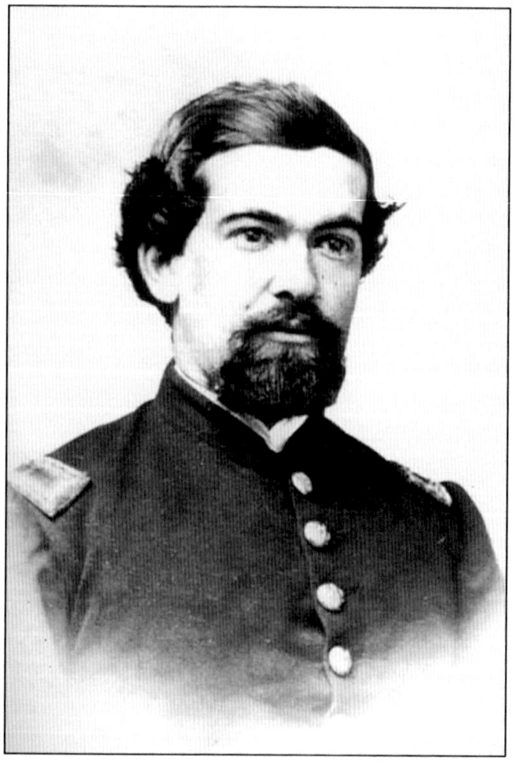

As the country went to war in 1862, local men joined the 150th Infantry Regiment and fought under the command of John H. Ketcham of Dover Plains. Shown is David Sleight, who was a first lieutenant in Company I. Other LaGrange families, including the Velies and Gidleys, also sent their sons off to battle. (JW.)

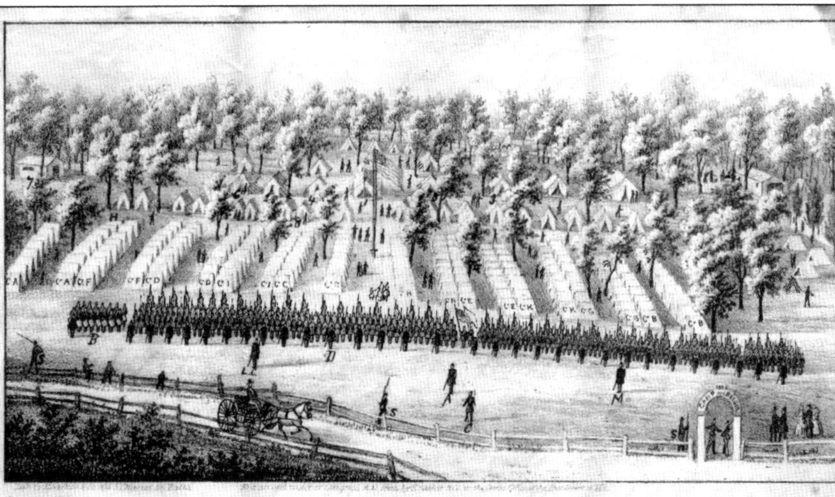

Lt. Col. Chas G. Bardett.
Major Alfred B. Smith.

CAMP BELGER BALTIMORE, MD

150TH REGT N Y VOLUNTEERS, FIELD & STAFF. COL JOHN H KETCHAM.

Baltimore, 186

This picture represents the Regiment on Dress Parade. The Adjutant has just taken his place in front of the Colonel and says: "Sir, the Parade is formed."

Explanation

C. Colonel. L.C. Lieutenant Colonel. M. Major. A. Adjutant B Band

The line of men in front of the ranks represents the position of the line Officers (Captains & Lieutenants) each in front of his own Company. Those in the rear are the file-closers or Sergeants. S.S, Sentinels a line of which is posted around the Camp at all times, night & day D is the position of your Cousin David with Captain Broas on the right and Lieutenant Titus on the left of him, Company I. being the fourth from the right when in line of battle

1 Colonel's tent. 2, Lt Col's. 3 Major's. 4 Adjutant's 5, Quartermaster's 6 Chaplain's 7 Hospital. 8 Tent of Lieuts Titus & Sleight with Capt Broas on left facing their Company street. This is the way all Camps are laid out.

This letter written by 1st Lt. David Sleight to his cousin in 1862 gives an excellent firsthand account of the Civil War experience. He describes the accompanying sketch of the muster formation and gives details of camp life but also shares some touching sentiments of a personal nature. His ancestors are in possession of a large collection of the letters he wrote to loved ones back home. David Sleight would be killed in action later that year at Averasbora, North Carolina. A large monument marks his grave site at the LaGrange Rural Cemetery.

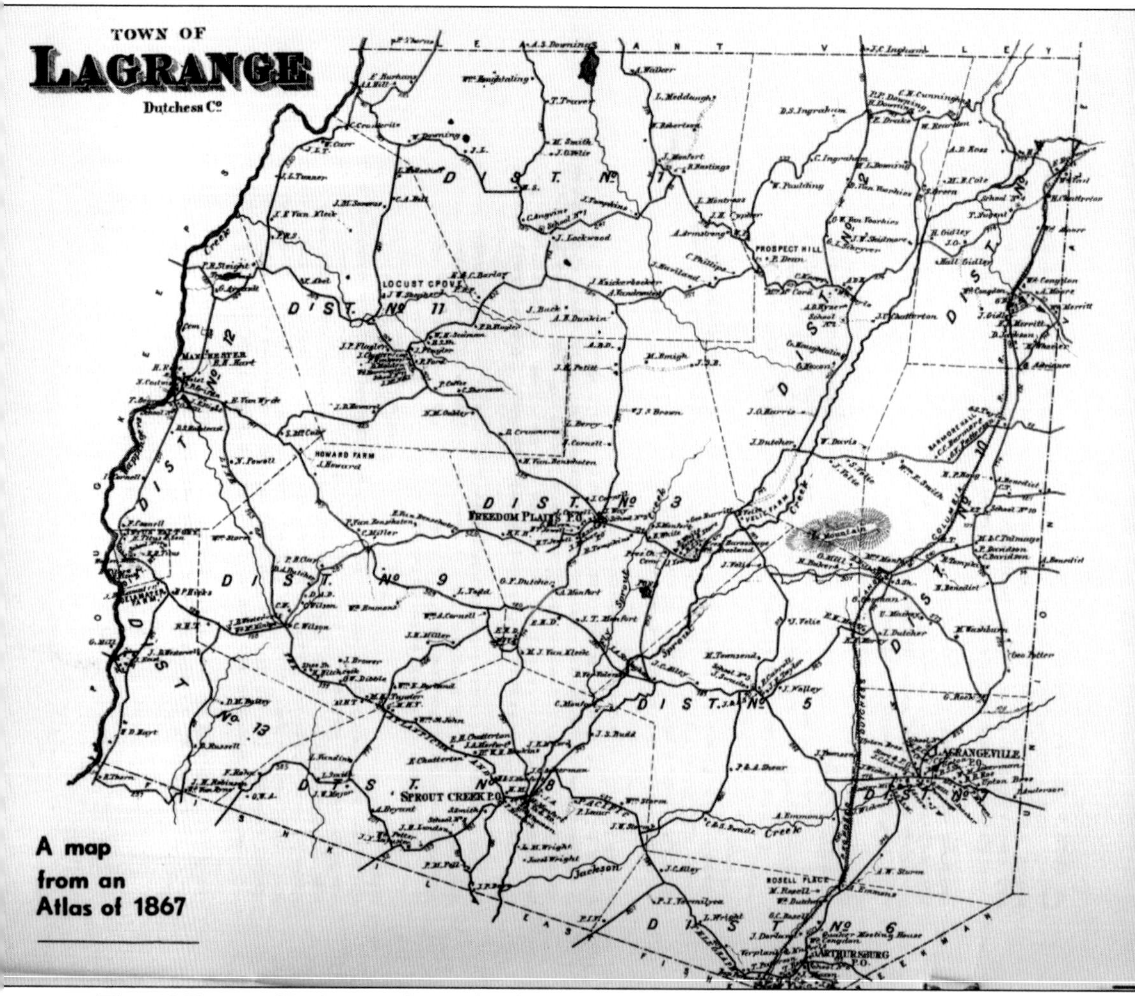

A map from an Atlas of 1867

This 1867 map of LaGrange shows the divisions of the districts, each of which had a least one school. Also noted are the homesteads that existed at that time; quite a few of the families mentioned still had descendants living nearby 100 years later. There were many farms, some over 100 acres, and various types of mills were established along Sprout and Wappingers Creeks. The coming of the railroad just a few years later would cause a shifting of town centers, with residents moving closer to the trains.

Two

THE RAILROAD ERA

Once the Civil War had ended, people's attention turned back to daily living. The introduction of the steam-driven locomotive brought tremendous change to the country, especially the small towns and villages. Reduced traveling time meant easier access to the country for those who wished to visit, whether for business or pleasure. The telegraph, another new invention, meant that people could more easily keep in touch. Both the LaGrangeville and Moore's Mills stations had telegraph offices.

Through the later part of the century, LaGrange continued to grow. Milk and apple production were logical choices for utilizing the natural resources of good soil and moderate climate. The railroad, coming through the town in 1869, enabled locally produced items to more quickly reach the markets of New York City and upstate. Various small businesses such as general stores and boardinghouses began to appear. LaGrange had become a thriving community, preserving its farming roots while looking ahead to a future of prosperity.

Many one-room schoolhouses had been established, as the law stated that no child should walk more than three miles to school. There were 14 districts within LaGrange, ensuring that every neighborhood had a school close by. The quality of education obtained in these quaint settings, with one teacher instructing several grades, is quite remarkable. Teachers often resided in the homes of local families, receiving their board as part of their compensation.

Houses of worship continued to be an important part of village life. There were still many Quakers in the town, holding services both in the meetinghouses and in members' homes. The Grange movement (the Order of the Patrons of Husbandry) was also becoming popular, offering farmers a sense of solidarity along with providing a needed social outlet.

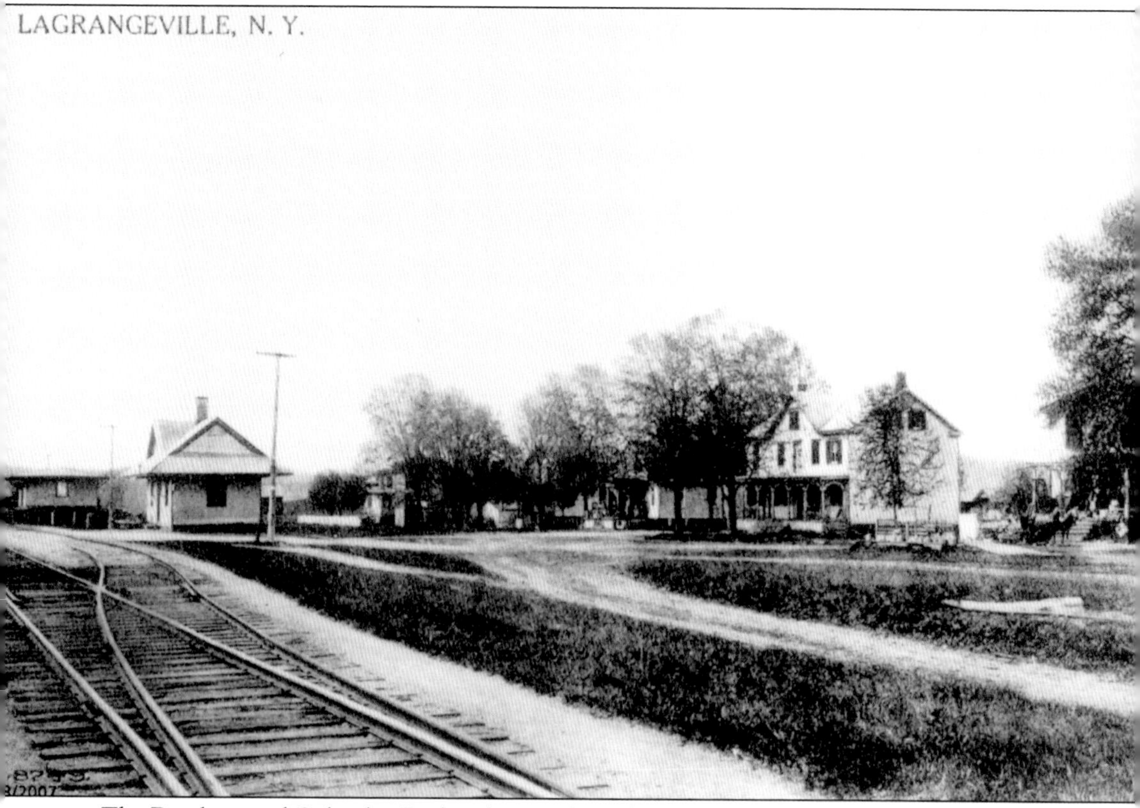

The Dutchess and Columbia Railroad came through LaGrange in the late 1860s. Freight trains enabled local farmers to deliver their goods (mostly fruit and dairy products) to the markets in Albany and New York City. The depot remains just off Noxon Road but is now privately owned. It served as an art gallery in the 1960s, when owned by the Hallocks.

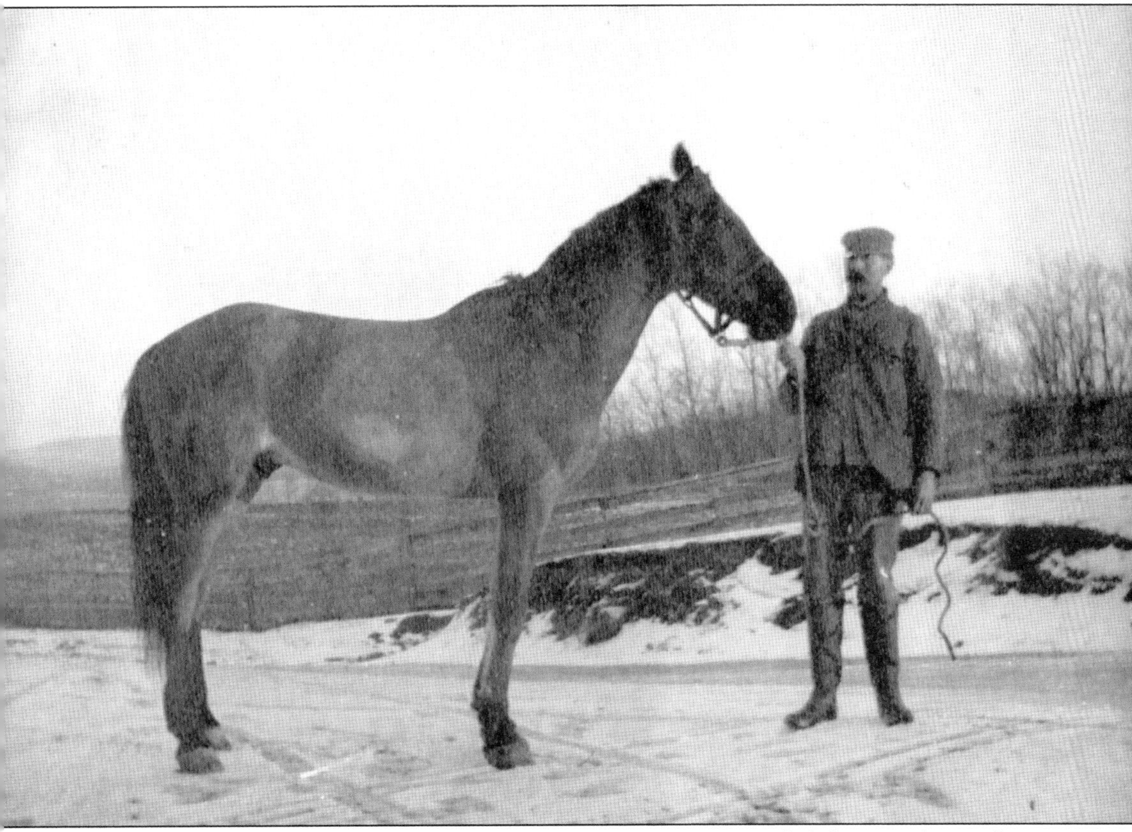

Andrew Skidmore is shown here with his horse, Pone. Skidmore attended the Friend's Academy in Locust Valley, Long Island, in 1888. He later married Jennie Gidley, just a few years after his brother Francis Jay was wed to her sister, Susie. A third brother, Herbert, married Ruth Storey, from Millbrook.

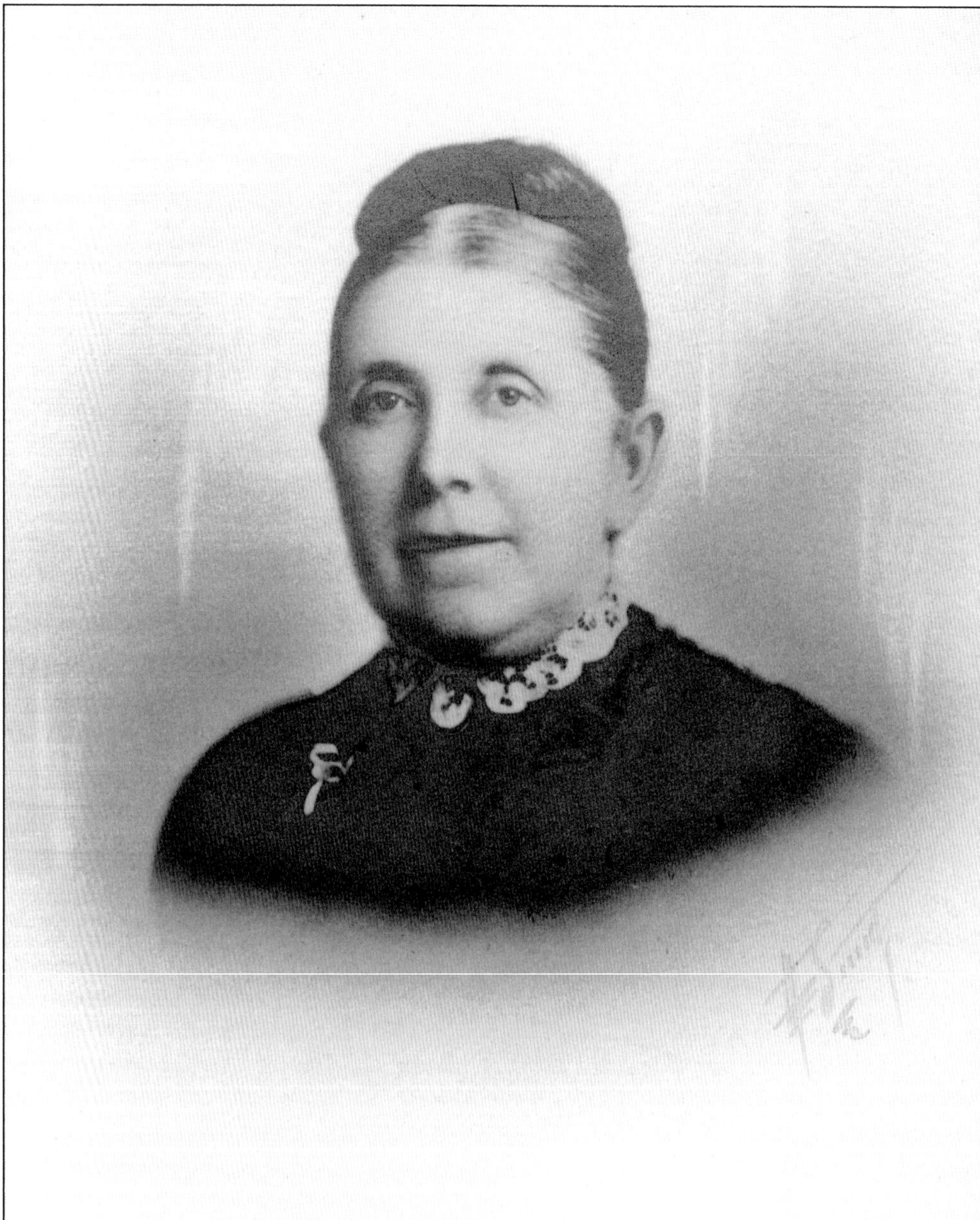

Susan Moore ran the Floral Home as a boardinghouse and hotel during the late 1800s. It was a popular spot for those seeking rest and the beauty of the rural countryside. Vassar students were among the guests who enjoyed the hospitality of Moore. Visitors were always welcome to attend the Quaker services on Sundays.

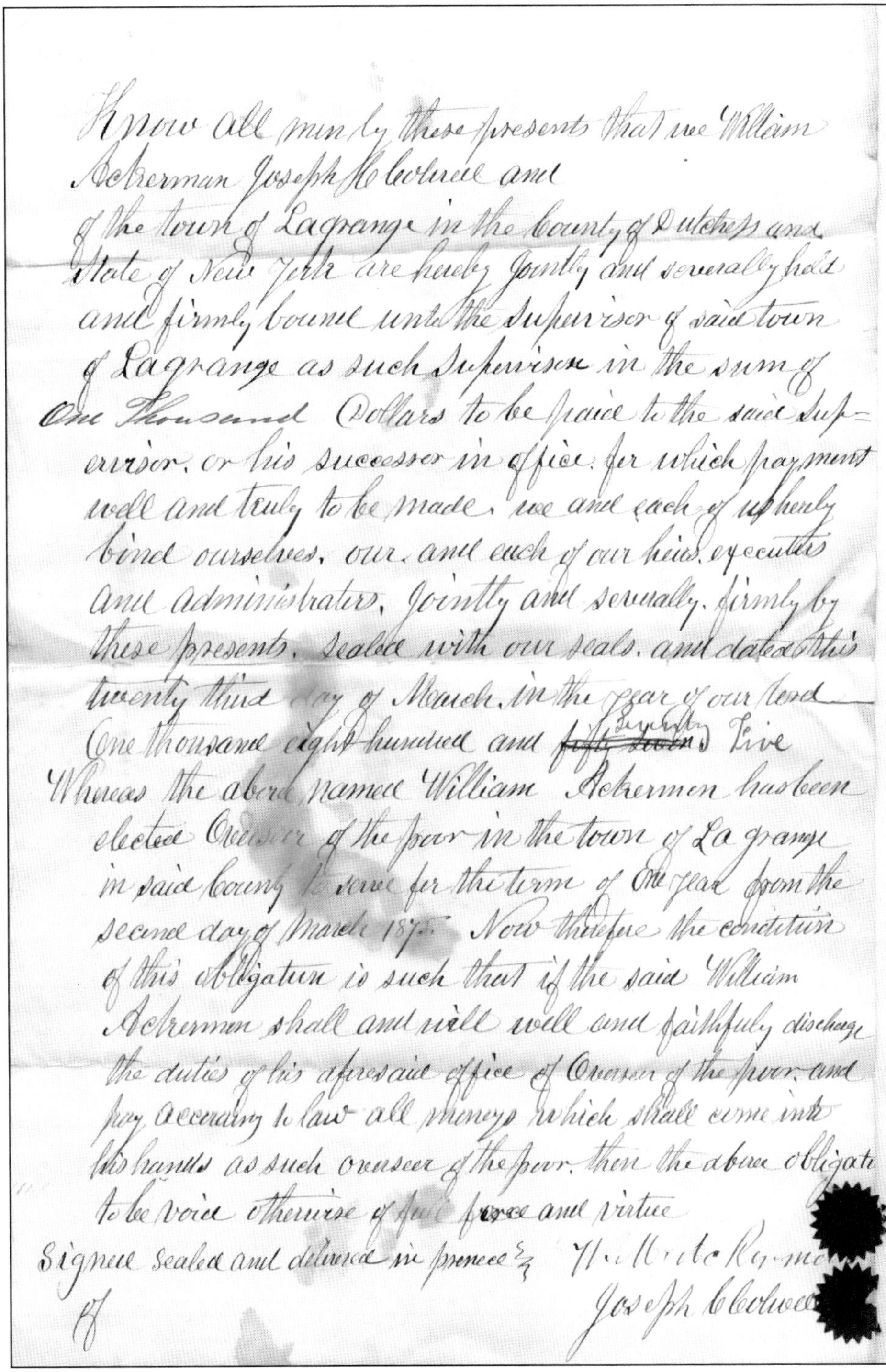

Know all men by these presents that we William
Ackerman Joseph H Colwell and
of the town of Lagrange in the County of Dutchess and
State of New York are hereby jointly and severally held
and firmly bound unto the Supervisor of said town
of Lagrange as such Supervisor in the sum of
One Thousand Dollars to be paid to the said Sup-
ervisor or his successor in office for which payment
well and truly to be made we and each of us hereby
bind ourselves our and each of our heirs executors
and administrators jointly and severally firmly by
these presents. Sealed with our seals and dated this
twenty third day of March in the year of our Lord
One thousand eight hundred and ~~fifty seven~~ Seventy Five
Whereas the above named William Ackerman has been
elected Overseer of the poor in the town of La grange
in said County to serve for the term of One year from the
second day of March 1875. Now therefore the condition
of this obligation is such that if the said William
Ackerman shall and will well and faithfully discharge
the duties of his aforesaid office of Overseer of the poor and
pay according to law all moneys which shall come into
his hands as such overseer of the poor then the above obligation
to be void otherwise of full force and virtue

Signed sealed and delivered in presence of

Wm Ackerman
Joseph Colwell

In 1875, William Ackerman was elected overseer of the poor in LaGrange, as recorded in this document. The salary was to be $1,000 for the year. Responsibilities probably included ensuring that destitute individuals had a roof over their heads, and enough to eat, but no details are mentioned.

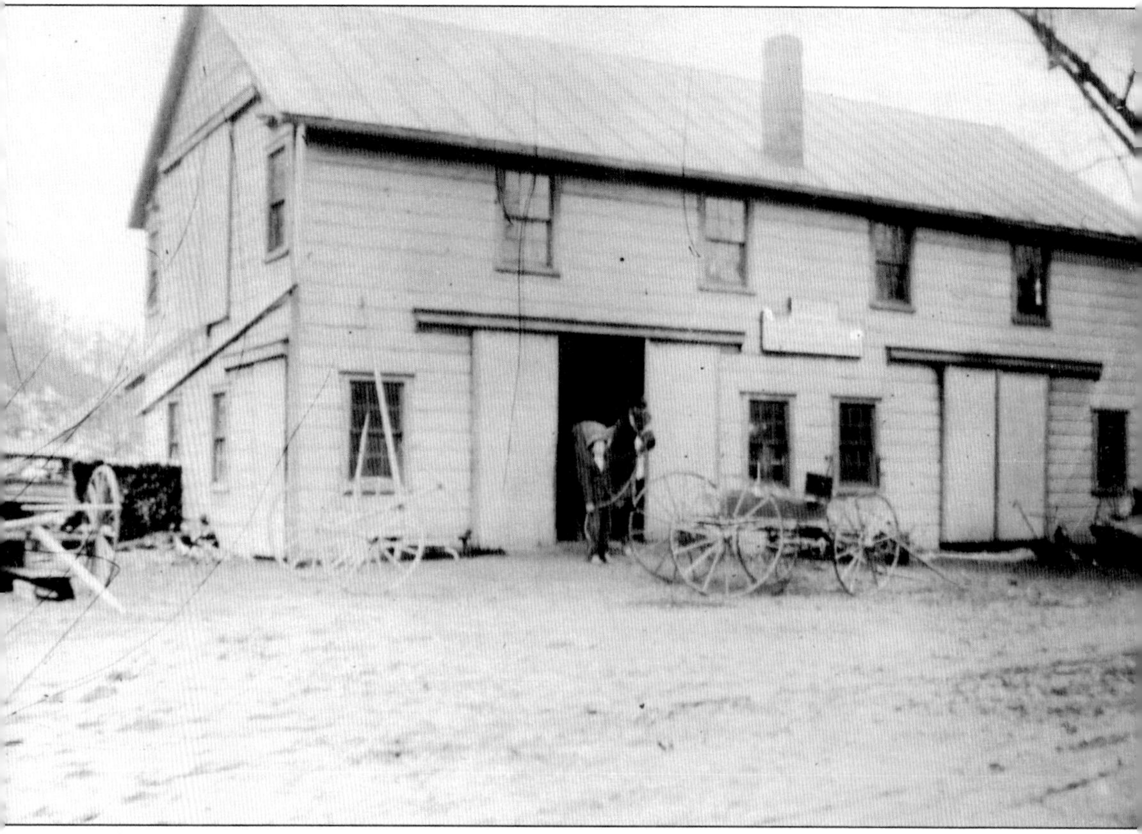

Blacksmiths were a necessity from the earliest days until the advent of the automobile. Several shops existed in LaGrange over the years, manufacturing many necessary tools and other items, along with shoeing horses. Pictured here is the establishment run by a Mr. Kelley, in the area of Moore's Mills.

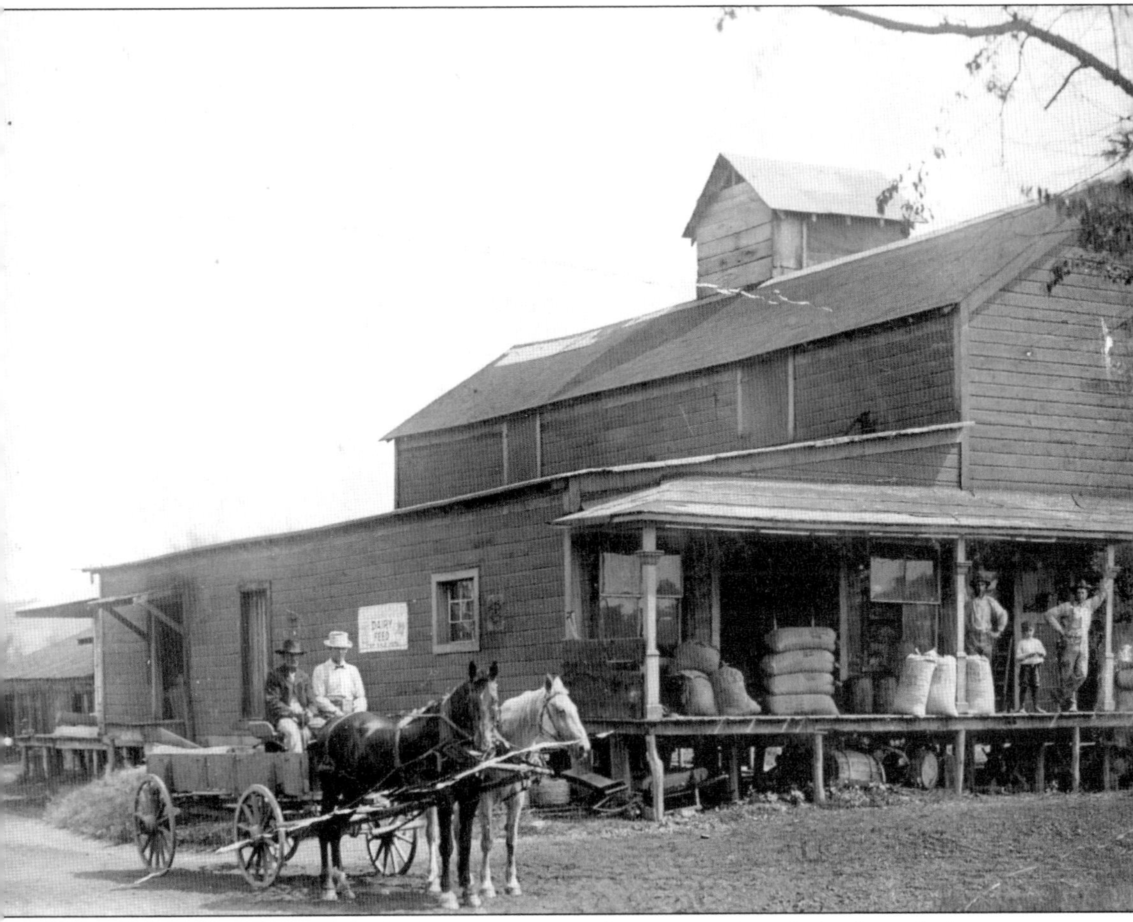

Local men gathered around the feed store to transact business, and no doubt shoot the breeze as well. This is probably the Budd's store, established in the late 1880s. George Budd owned a steam tractor and traveled with it to local farms during threshing season; it was also occasionally used for running small sawmill operations.

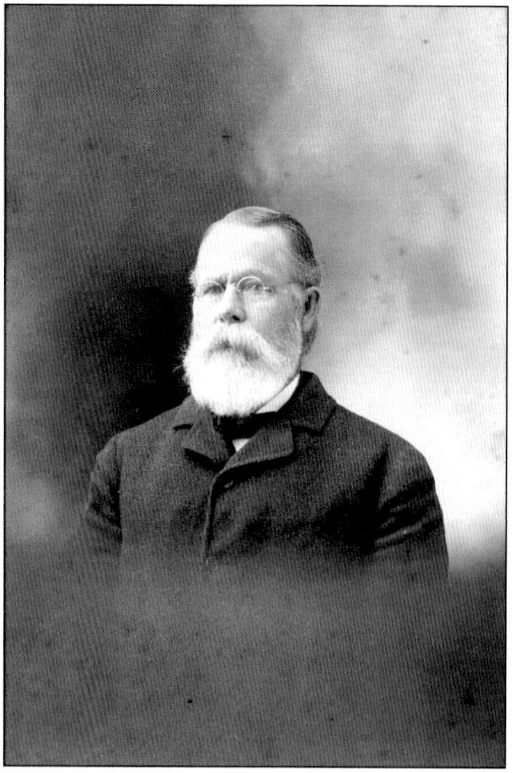

Williams A. Wells served as treasurer and accountant for the Newburgh, Dutchess and Columbia Railroad for 30 years, starting in 1870. He was married to Hannah (Stevens) for over 50 years; a newspaper item from 1898 mentions that the well-respected couple celebrated their golden anniversary at a party given by their neighbors in Moore's Mills.

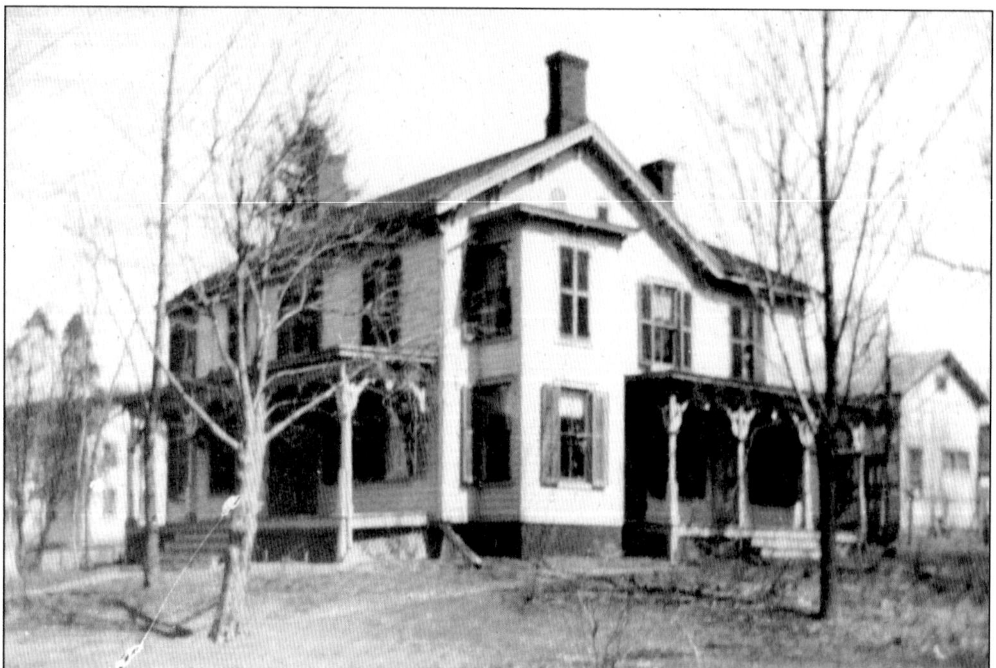

The Wells Manor was the business office of the local railroad for a short time, when it was owned by a General Schultz; later on the office was run from the village of Matteawan (now Beacon). George Stevens Wells, son of William and Hannah, was the station agent for most of his life.

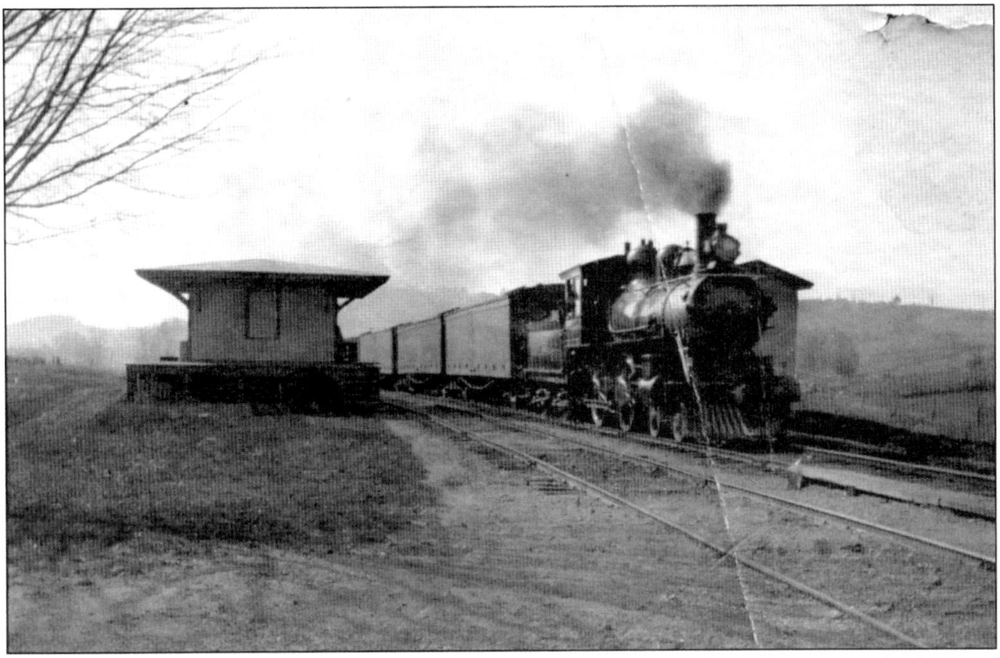

A freight train like this came through Moore's Mills three times daily, picking up and delivering goods such as produce. According to a document shared by resident Sara Wells, local men who worked taking care of the train tracks were paid a salary of $9 a week, considered a good wage at the time.

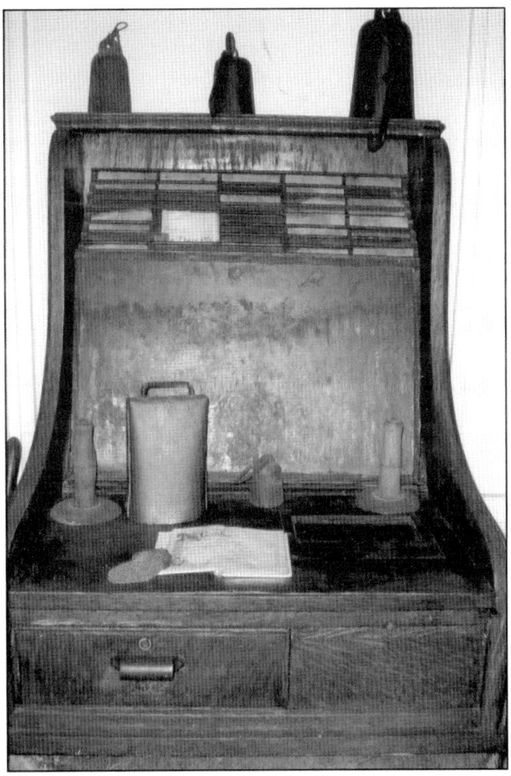

This wooden cash register was used by the Wade family in their meat market during the 1800s. Money was kept in the drawer at the bottom, and account slips were stored in the slots at the top—quite a change from today's high-tech laser scanner at the supermarket. (GW.)

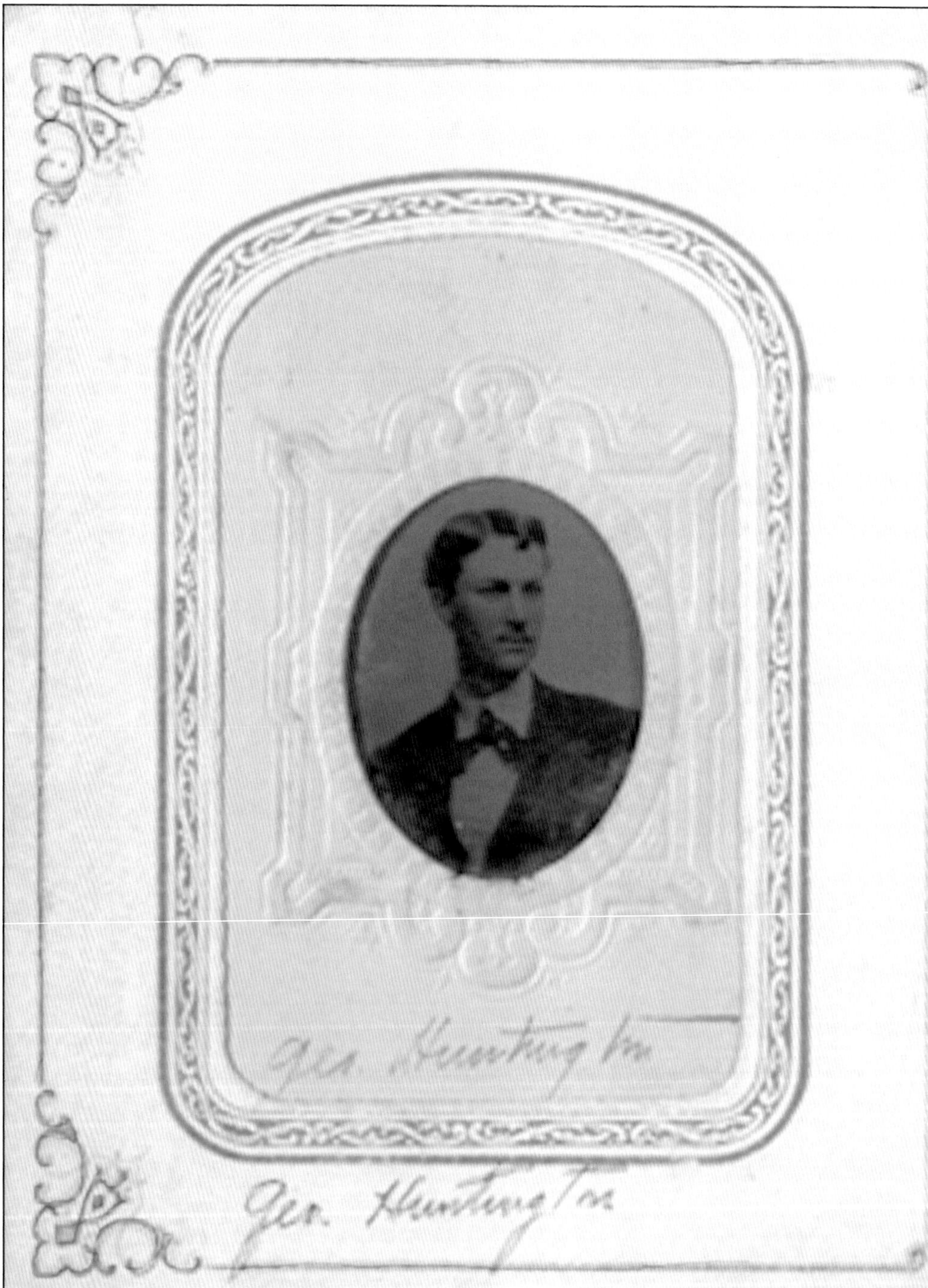

Dr. George Huntington was a resident from 1874 to 1901, living in the area of Morey's Corners. Originally from East Hampton, Long Island, he was a well-loved physician who himself suffered from poor health due to severe asthma. It was noted that he often took his payment in grain, chicken, and other farm products. The price for a house call was $1, and that included medicine. (LIC.)

This cherubic young lady is Margaret Smith, daughter of Mr. and Mrs. Robert Smith. She married Monfort Wade, and they settled on Freedom Road. They were known for taking in children (probably orphans) for many years, as related by students who attended the nearby Freedom Plains school. (GW.)

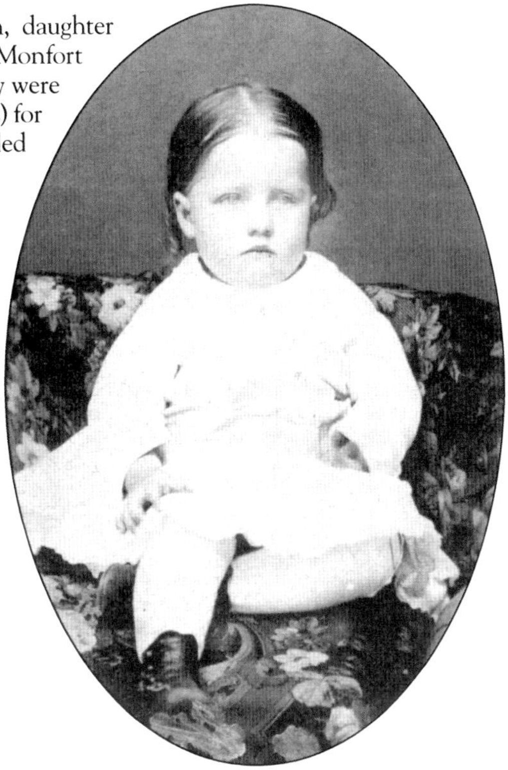

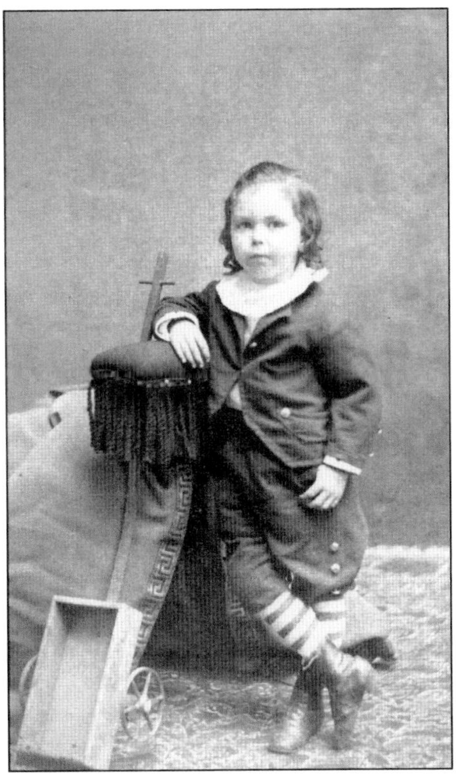

Monfort was the son of George Wade and Mary (Van Kleeck) Wade. He and his son George continued running their family meat market through two world wars. They delivered door-to-door on two routes, first by horse and wagon and later by car. (GW.)

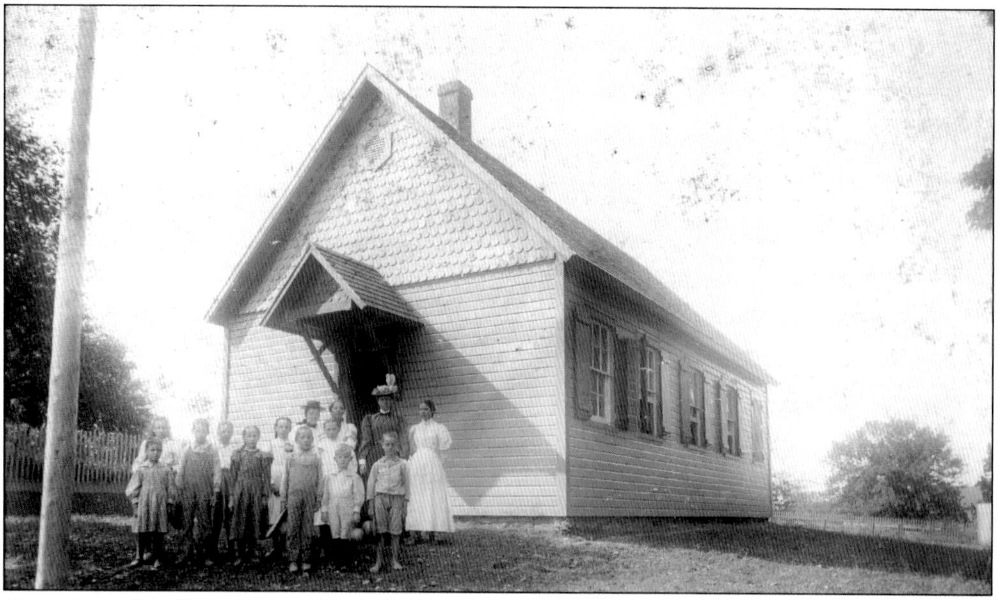

One-room schoolhouses were located throughout LaGrange at each hamlet or village. Here is the school in Moore's Mills, around the dawn of the 20th century. All the boys have dutifully removed their hats to have their picture taken. The school was used up until the 1930s, when the children of the few families still living in the hamlet could attend larger nearby schools.

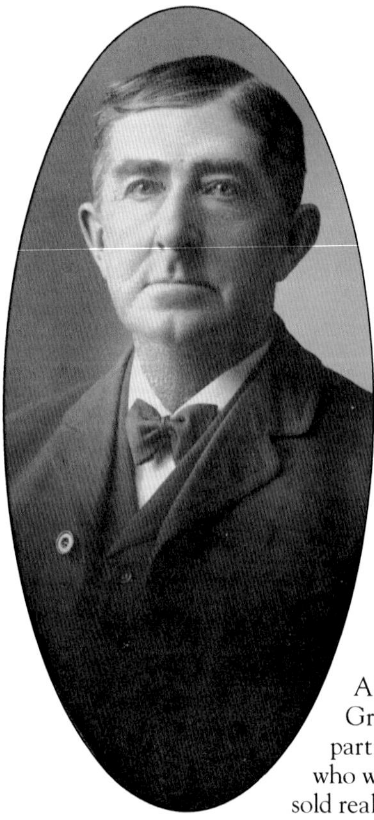

Alfred H. Moore and his second wife, Mattie (Alley), were Grange members in the later part of the 18th century, participating in various posts. Mattie was one of the delegates who went to Cortland for the Grange session in 1904. Alfred also sold real estate and was a lifelong member of the Quaker faith.

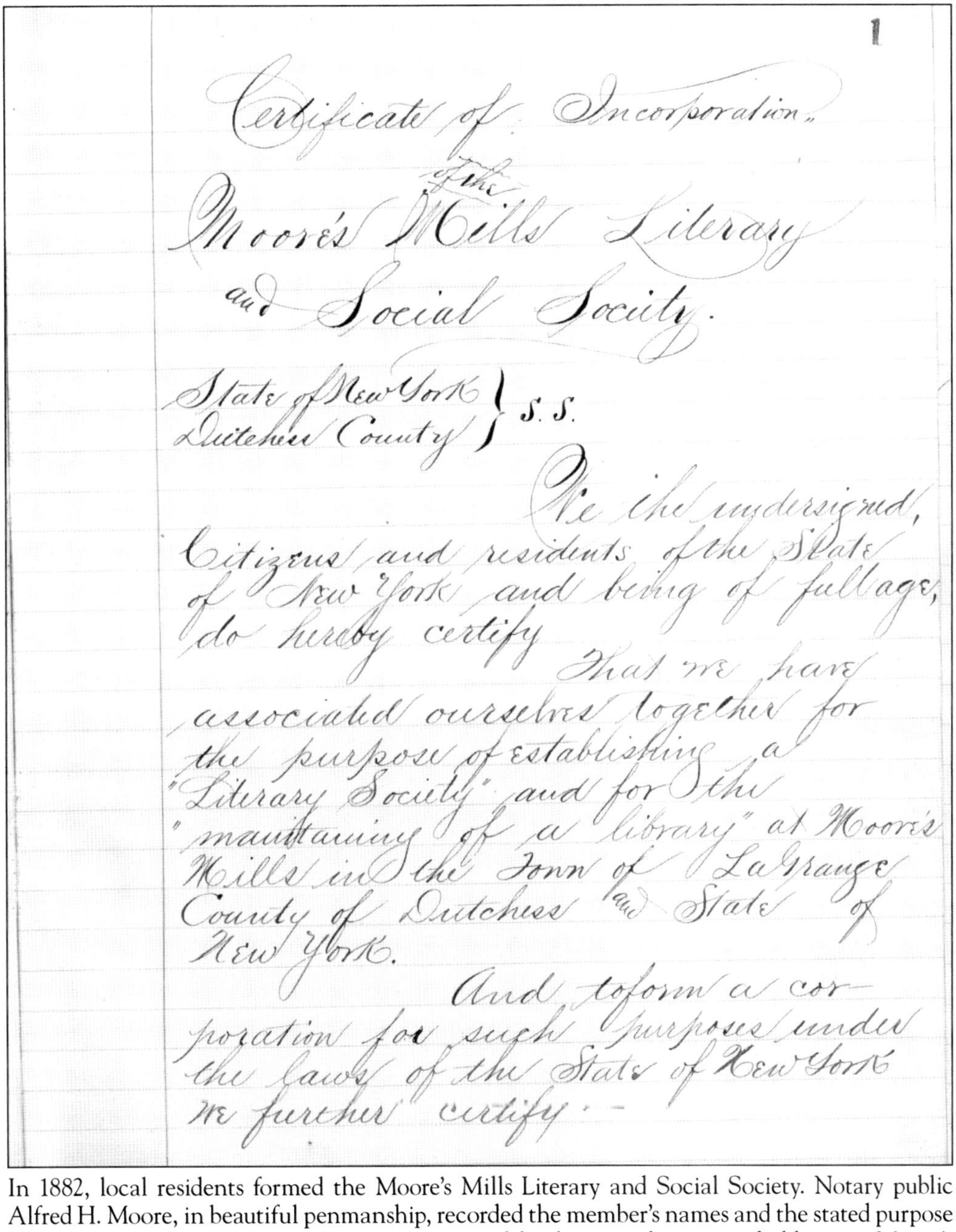

1

Certificate of Incorporation.

of the

Moore's Mills Literary and Social Society.

State of New York }
Dutchess County } S. S.

We the undersigned, Citizens and residents of the State of New York and being of full age, do hereby certify

That we have associated ourselves together for the purpose of establishing a "Literary Society" and for the "maintaining of a library" at Moore's Mills in the Town of La Grange County of Dutchess and State of New York.

And to form a corporation for such purposes under the laws of the State of New York we further certify:–

In 1882, local residents formed the Moore's Mills Literary and Social Society. Notary public Alfred H. Moore, in beautiful penmanship, recorded the member's names and the stated purpose of the group: "for establishing a literary society and for the manufacturing of a library in Moore's Mills." Judging by the later entries, they did indeed accomplish their goal.

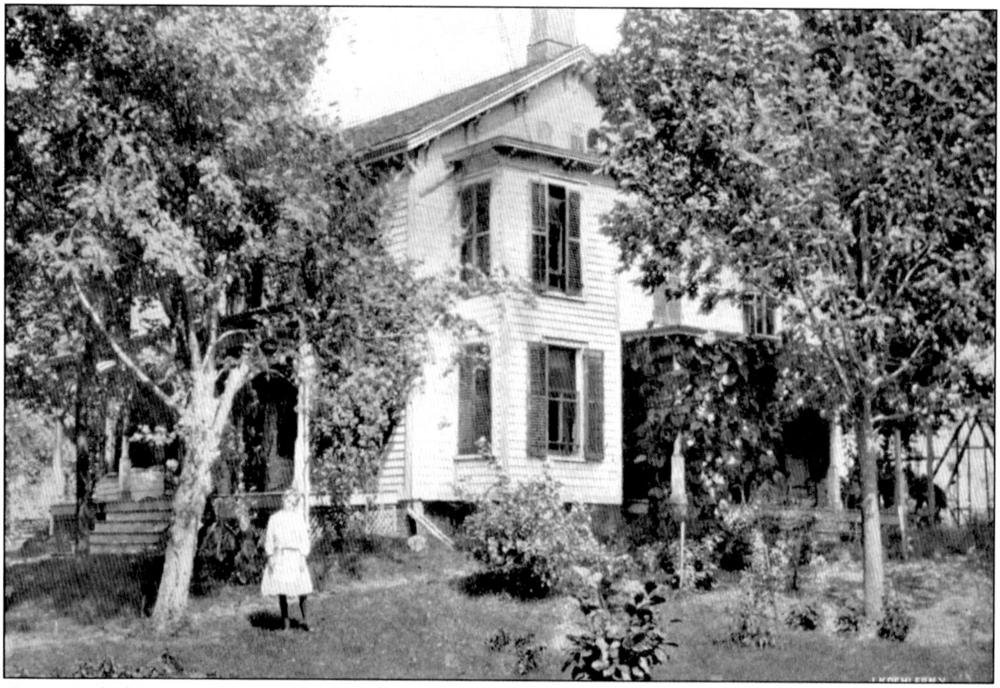

A young lady stops to pose for this shot of the Wells Cottage, as the locals referred to it. It was certainly a substantial cottage, and a lovely one, with morning glories climbing up the porch posts. The Wells family was a fixture in Moore's Mills for several generations.

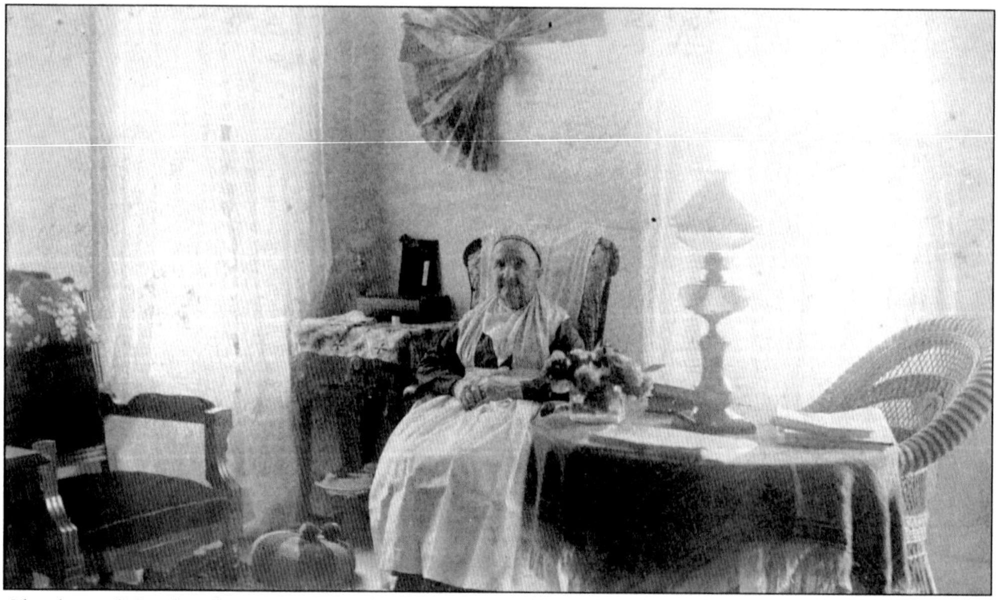

Charlotte (Haviland) Moore was the mother of Susan, Alfred, and Ruth Moore. She is seen here in a photograph from the late 1800s, likely a room in the Floral Home, with clothing and furnishings typical of the period. The Havilands were originally from the Quaker Hill area in Pawling.

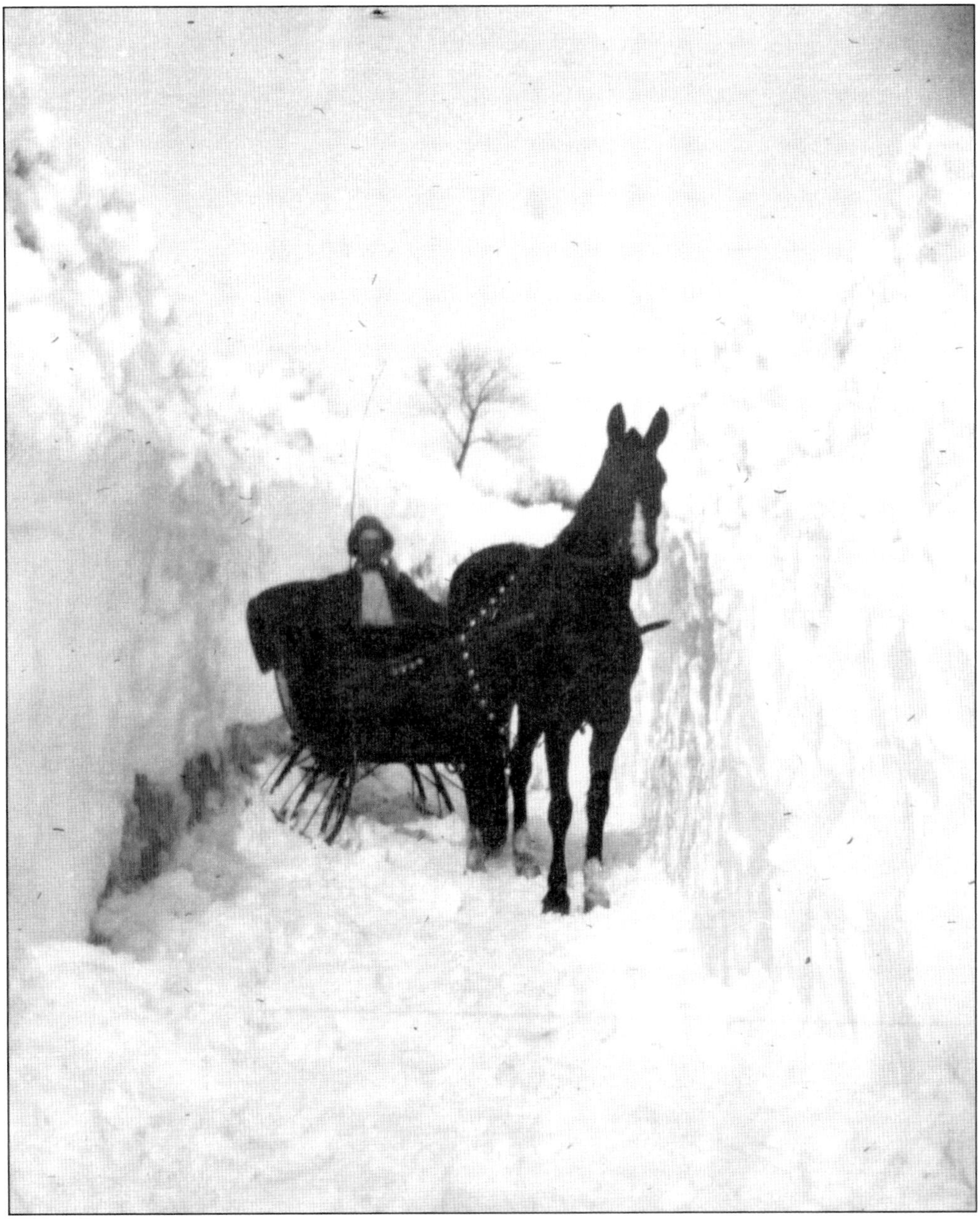

The winter weather was often brutal, and before snowplows existed, horse-drawn sleighs had to be depended on to get milk to the creamery, wheat to the mill, and doctors to their patients. The blizzard of 1888 must have presented a challenge to local residents, to say nothing of the poor "hosses."

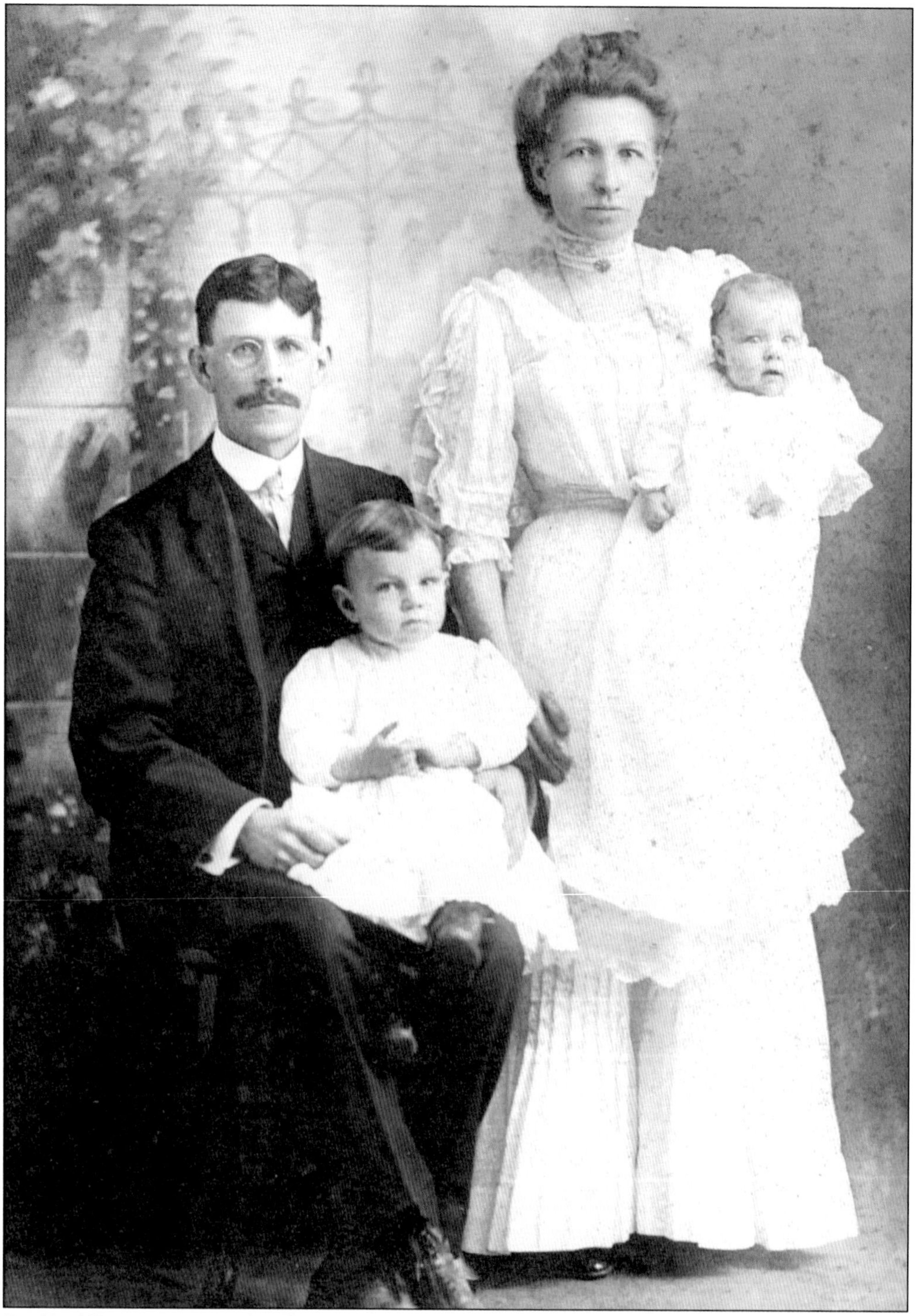

Bradford Yeomans married Lydia Houghtaling and had three children. Pictured here are Harold and Agnes. The Yeoman and Houghtaling families were some of the earliest settlers in Moore's Mills. Lydia was a teacher in the one-room schoolhouse, presumably before she was married, since it was generally required in those days that teachers be single women.

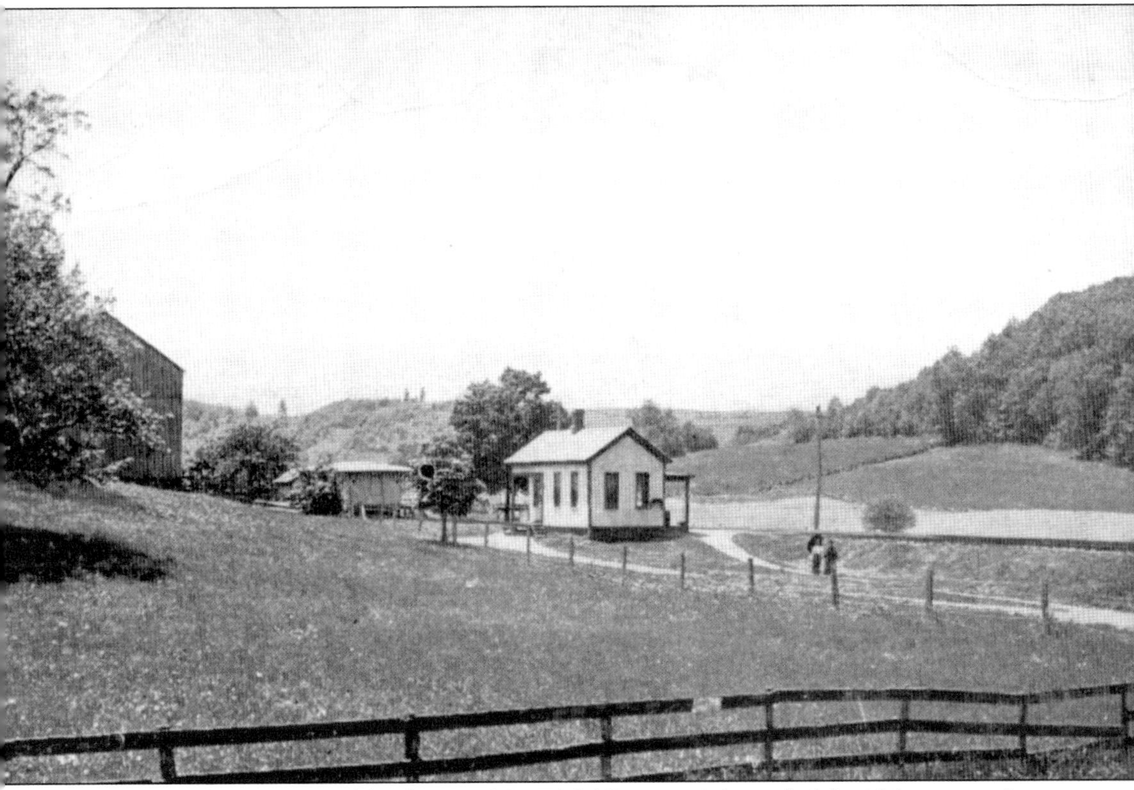

This postcard shows a view of the depot at Moore's Mills toward the end of the 19th century. Just down the tracks was a storage tank for water, for the trains to use as they came through. Telegrams were sent and received here also, at the American Express Office. Young William Wells was the delivery boy for messages, often taking his bicycle. There was a freight house with a scale on the opposite side of the tracks. Behind the office was another necessity—the outhouse.

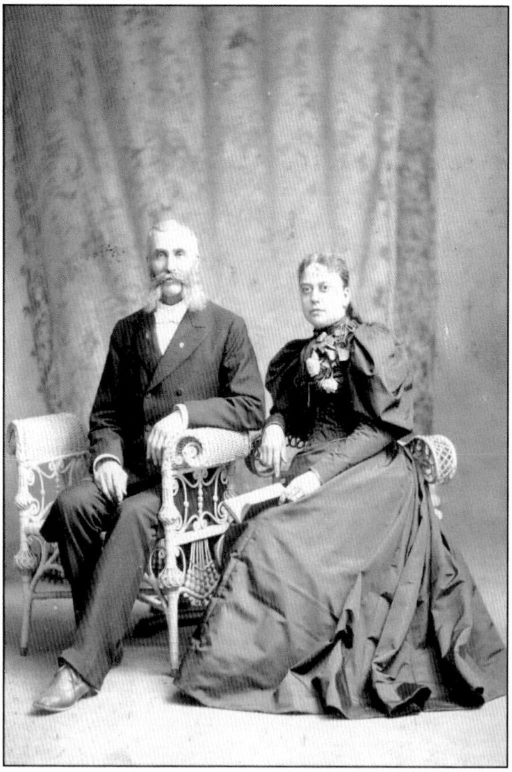

Joining two established families of LaGrange, Ruth Moore married Peter Akin Skidmore in 1895. Note the lovely Victorian wicker furniture and the flowing sideburns! Peter was the son of Jesse Skidmore; Ruth was the sister of Alfred and Susan Moore. She and her husband lived in Beekman after they were married.

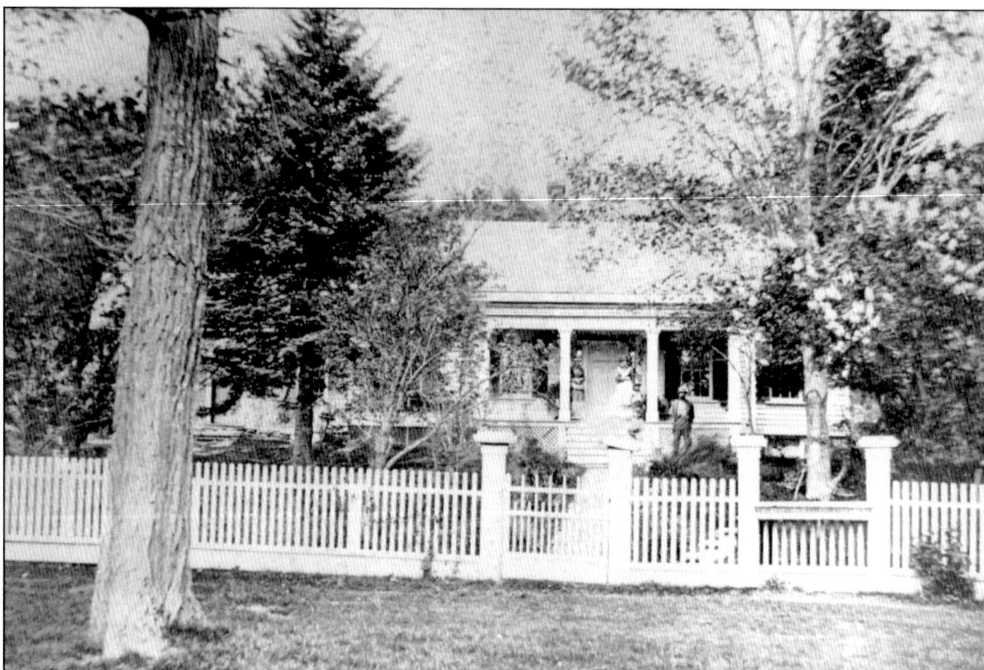

Although not identified, this was probably the parsonage on Dr. Fink Road. The surrounding fence had a feature that many of the era possessed, an opening with steps to assist the ladies in their long dresses to dismount gracefully from carriages.

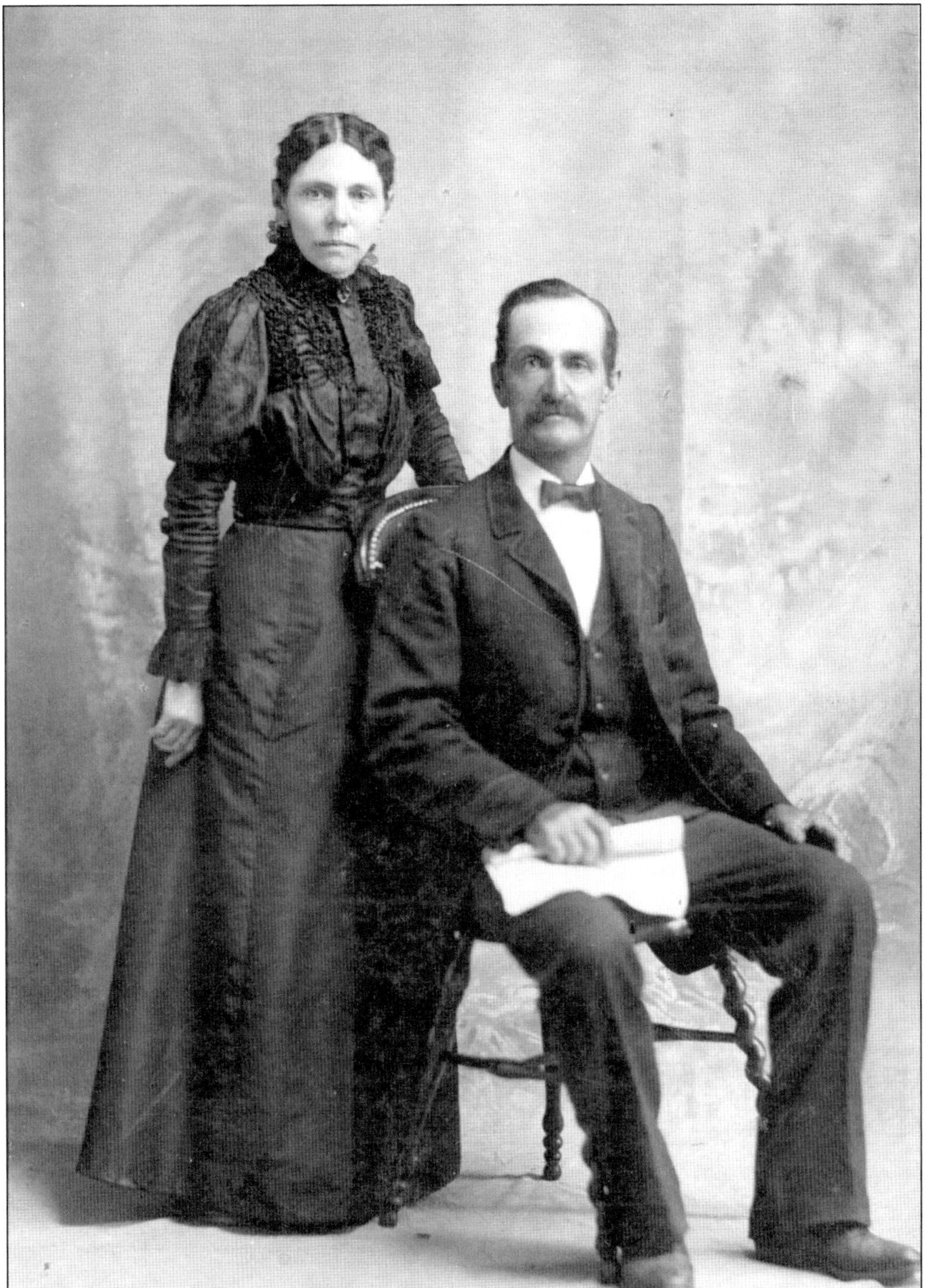

Henry and Rebecca Gidley pose for this formal portrait from the late 1870s. Henry brought his bride Rebecca (Jewell) to his family home on Gidley Road after they were married. Their children were Ida, William, Susie, George, and Jane (known as Jennie). An unnamed son died in infancy.

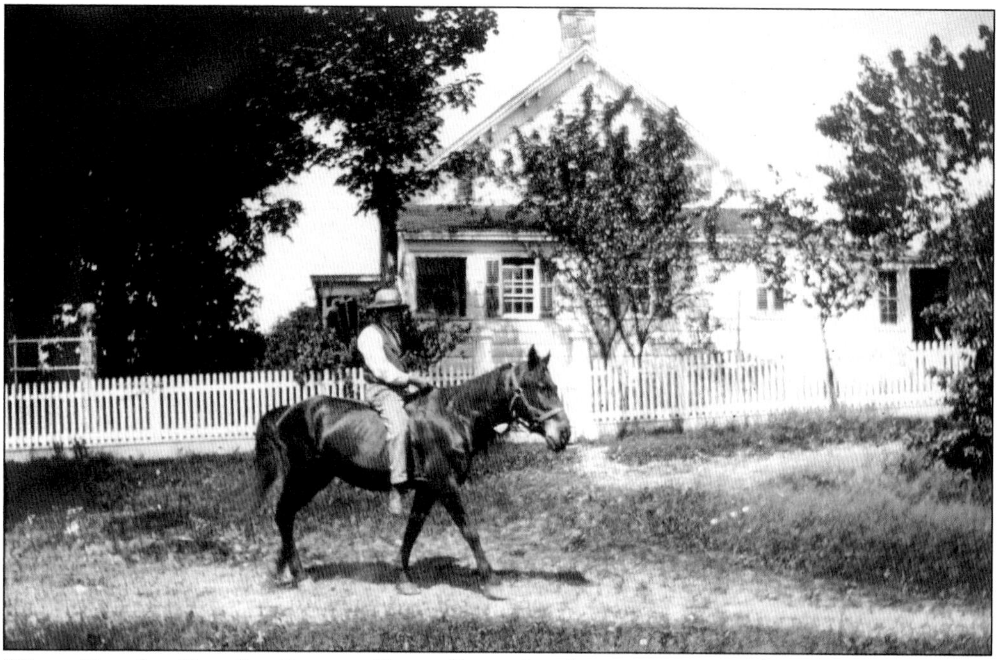

"Great-Grandpa Cromline Dean and horse George" is the inscription on this *c.* 1889 photograph taken on the Prospect Hill farm. It is part of a scrapbook assembled by a family member, showing many different views of the lovely property on Barmore Road, including one taken from the top of the windmill and one of the yearly hay gathering.

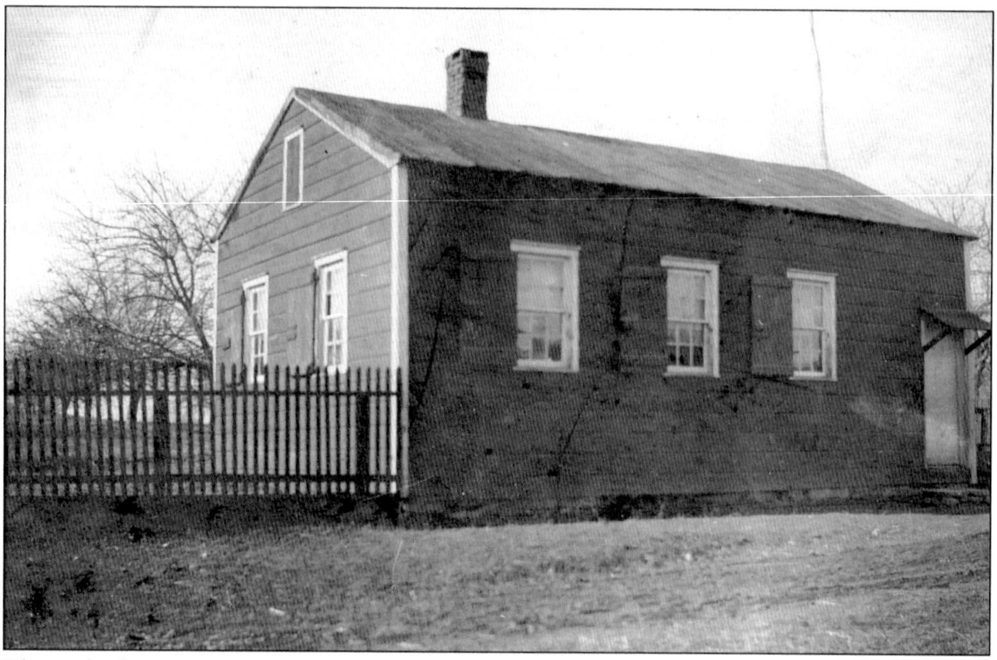

This is the first one-room schoolhouse in Manchester Bridge, torn down in 1902. A new building was then erected. This little country school had a moment of fame in 1937 when Eleanor Roosevelt paid a visit. She was impressed by the abilities of the school's teacher, Bessie Thatcher, as she later wrote in her column, "My Day."

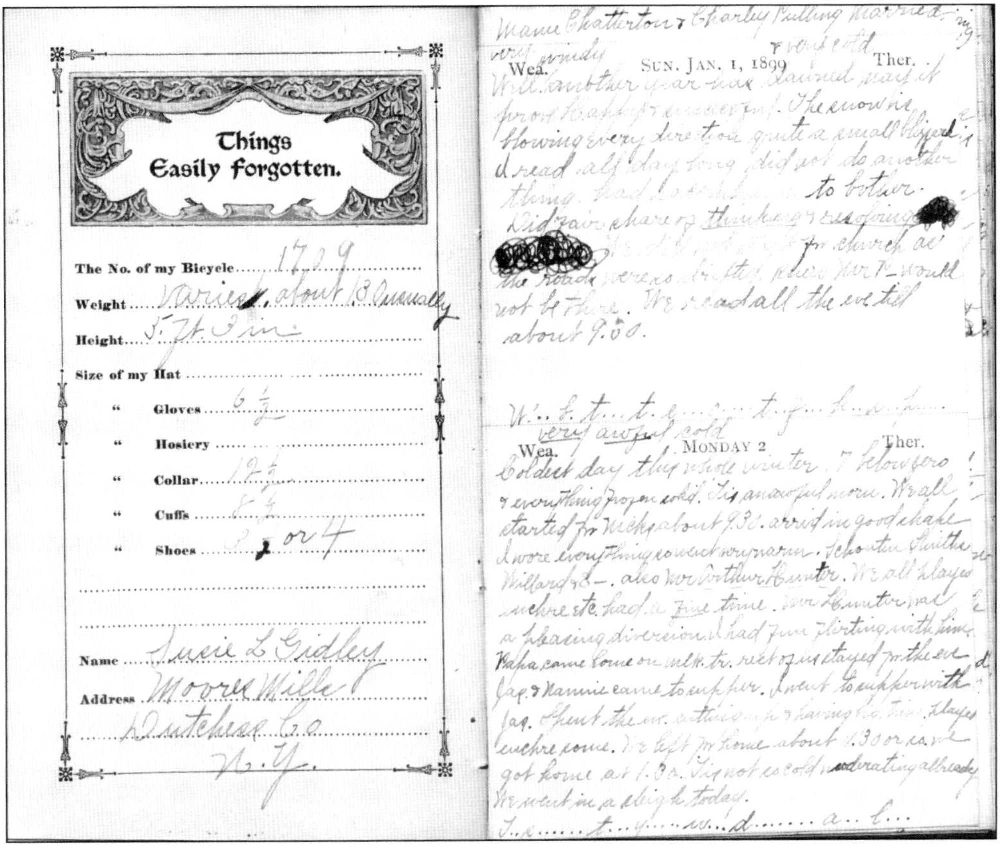
Things Easily Forgotten.

The No. of my Bicycle 1709

Weight varies, about 13[illegible]

Height 5 ft 3 in

Size of my Hat

" Gloves 6 1/2

" Hosiery

" Collar 12 1/2

" Cuffs 8 1/2

" Shoes 3 1/2 or 4

Name Susie L. Gidley

Address Moores Mills Dutchess Co. N.Y.

Wea. SUN. JAN. 1, 1899 Ther.

Wea. MONDAY 2 Ther.

This journal was kept by a teenaged Susie Gidley for the year 1899. She records the many visits paid by neighbors, parties and dances attended, and letters received during the year as well as some town gossip. Susie, her husband Francis Jay Skidmore, and daughter, Hazel, all kept daily diaries throughout their lives.

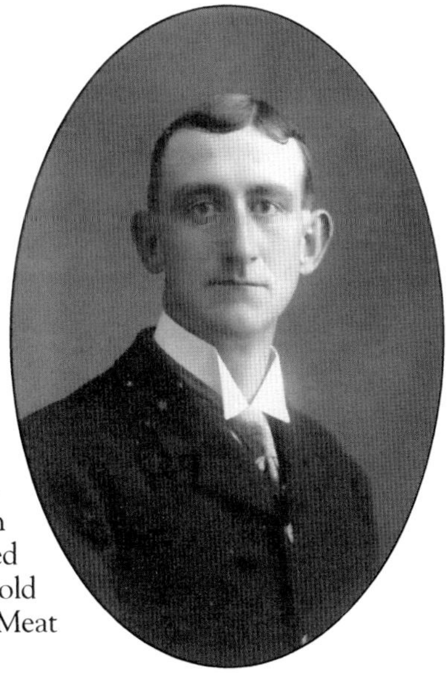

Jesse Alley wore many hats during his years in LaGrange; in addition to running a feed store, he grew apples with business partner George Kuchler, raised sheep, and acted as postal carrier. He also raised fattened calves that he sold for slaughter. One of his steady customers was Wade's Meat Market. (MD.)

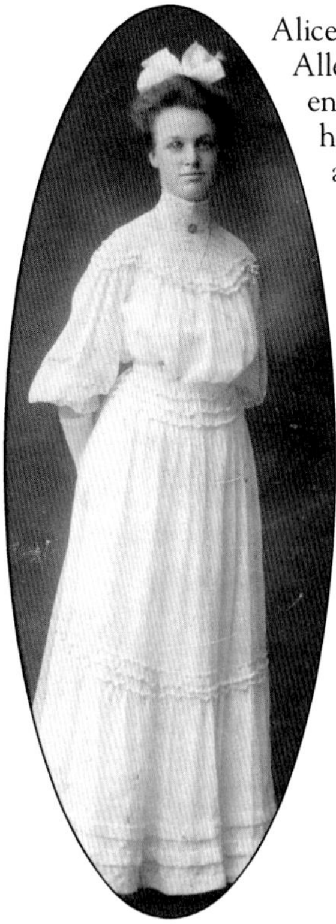

Alice Jane Townsend's family had a home on Long Hill. She married Jesse Alley in 1889, and they raised their family in a house at the western end of Alley Road. Alice was a teacher at the Billings school before her marriage. The Townsends, all Quakers, have a long history in the area. (MD.)

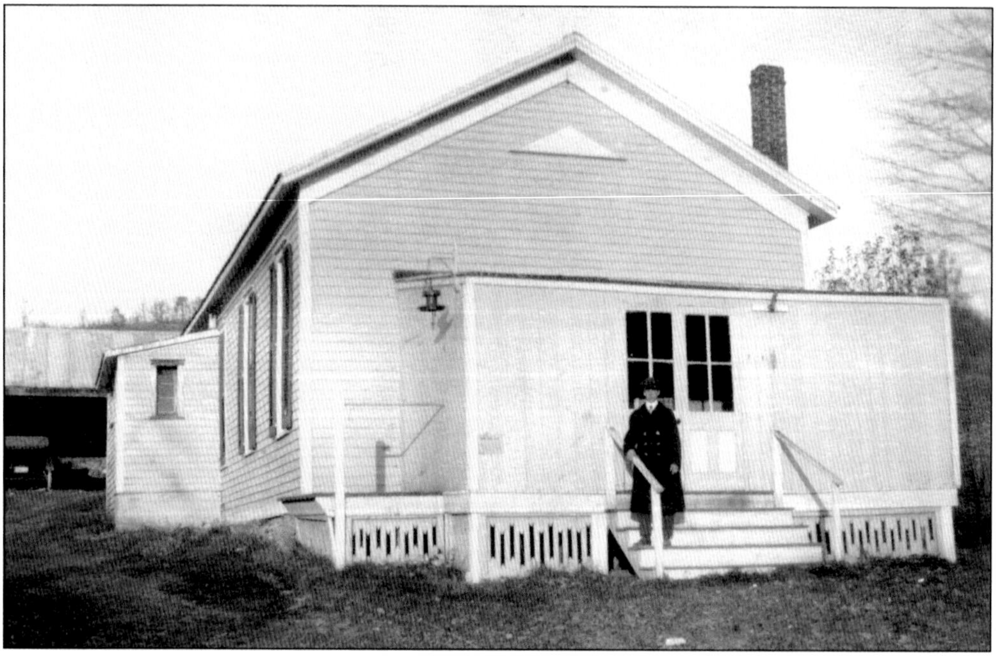

The William Wells Community House in Moore's Mills was used for town activities such as lectures and meetings. Even the smallest communities usually had such a place, referred to as the community hall or lyceum, as people preferred not to have to travel too far from home for their entertainment.

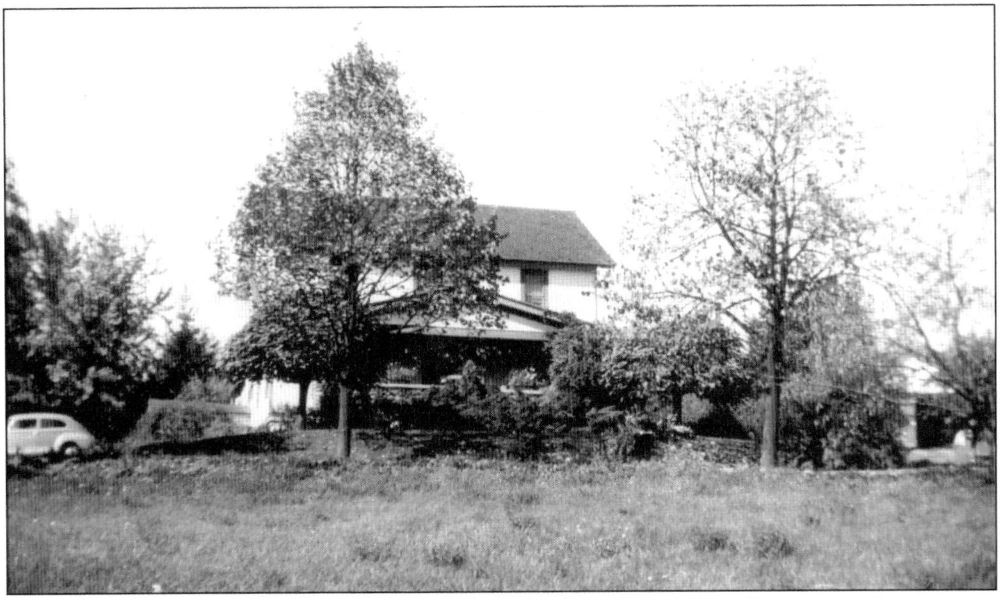

This home on the western end of Alley Road was built by Jesse Alley, along with a feed store to the left that was later torn down. The house remains, although somewhat altered. Nearby fruit orchards were also owned by the Alleys and were another source of income. (MD.)

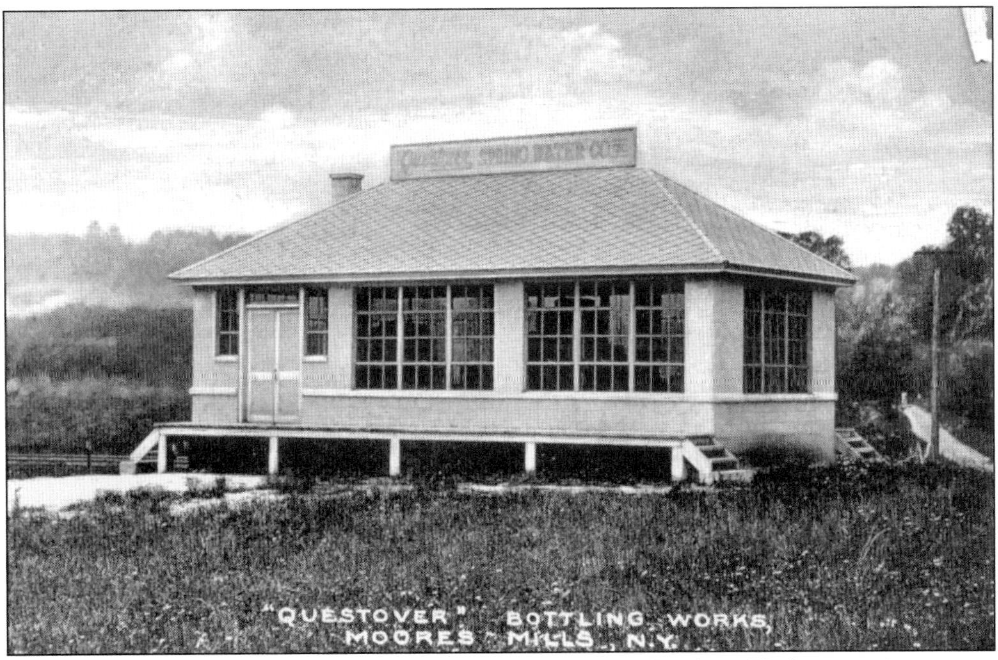

What resembles a train depot was home of the Questover Bottling Works near the present Rockledge Herb Farm. A local spring supplied the water that was bottled here, near the railroad, which made for easy distribution. Local collector Art Church has an original bottle from the Questover plant.

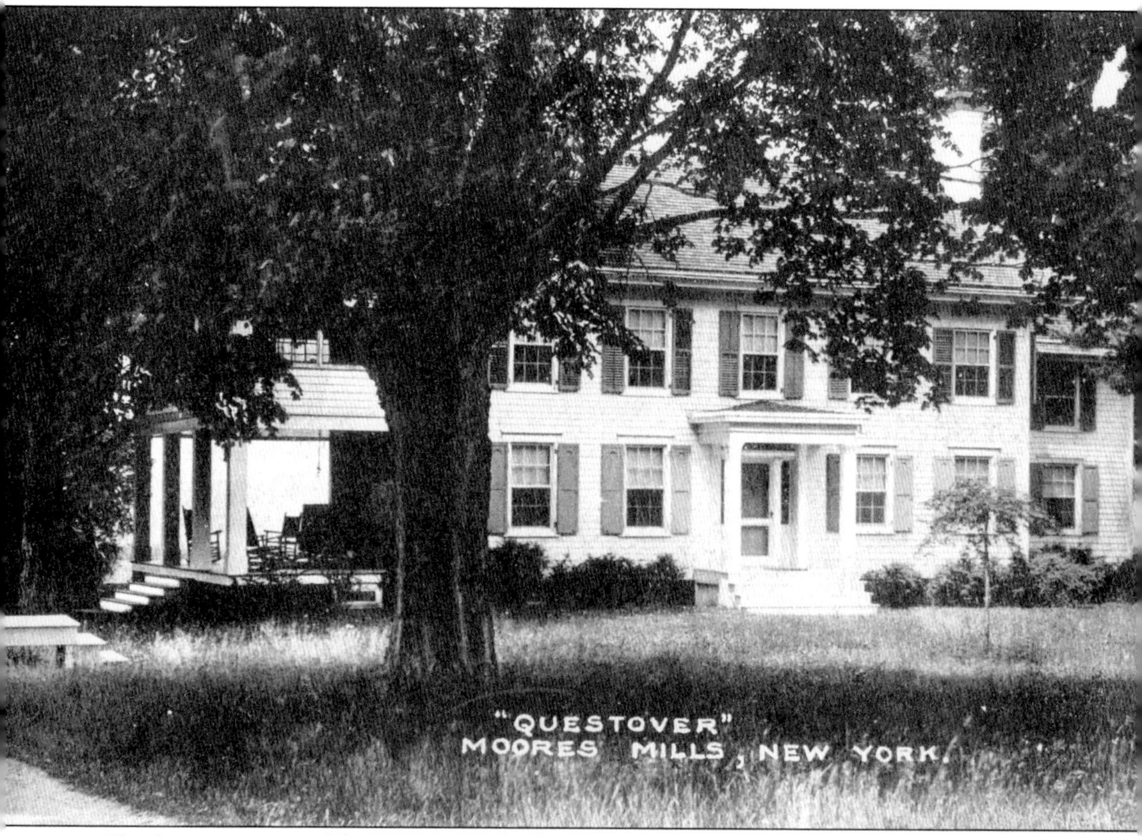

This house was part of the property of the Questover bottling center and stills stands on Route 82 near Moore's Mills. Formerly owned by both the Crosby and Williams families, it is an attractive home, with a unique second-story porch.

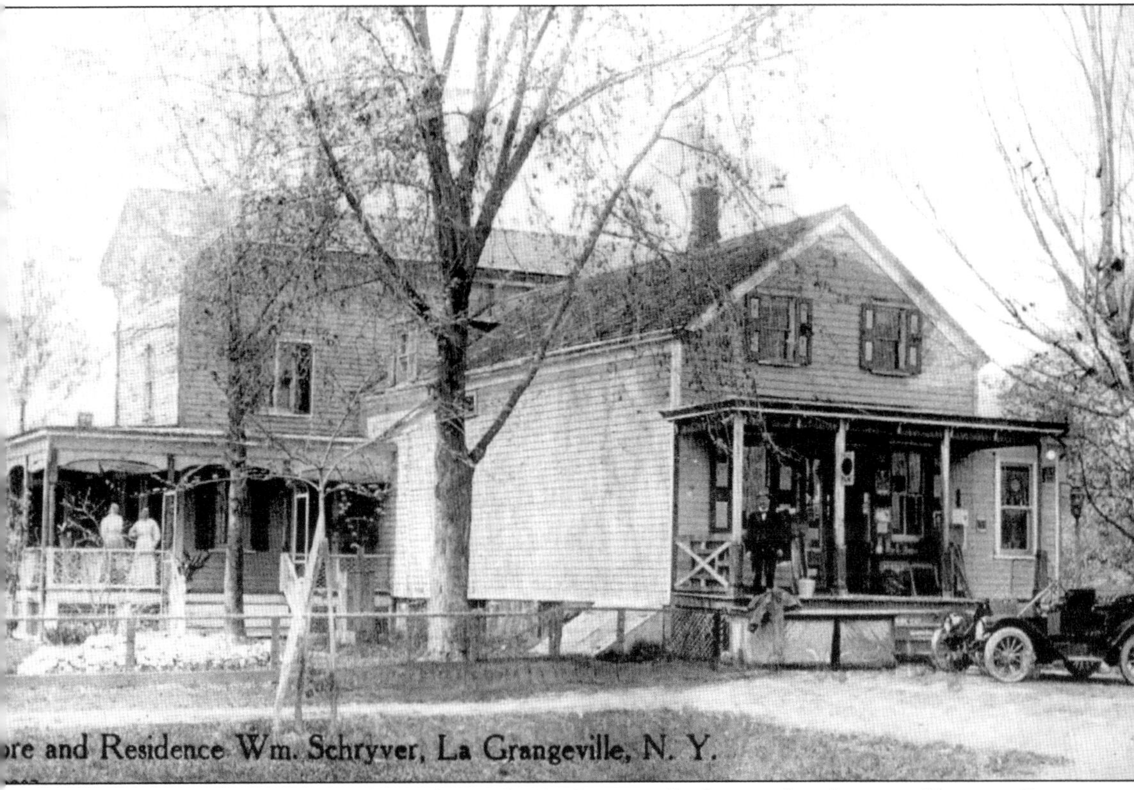

William Schryver ran a general store located in LaGrangeville. It served as the post office as well, beginning in 1914. William's wife Alice Schryver acted as postmistress behind the counter, while the postmasters braved the weather to make the mail deliveries. It is said that the postmasters always belonged to the political party that was in office at that time. (AC.)

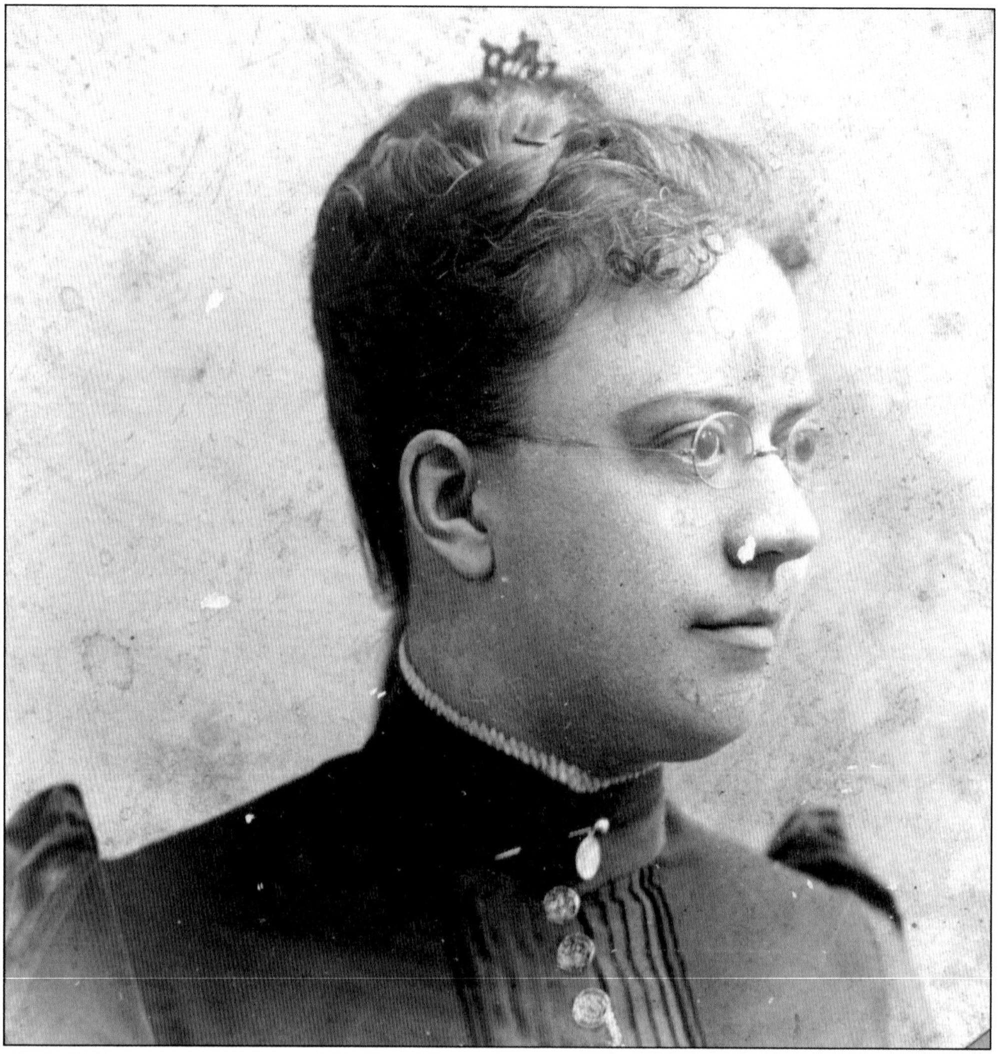

Phebe Osborn was a cousin to Alfred and Susan Moore. She was the daughter of William Osborn and his wife Content (Moore). The Osborns were from the Pawling area, and both William and Content are buried in the Quaker Hill cemetery. Phebe married Seneca Stevens.

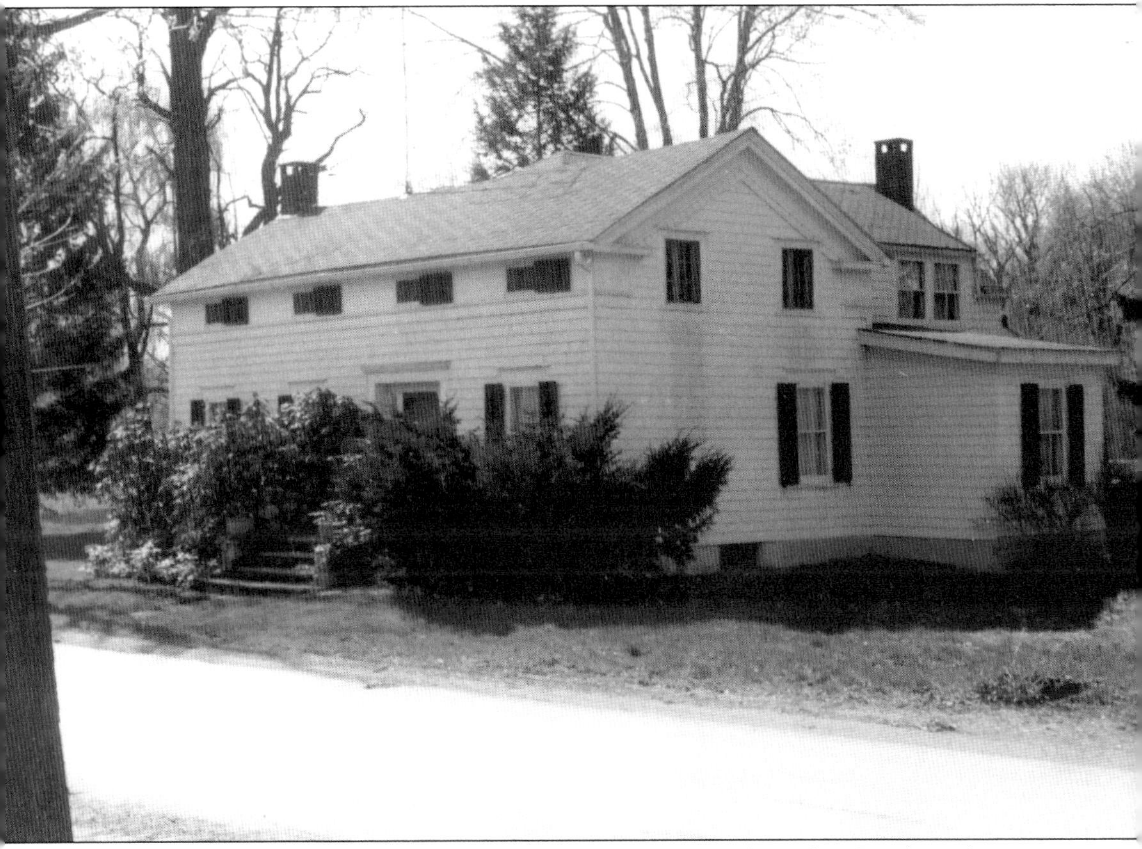

The home of Dr. Austin Fink stood at the corner of Route 55 and Freedom Road, until it was torn down in the late 1990s. Dr. Fink was a popular local physician who was known for his kindness and generosity. His house served as a post office just before the dawn of the 20th century. The mailboxes were still there and intact in the 1950s, when the home was purchased by the Burdick family.

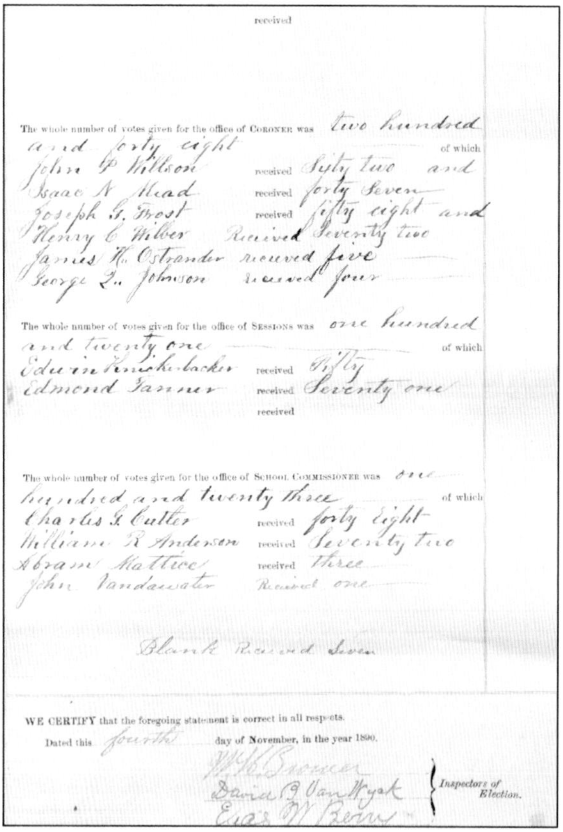

received

The whole number of votes given for the office of CORONER was two hundred and forty eight of which

John P Willson received Sixty two and
Isaac N Mead received forty seven
Joseph G. Frost received fifty eight and
Henry C Wilber Received Seventy two
James H. Ostrander received five
George L. Johnson received four

The whole number of votes given for the office of SESSIONS was one hundred and twenty one of which

Edwin Knickerbacker received Fifty
Edmond Tanner received Seventy one
received

The whole number of votes given for the office of SCHOOL COMMISSIONER was one hundred and twenty three of which

Charles G. Cutter received forty eight
William R Anderson received Seventy two
Abram Mattice received three
John Vandawater Received one

Blank Received Seven

WE CERTIFY that the foregoing statement is correct in all respects.

Dated this fourth day of November, in the year 1890.

W. H. Brower
David G Van Wyck
Elias M Benn
} Inspectors of Election.

This certificate of canvass is dated November 1890. It shows the votes received by candidates for the offices of court of appeals judge, assembly members, congressional representative, school commissioner, and coroner. Most of the offices were won by a landslide—in one case, by 119 to 1.

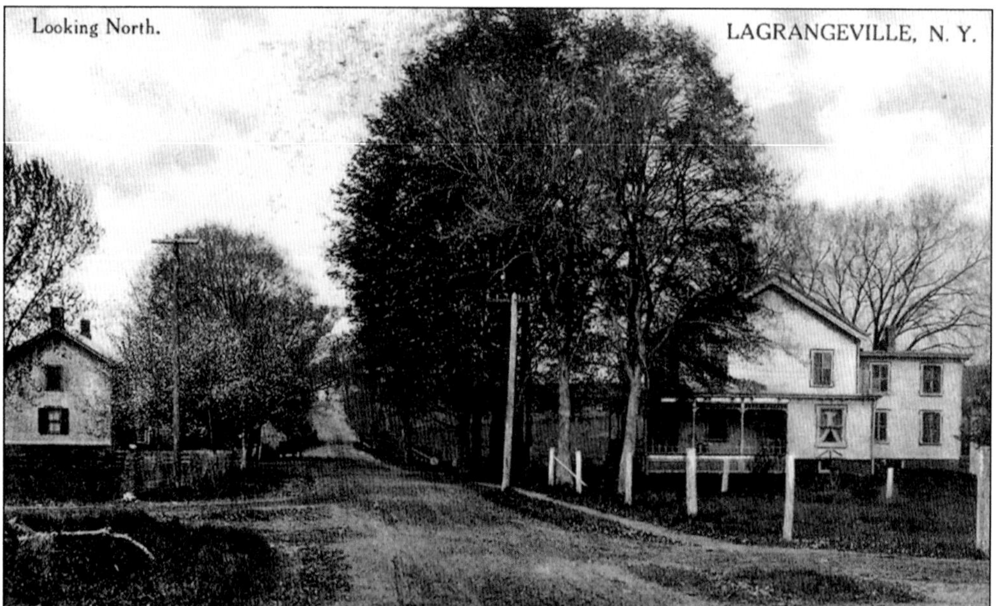

Here is a view of LaGrangeville looking north. At the south end of Budd Lane can still be seen the barn that was once a blacksmith shop. The house on the right belonged to the Benedicts. Parts of the hamlet still look similar to this scene from the dawn of the 20th century. (AC.)

Three

From Prosperity to the Great Depression

As the Victorian era ended, modern times brought social changes, one of which was the temperance movement. Political parties in LaGrange campaigned as being either for or against Prohibition. Most towns had temperance societies, as did LaGrange, in which members agreed to abstain from the use of alcohol. This movement seemed to have a lasting effect on the town, as it has never had many drinking establishments within its borders.

Soon World War I was looming. Many local families said goodbye to their young sons as they left for the European battleground. Residents sought to divert themselves from the uncertainty with patriotic festivals and other entertainment.

The troubles continued with the stock market crash of 1929, bringing on the Depression. Many residents of LaGrange were still able to grow much of their food and fare a little better than those in the cities. Nevertheless, it was a challenging time for farmers, with the prices dropping continuously. These difficulties, and rising taxes, would force many to give up land that their families had farmed for generations.

LaGrange remained a close-knit community during these difficult times. Quaker membership had decreased, but both the Methodist and Presbyterian Churches had large fellowships. Evenings were often spent attending a church supper, school play, or other special event. The Grange hall, constructed in 1925, often held dances or recitals, as did the lyceum in Arthursburg.

In the late 1930s, plans were being made for what would have a major impact on LaGrange—the building of the Taconic State Parkway. Originally designed as a scenic drive, the parkway had few travelers in its early days. No one could have guessed then how numerous the newfangled automobiles would eventually become, and how a steady stream of southern neighbors would soon make LaGrange their home.

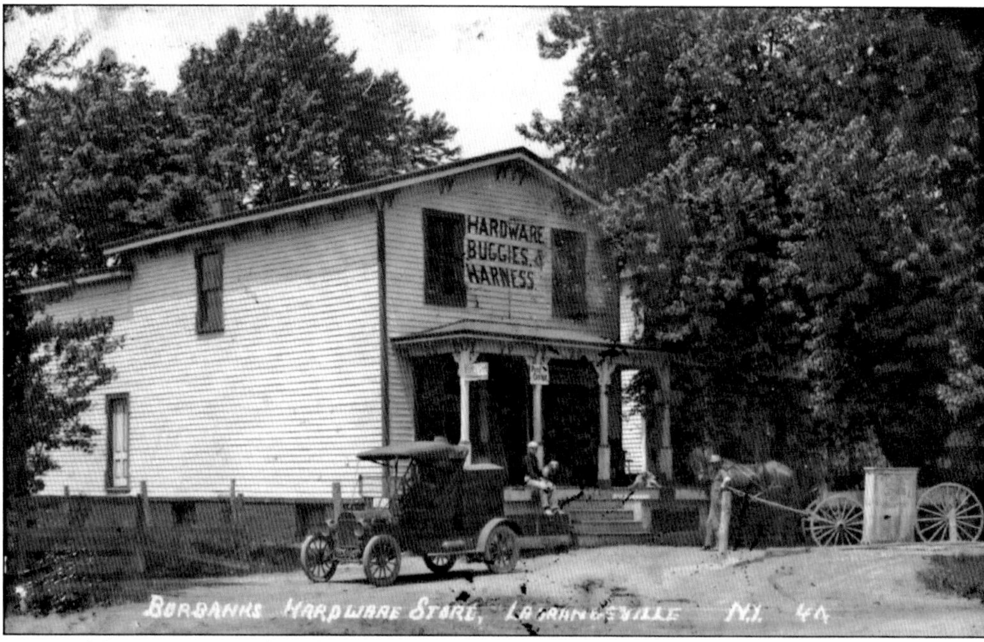

Past and future meet in this photograph of the local hardware store. Automobiles were all the rage in the early part of the century, but there were still plenty of horses being used, so this establishment provided for those needs as well. A customer relaxes on the porch as a pair of dogs laze nearby. (AC.)

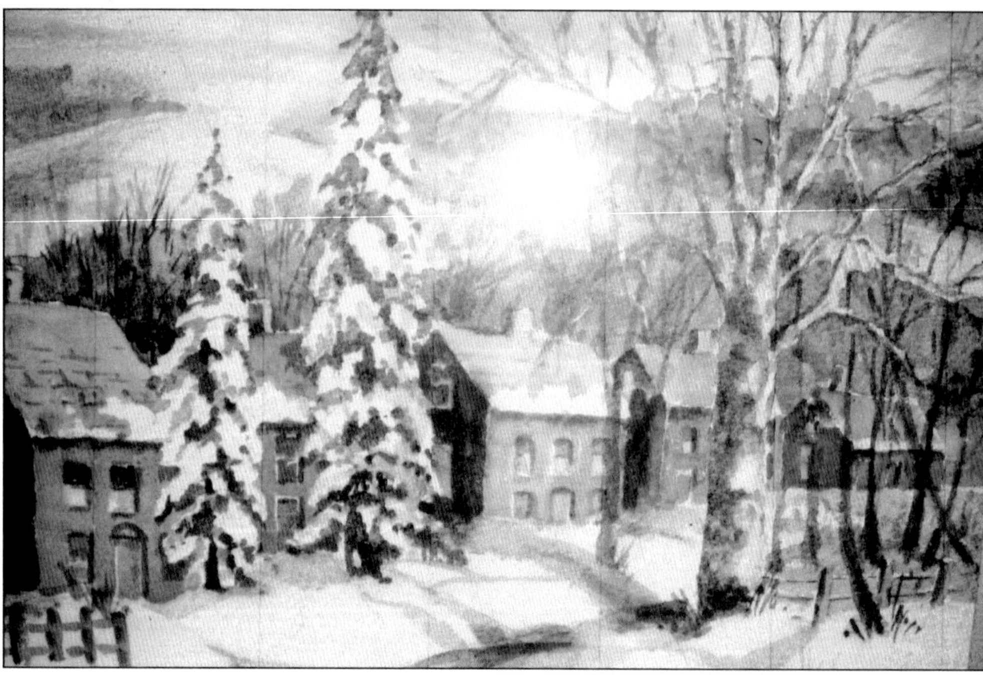

Artist Kay Gardner captured the brick row before it was torn down. The 1875 structures, situated on the east side of Route 55 near the present trailer park, were home to employees of the nearby Titus mills. A tale is told that efforts were made to save the ancient tree in the foreground, when the road was being widened. But it, too, is now long gone. (WH.)

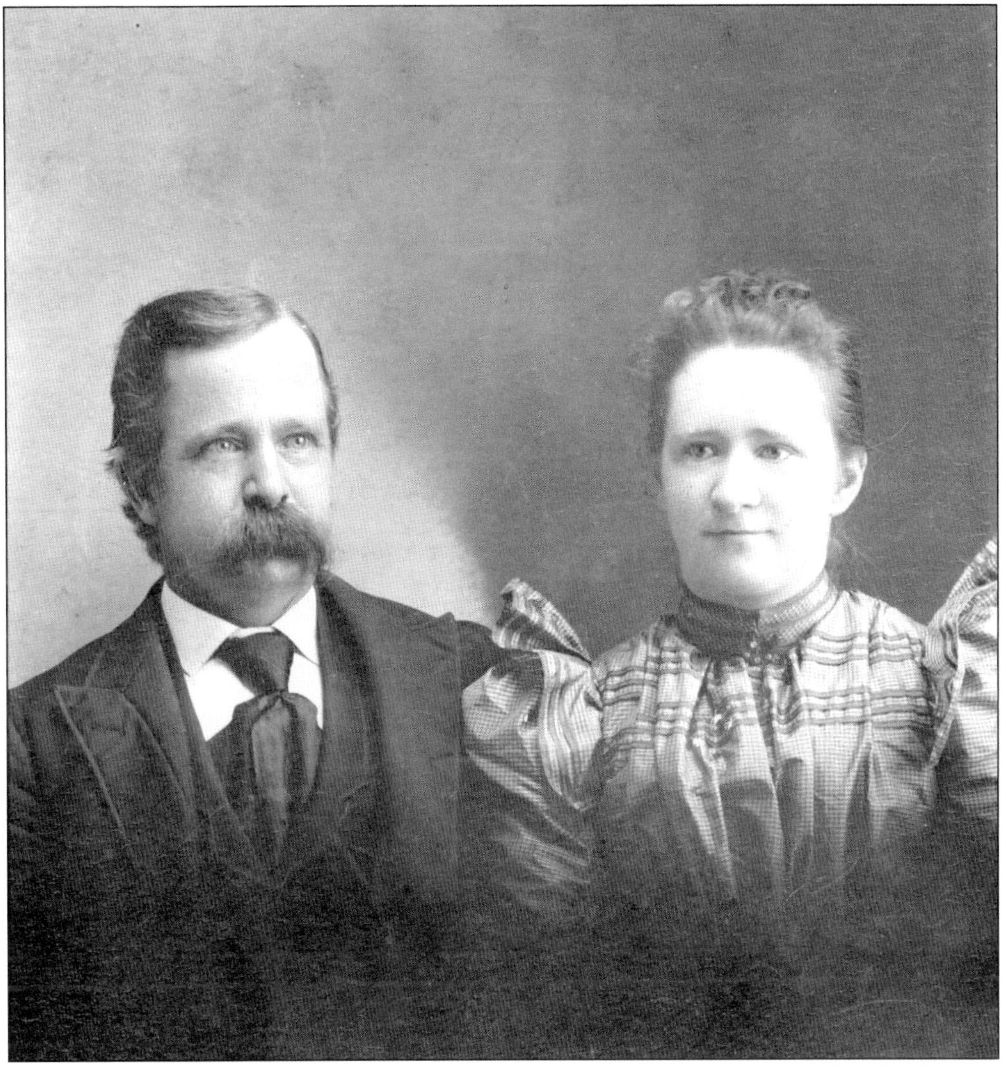

George Stevens Wells and Nellie (Haviland) Wells married in 1893 and ran the Floral Home after the death of Susan Moore, Nellie's cousin. George was the telegrapher at the Moore's Mills station for 40 years, while Nellie was very active in the Women's Christian Temperance Union. She was vice president when she died in 1922.

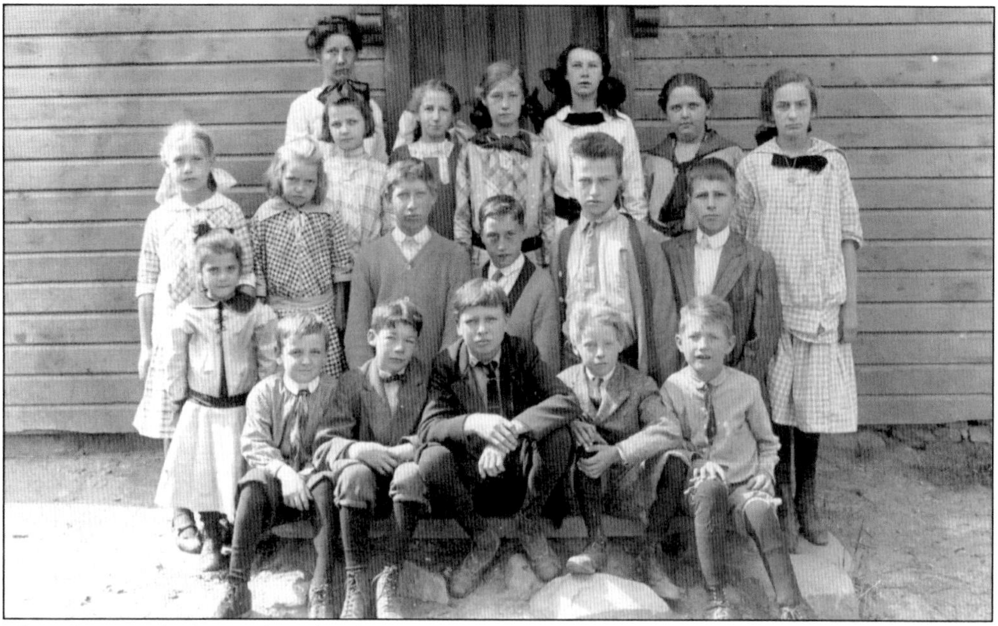

This photograph shows the school in Moore's Mills around 1905. Attending at that time were children of the Melgaard, Page, and Shafer families, and one student named Mary Christmas!

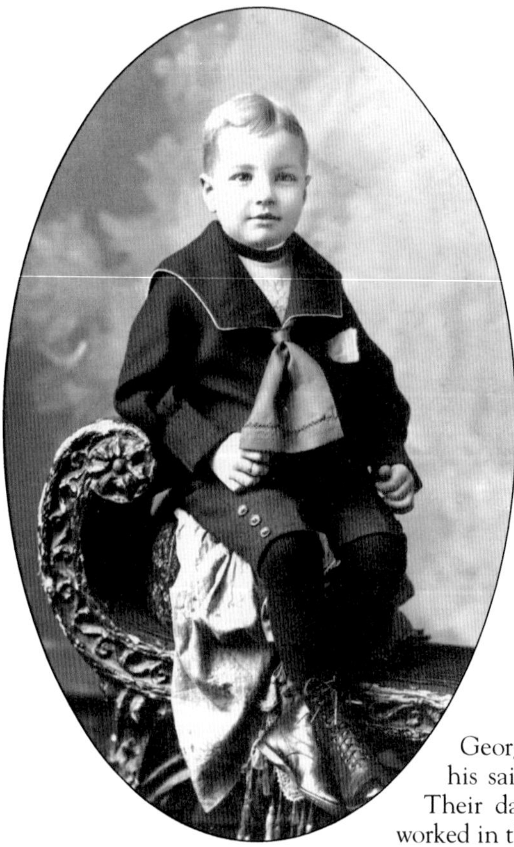

George Wade II was quite a dashing young man in his sailor suit. He married Ada Post in the 1930s. Their daughter Lois married Everett Clement, who worked in the meat market with the Wades. (GW.)

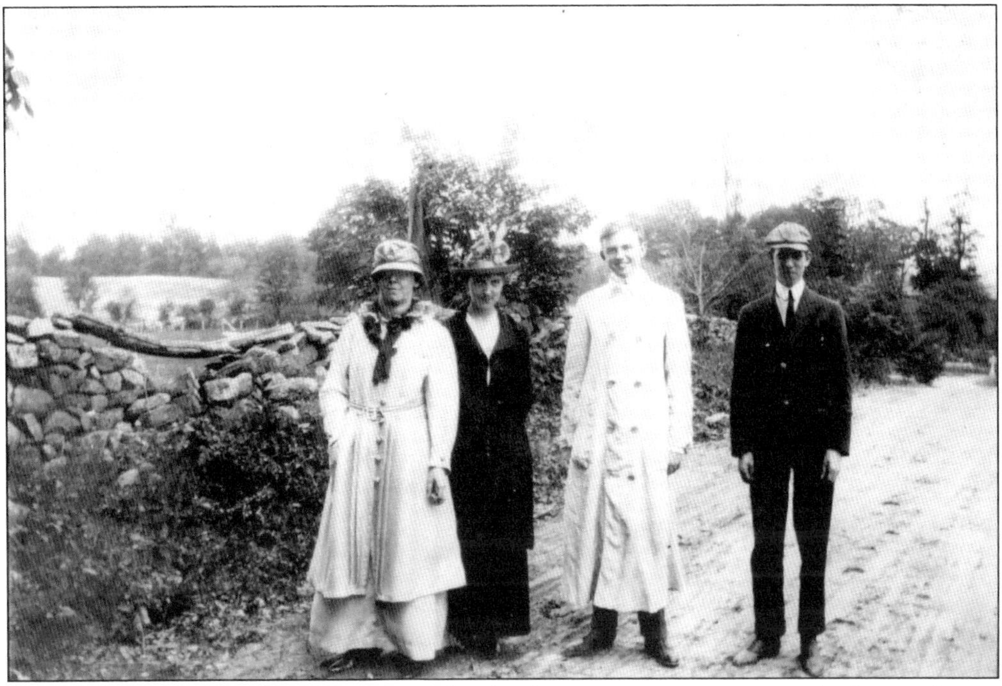

The rural countryside of LaGrange was a lovely place to get some exercise, whether on foot or bicycle. This group got dressed up for their walk, the woman on the far left wore her fox stole for the outing. Some favorite hikes included Sunset Hill and Oswego Road.

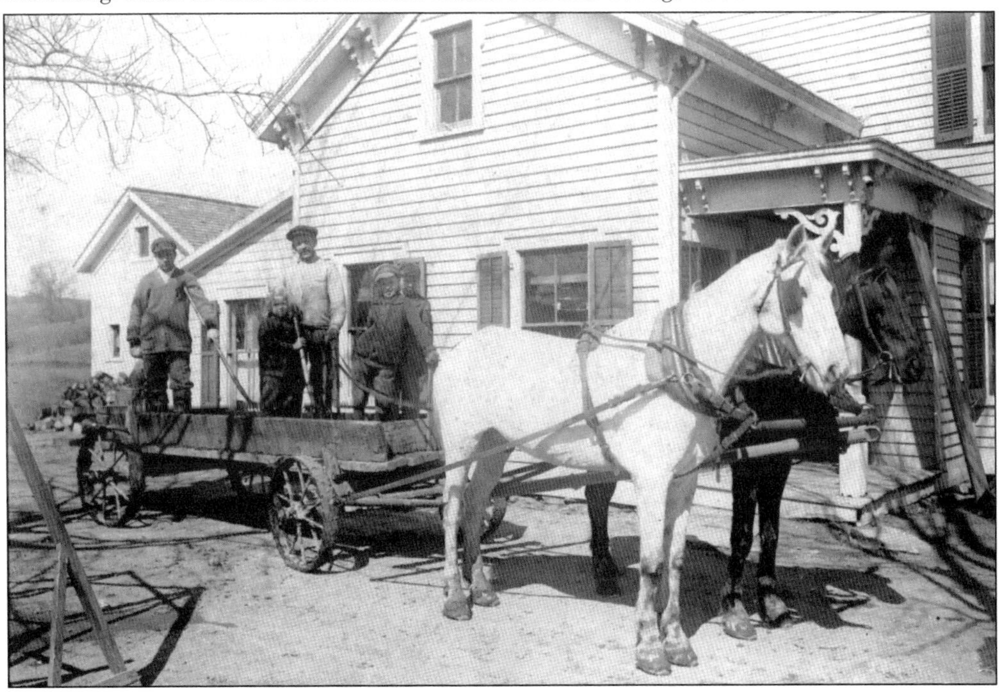

The young Wade boys, along with Charlie McCabe, have the horses harnessed and ready to go in front of the Wade homestead in this c. 1920 photograph. The house was on Freedom Road and is now owned by the Trott family. (GW.)

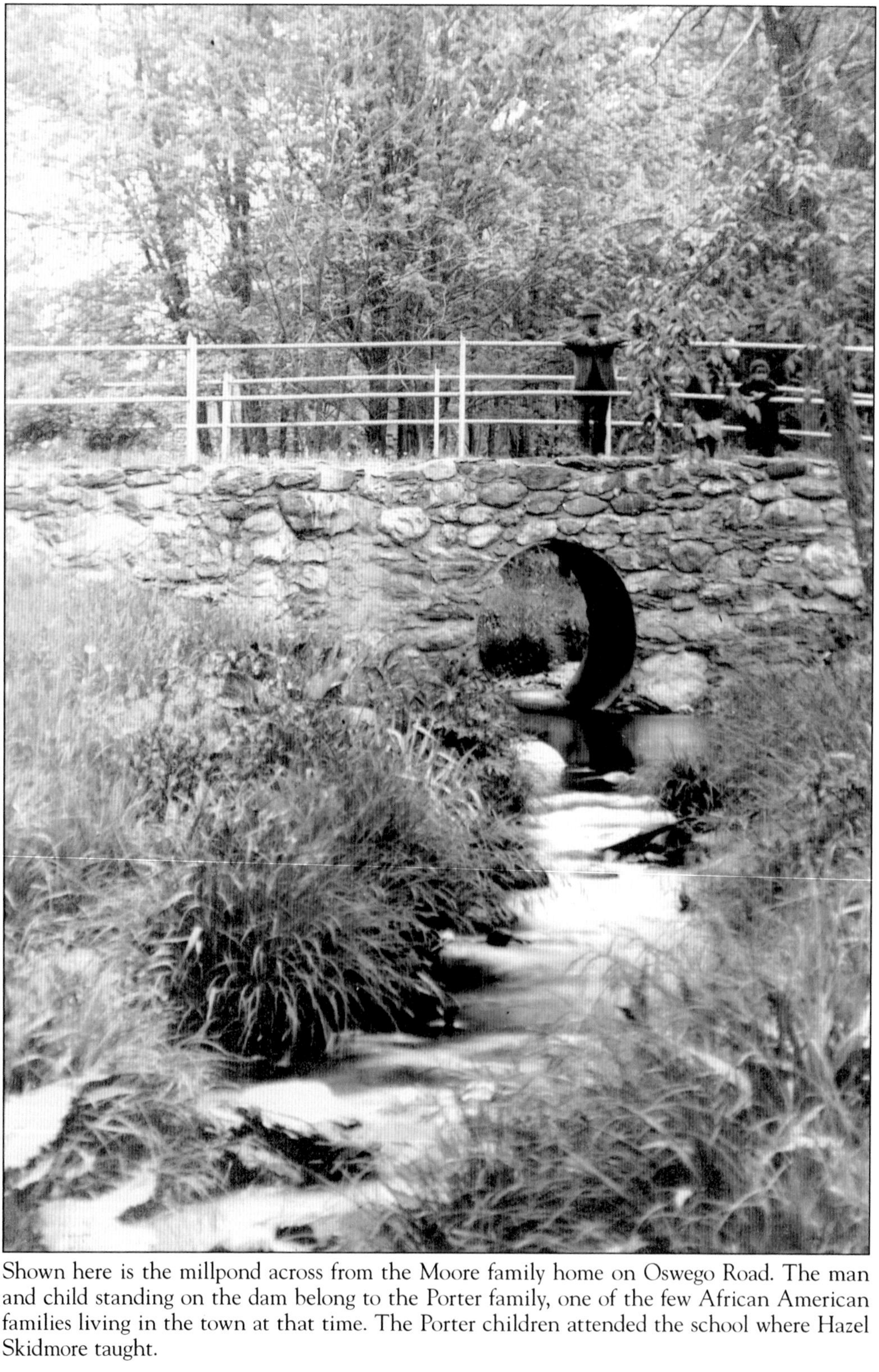

Shown here is the millpond across from the Moore family home on Oswego Road. The man and child standing on the dam belong to the Porter family, one of the few African American families living in the town at that time. The Porter children attended the school where Hazel Skidmore taught.

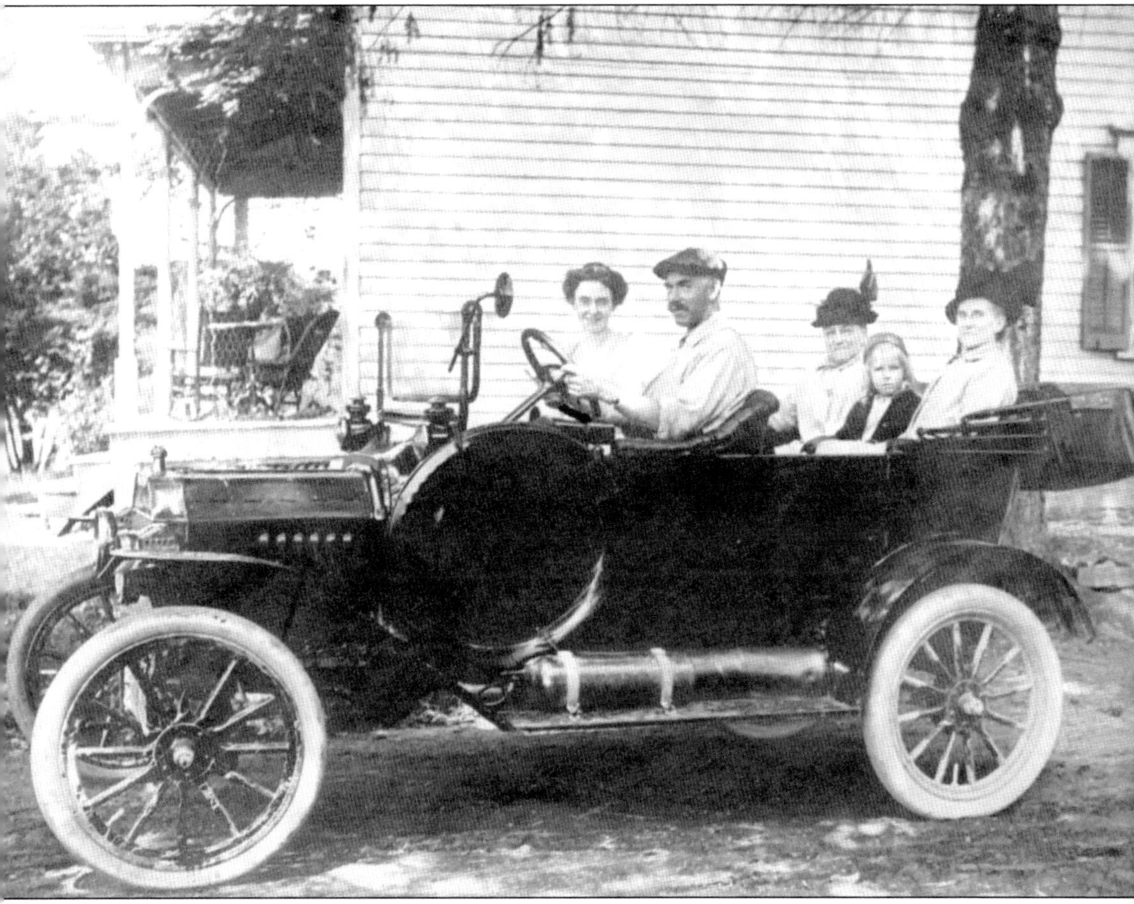

The Wade family is enjoying its snazzy new automobile in the 1920s, with Monfort at the wheel. Young George II sits in back between his grandmother and aunt, wearing the long curls that were common on little boys at the time. Cars were still a novelty then, as evidenced by the excited expressions. (GW.)

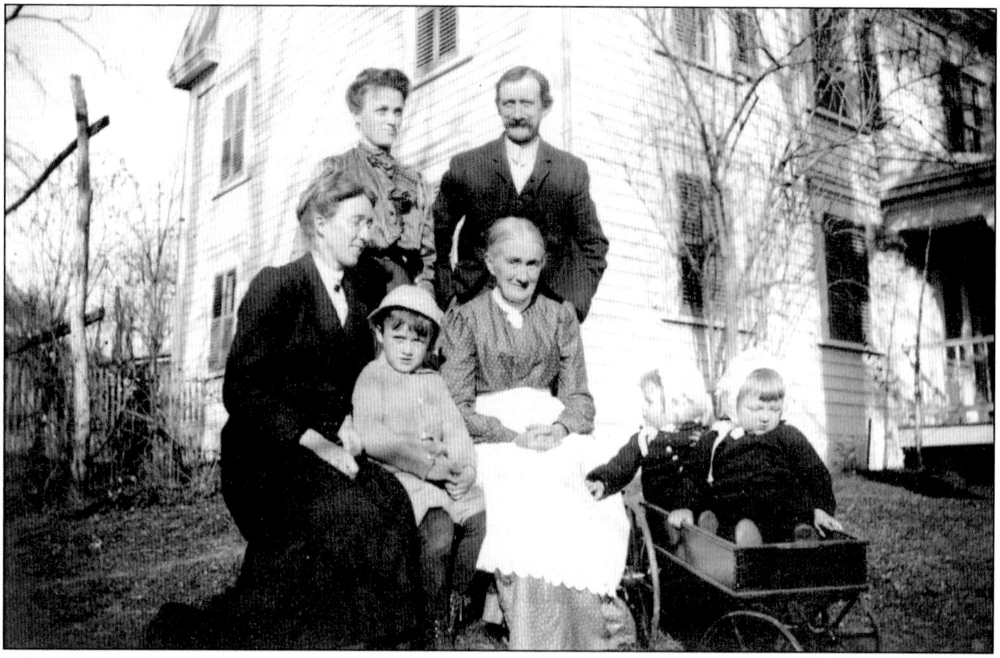

The Alleys are shown on the lawn of the family farmhouse on Noxon road. The property belonged to Jesse's father, Henry, and was a sheep farm for many years. Pictured seated in front of Alice and Jesse are Jesse's sister (possibly Ida) and his mother Ester, with young Franklin sitting between. The twins, Milton and Mildred, sit patiently in their wagon. (MD.)

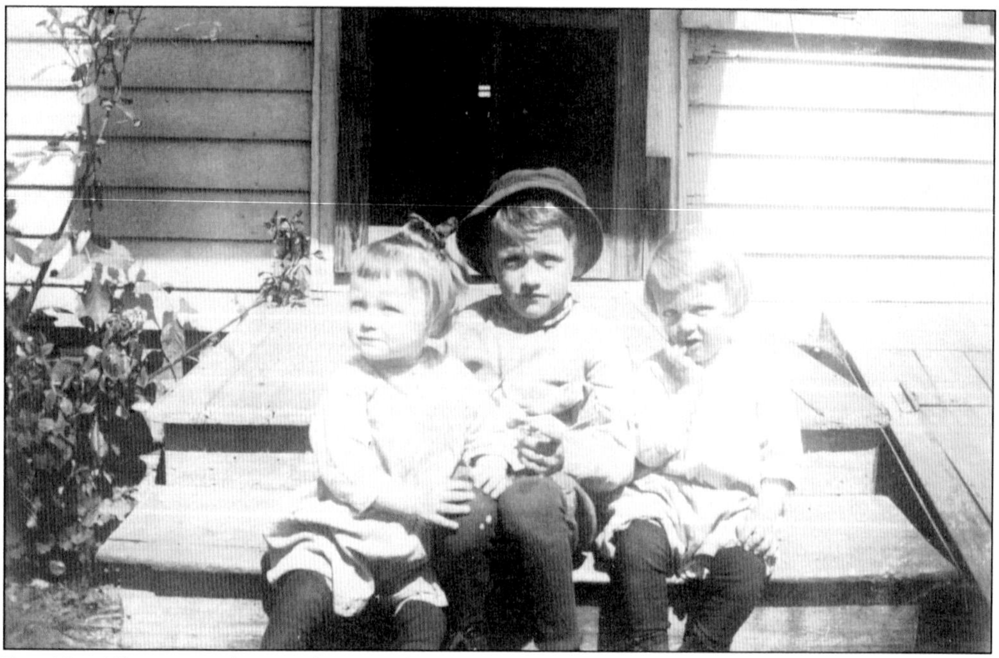

Franklin Alley sits on the steps between his siblings Mildred and Milton. Franklin later succumbed to leukemia and passed away before he reached his teens. His sister Mildred remembers him receiving blood transfusions, but in those days of few medical options it was not enough to save him. (MD.)

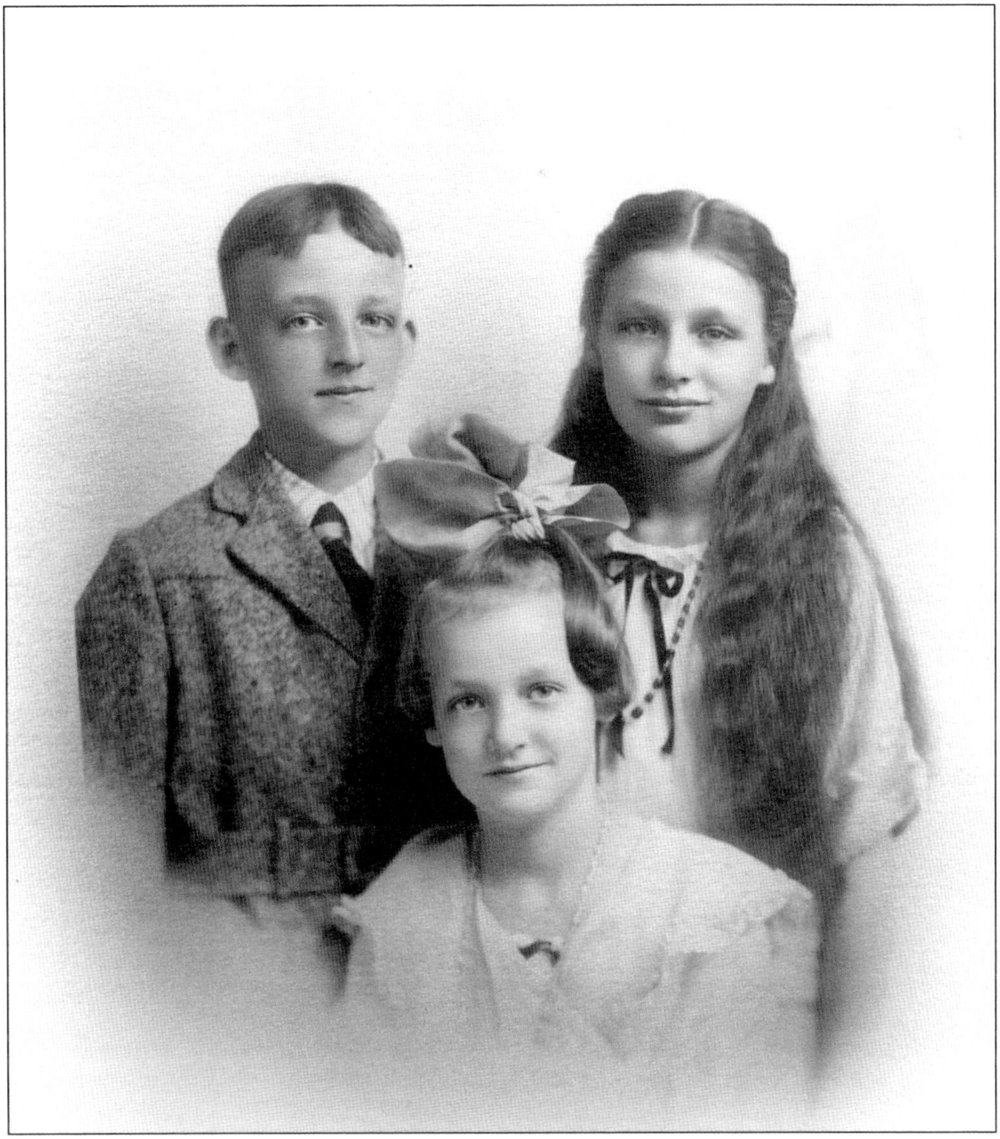

Twins Mildred and Milton Alley are shown here with their blond sister Dorothy. Milton went to Boston as a young man, to study engineering, and then returned home to work in the family business that later became Milton Alley Agway. Mildred became a teacher, teaching at the schoolhouse on Velie Road for several years. She later married Louis Doughty, from Hopewell. (MD.)

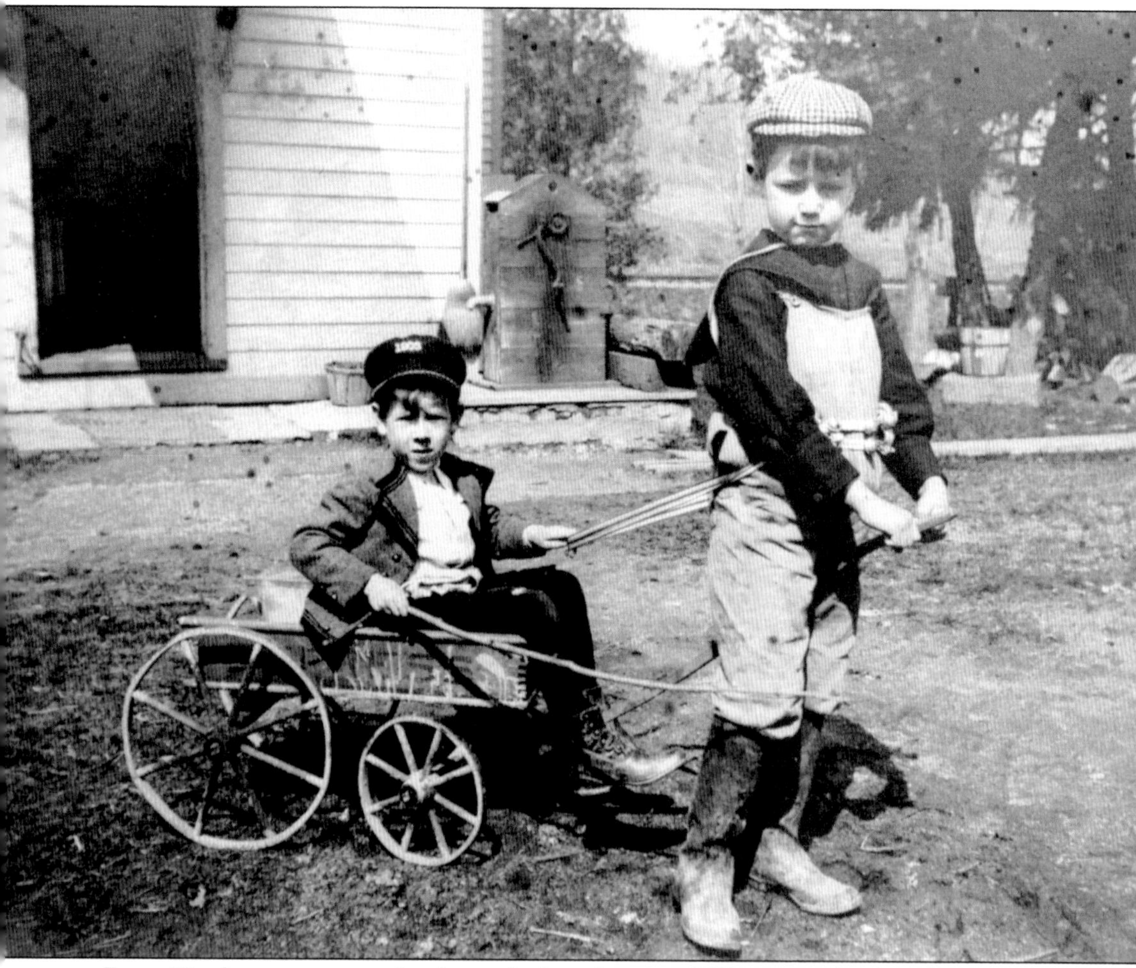

Evart Watchorn agrees to play horse for his playmate William Haviland Wells as they pose for this photograph. Evart's parents had purchased the former Floral Home from George and Nellie Wells. Both boys later served in World War I. Evart, a pilot, died at age 26 from war-related injuries.

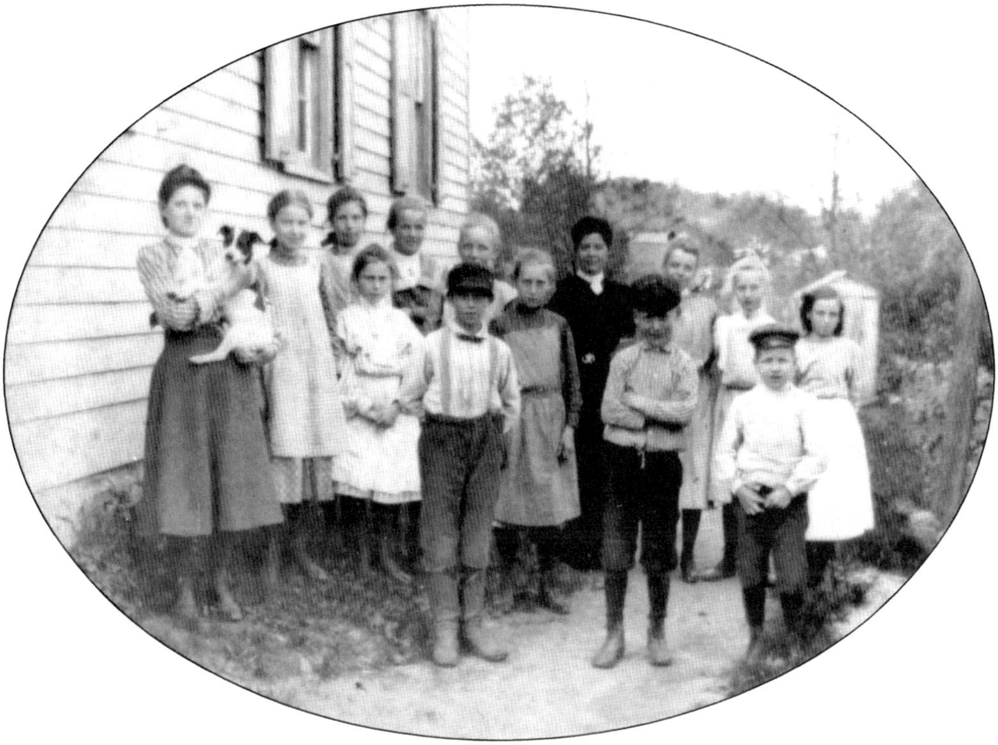

George Wade II is the young man on the right in the first row in this picture of a class at the Freedom Plains school. Perhaps the little dog that the girl on the left is holding followed someone to school that day. The outhouse seen in the background can still be found by following the path on the north side. (GW.)

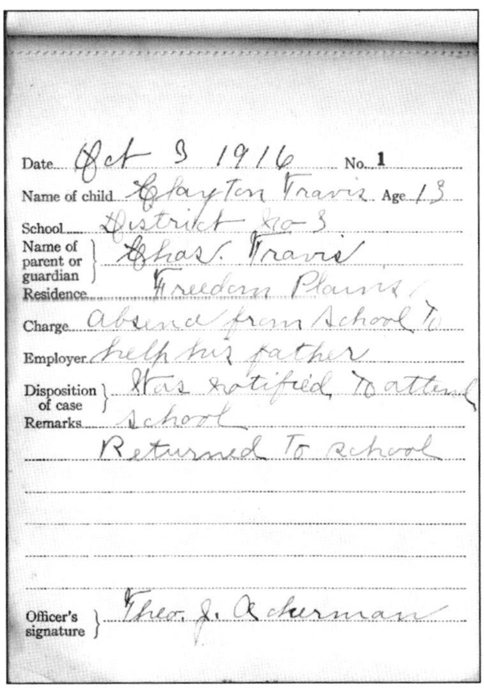

Date Oct 3 1916 No. 1
Name of child Clayton Travis Age 13
School District No 3
Name of parent or guardian Chas. Travis
Residence Freedom Plains
Charge absence from school to
Employer help his father
Disposition of case Was notified to attend
Remarks school
Returned to school
Officer's signature Theo. J. Ackerman

Theodore Ackerman kept this log while serving as school attendance officer in 1916–1917. A record was made whenever a student failed to appear for class. He notes here that a young Clayton Travis was absent on this day in order to help his father, no doubt with chores. He was nevertheless instructed to report to school, education being the priority.

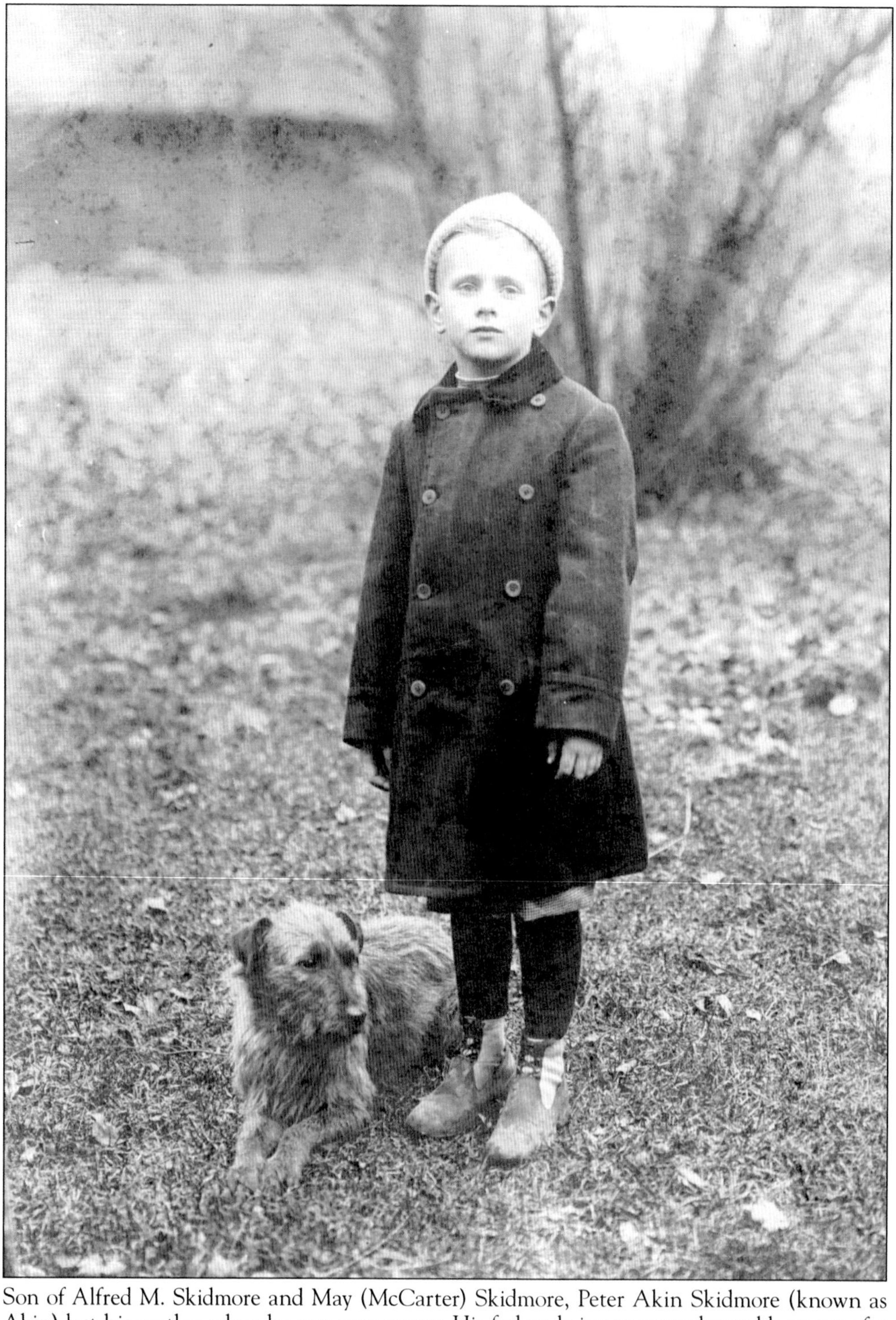

Son of Alfred M. Skidmore and May (McCarter) Skidmore, Peter Akin Skidmore (known as Akin) lost his mother when he was very young. His father, being apparently unable to care for him, sent Akin to be raised in the Floral Home by family friend Jennie Rhinehart. Akin is shown here at five years of age, with another good friend.

Jennie Rhinehart and Akin Skidmore are seen here standing in front of the barn at the Floral Home. Akin would grow up to marry a young lady from Millbrook, Tryntje Selderbeck. He remained active in the Quaker faith, attending the 1937 Friends World Conference in Pennsylvania.

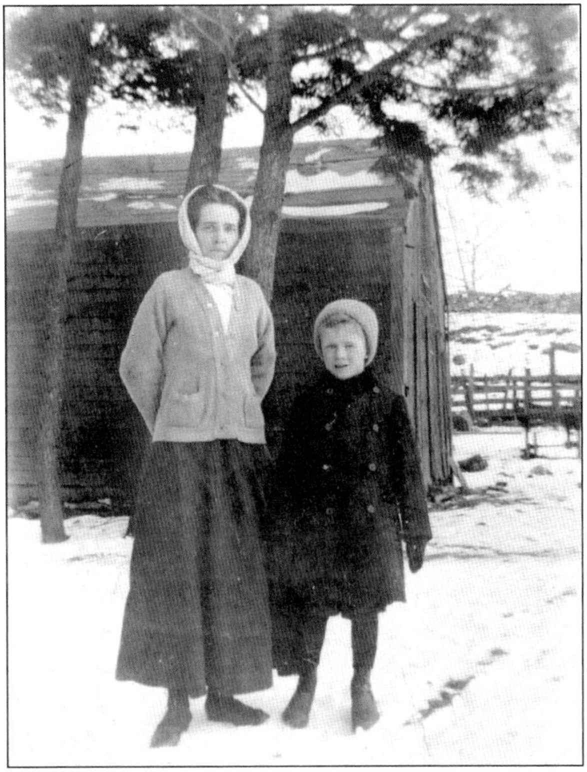

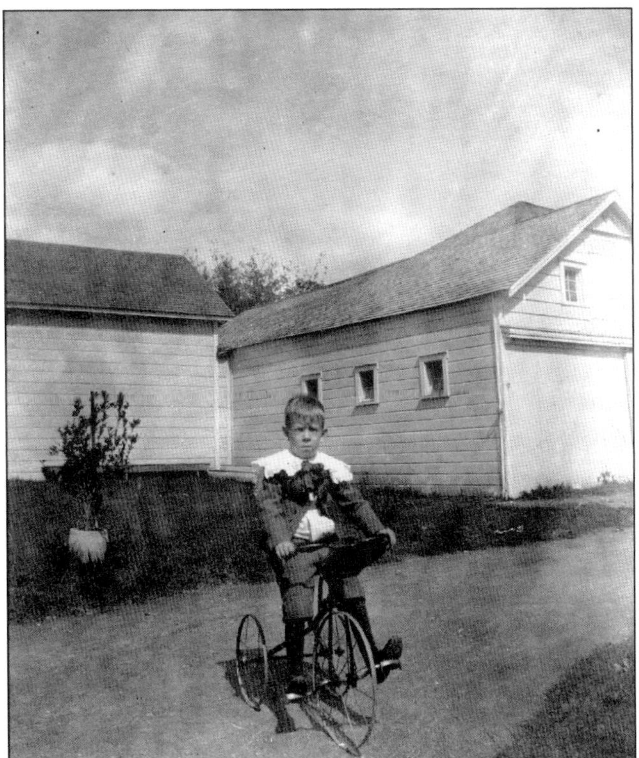

William H. Wells is the young gentleman riding his tricycle in this photograph, with the icehouse and wagon house of the Floral Home in the background. William was the son, and only child, of George and Nellie Wells. He survived World War I but died a few years later, leaving his young wife Sarah with three children.

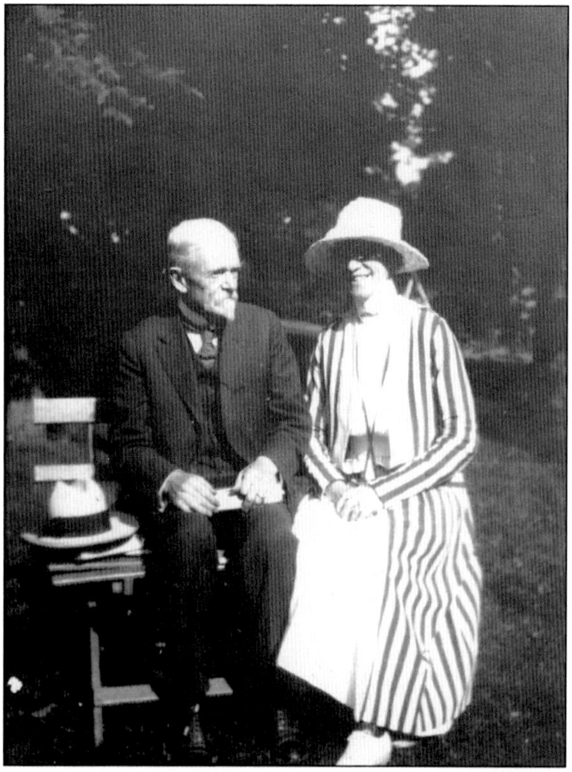

The distinguished-looking gentleman is Dr. Ridgley Lytle, with his wife Ethel, seen here relaxing at the Floral Home in 1919. The couple came to Moore's Mills as a respite from his busy career. The doctor was buried in his native Tennessee after his death in 1931.

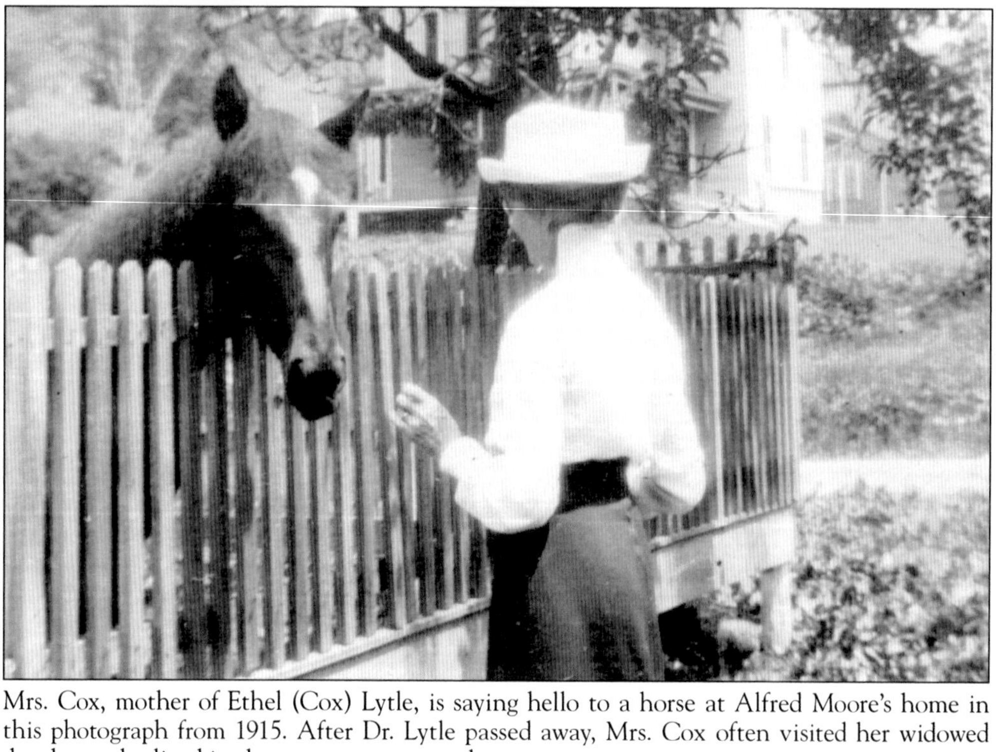

Mrs. Cox, mother of Ethel (Cox) Lytle, is saying hello to a horse at Alfred Moore's home in this photograph from 1915. After Dr. Lytle passed away, Mrs. Cox often visited her widowed daughter, who lived in the stone cottage nearby.

In 1911, the ladies of the Freedom Plains Presbyterian Church had already been busy saving souls for many years, both here and abroad. Part of the scheduled entertainment for the missionary celebration included a hymn written by Pastor Wilcox, titled "Our Christian Commission," which urges bringing the gospel to "the heathen [that] in darkness now dwell." (FPC.)

1886 -- 1911

The 25th Anniversary

OF THE

Women's Home and Foreign Missionary
Society of the
Freedom Plains Presbyterian Church,

ON

Sunday, October 1st, 1911.

At 2:30 p. m.

REV. WM. H. WILCOX, Pastor.

Mrs. W. H. Wilcox, Pres.
Mrs. Frank Tompkins, 1st Vice-Pres.
Mrs. Godfrey Wolven, 2nd Vice- Pres.
Mrs. O. D. Daley, Sec'y.
Mrs. Emma L. Brownell, Treas.

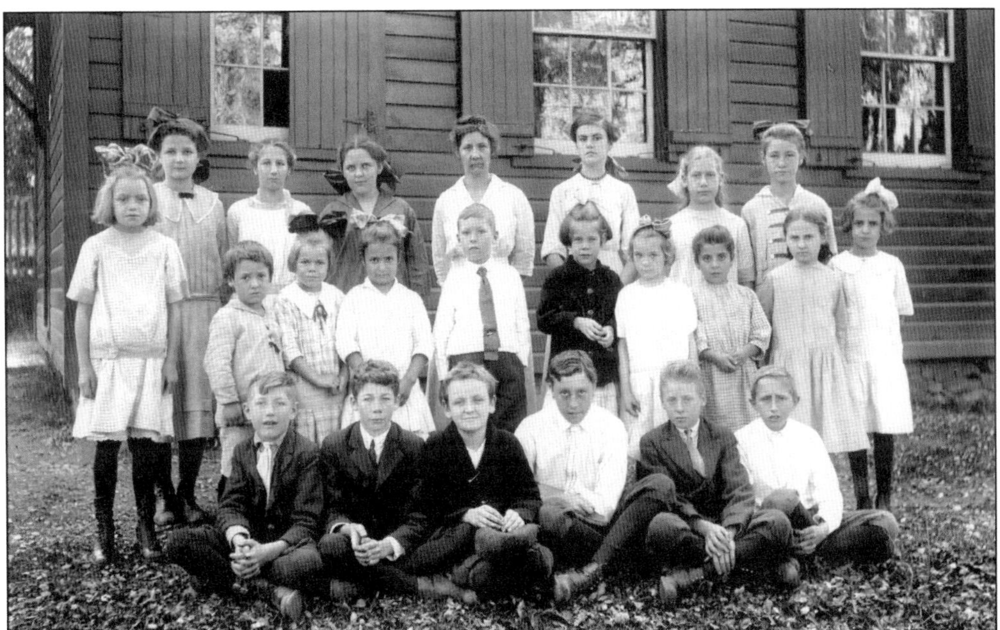

Some of the students look as somber as the teacher in this *c.* 1915 photograph of a class at the Moore's Mills school. For the girls of that era, a large bow was a must, whether worn in the hair or as part of her dress. The teacher, appearing in several class pictures of the era, may have been a Miss Van Wyck.

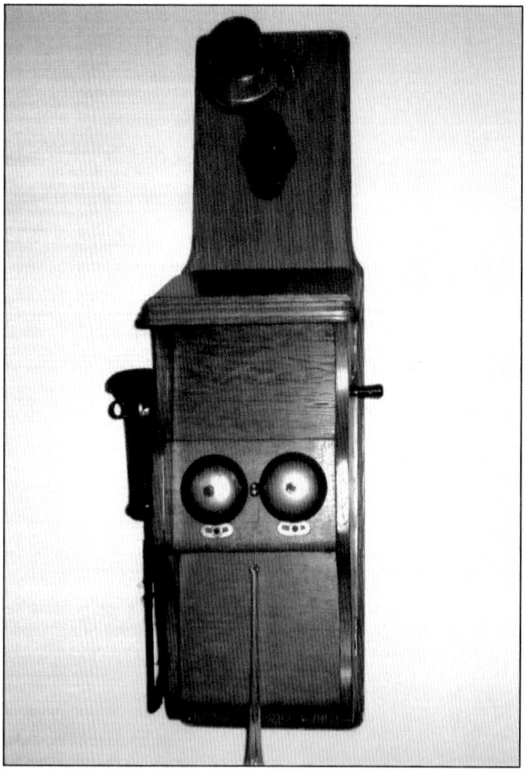

This telephone was the first to be in use in LaGrange. George Wade displays it in his home, along with the document that records its purchase in 1912. New York Telephone Company charged $18 per year for service. (GW.)

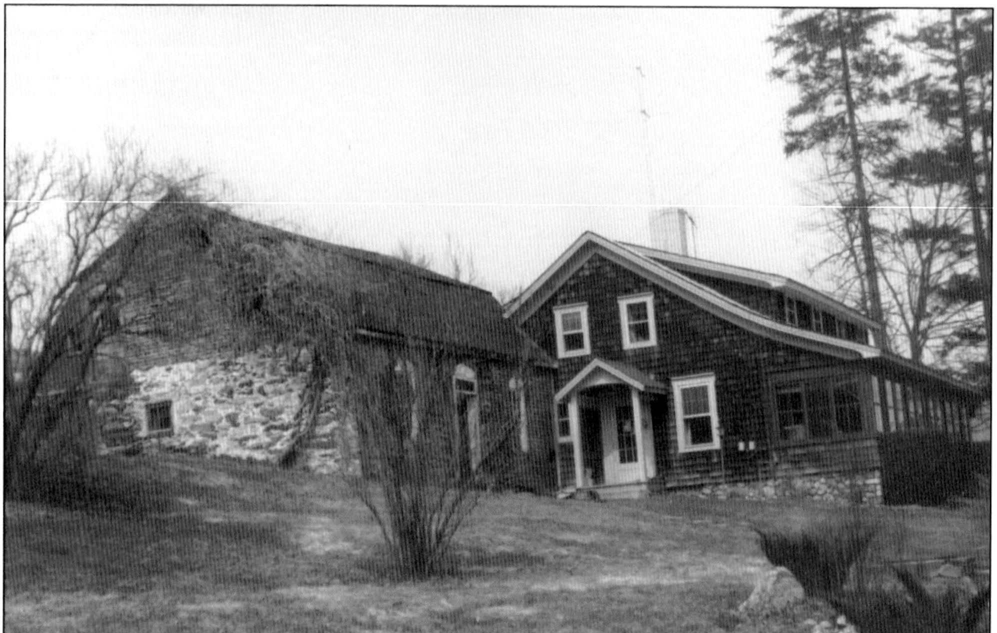

The brick section of the Skidmore home dated from around 1780 and was originally used as a school for the village; it was later removed, but the frame section remains on Skidmore Road. Family records show that Libby Downing was the first teacher, instructing several neighbor children as well as the Skidmore family.

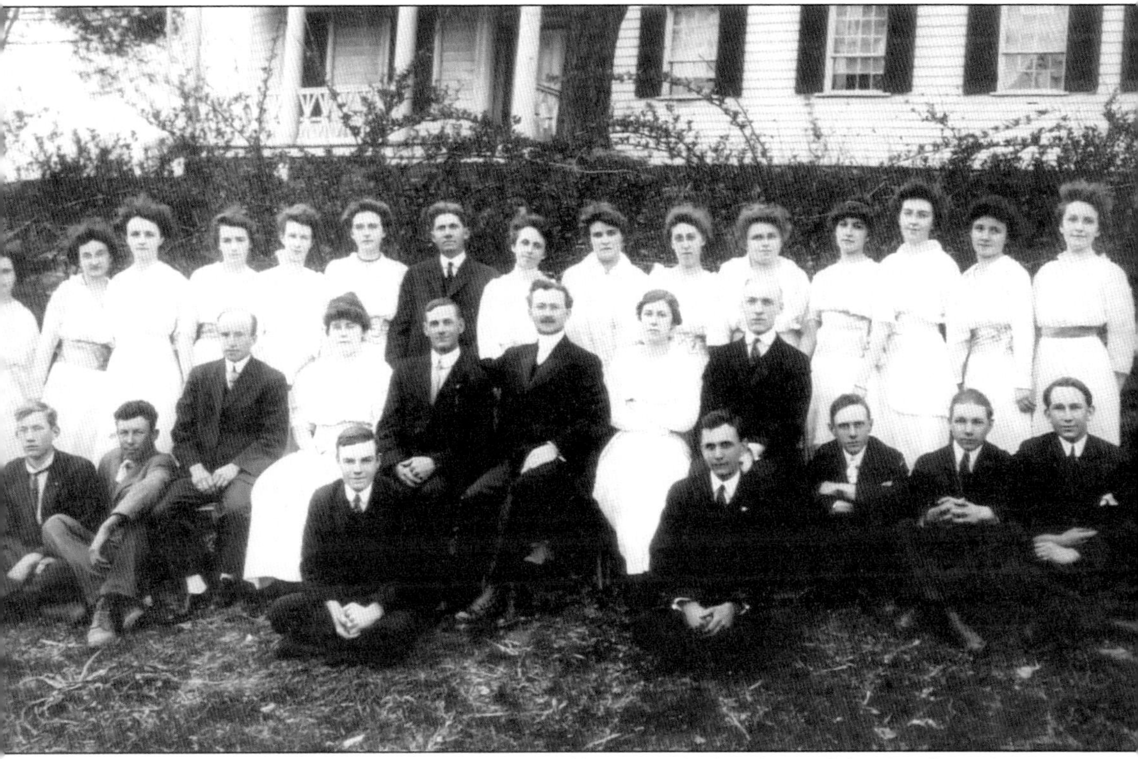

This photograph from the 1920s shows Pastor William Hanford Wilcox of the Freedom Plains Presbyterian Church with the "Willing, happy workers" (as the young men were called) and the "Bethany Girls." Presumably it was a type of youth group that also offered a chance to socialize. The house in the background was the parsonage on Skidmore Road. (GW.)

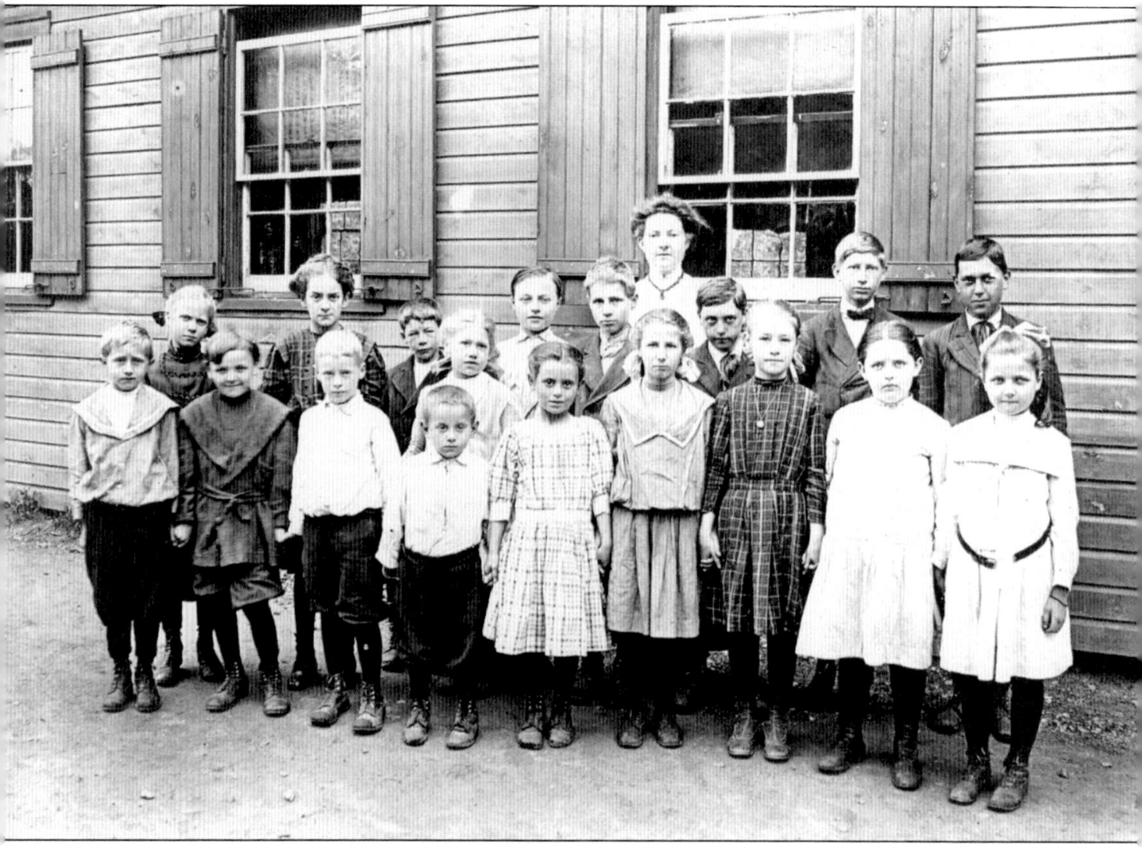

These children pose for their photograph in 1917 in front of the Manchester Bridge school. They were probably told to join hands in order to eliminate fidgeting while the picture was taken. Frances Rensley was the teacher at the time and presented copies of the photograph to the families of the students.

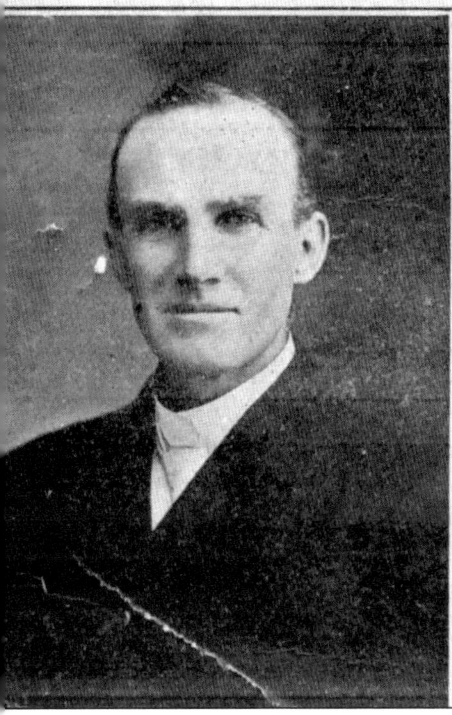

To Voters of the First Assembly District,

Gentlemen: If you want a clean man to represent you in the Assembly — clean morally, physically and politically—who will endeavor to be on the right side of every question, who will never dodge, but will honestly represent his constituency, cast your vote for **Mr. Vincent M. Buck** *of LaGrange, a man of unquestioned integrity and ability.*

Respectfully yours,

Prohibition Executive Committee,

C. H. BAKER, *Chairman.*

During the early part of the 20th century, the issue of alcohol consumption was taken very seriously. Temperance was considered by many citizens to be a necessary virtue. When Vincent Buck ran for assemblyman in the 1920s, he stressed his support of Prohibition, appealing to those who were "opposed to the Saloon."

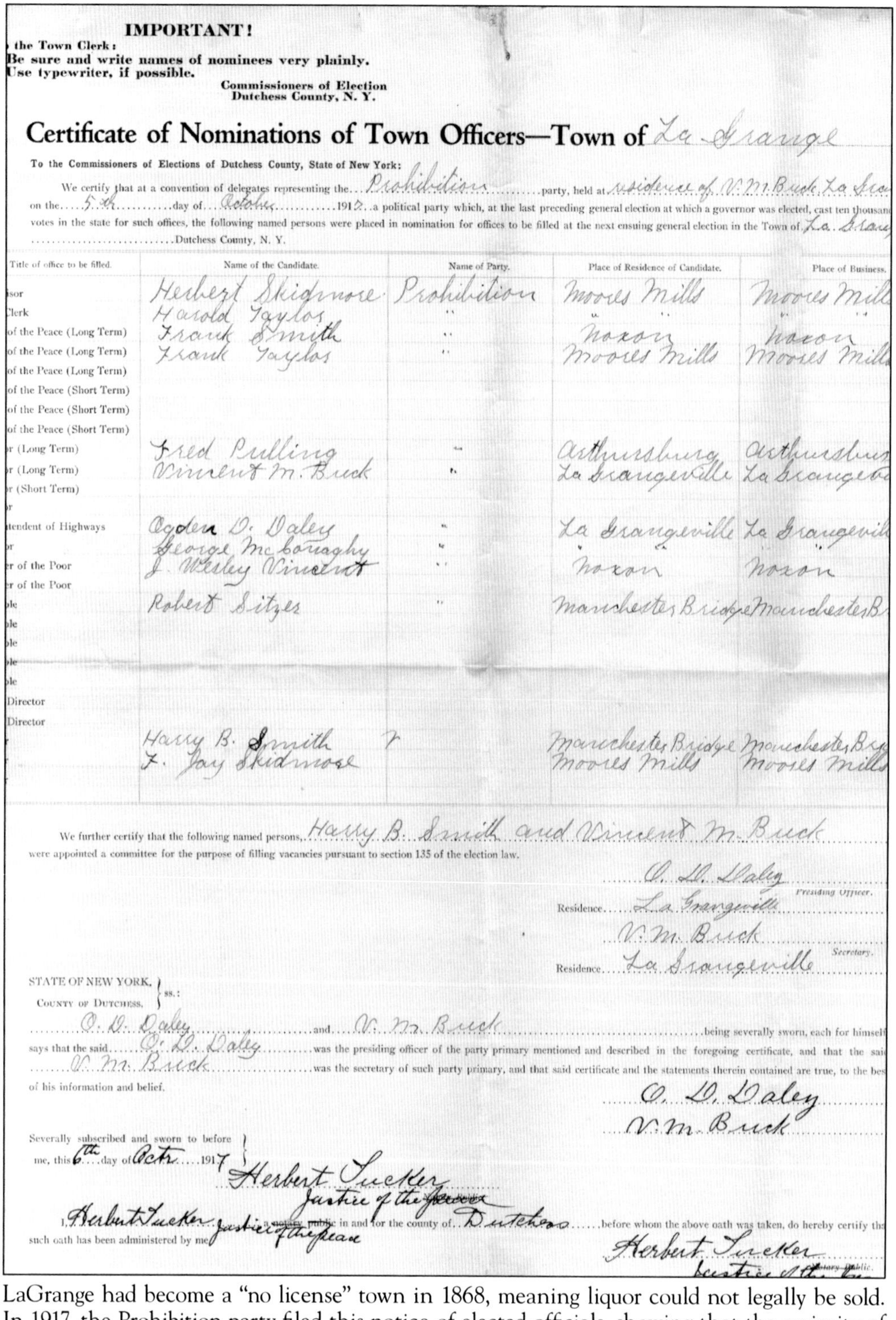

IMPORTANT!

the Town Clerk:
Be sure and write names of nominees very plainly.
Use typewriter, if possible.

Commissioners of Election
Dutchess County, N. Y.

Certificate of Nominations of Town Officers—Town of La Grange

To the Commissioners of Elections of Dutchess County, State of New York:

We certify that at a convention of delegates representing the... Prohibition ...party, held at residence of V. M. Buck La Gra[nge] on the... 5th ...day of... October ...1917...a political party which, at the last preceding general election at which a governor was elected, cast ten thousan[d] votes in the state for such offices, the following named persons were placed in nomination for offices to be filled at the next ensuing general election in the Town of La Gran[ge] ...Dutchess County, N. Y.

Title of office to be filled.	Name of the Candidate.	Name of Party.	Place of Residence of Candidate.	Place of Business.
[Superv]isor	Herbert Skidmore	Prohibition	Moores Mills	Moores Mill[s]
[C]lerk	Harold Taylor	"	" "	" "
[Justice] of the Peace (Long Term)	Frank Smith	"	Noxon	Noxon
[Justice] of the Peace (Long Term)	Frank Taylor	"	Moores Mills	Moores Mill[s]
[Justice] of the Peace (Long Term)				
[Justice] of the Peace (Short Term)				
[Justice] of the Peace (Short Term)				
[Justice] of the Peace (Short Term)				
[Assesso]r (Long Term)	Fred Pulling	"	Arthursburg	Arthursbur[g]
[Assesso]r (Long Term)	Vincent M. Buck	"	La Grangeville	La Grangevi[lle]
[Assesso]r (Short Term)				
[Collecto]r				
[Superin]tendent of Highways	Ogden D. Daley	"	La Grangeville	La Grangevi[lle]
[Collecto]r	George McConaghy	"	"	"
[Oversee]r of the Poor	J. Wesley Vincent	"	Noxon	Noxon
[Oversee]r of the Poor				
[Consta]ble	Robert Sitzer	"	Manchester Bridge	Manchester B[ridge]
[Consta]ble				
[Consta]ble				
[Consta]ble				
[Consta]ble				
Director				
Director				
	Harry B. Smith	"	Manchester Bridge	Manchester Br[idge]
	F. Jay Skidmore		Moores Mills	Moores Mills

We further certify that the following named persons, Harry B. Smith and Vincent M. Buck were appointed a committee for the purpose of filling vacancies pursuant to section 135 of the election law.

O. D. Daley
Presiding Officer.
Residence... La Grangeville

V. M. Buck
Secretary.
Residence... La Grangeville

STATE OF NEW YORK, } ss.:
COUNTY OF DUTCHESS, }

O. D. Daley ...and... V. M. Buck ...being severally sworn, each for himsel[f] says that the said... O. D. Daley ...was the presiding officer of the party primary mentioned and described in the foregoing certificate, and that the sai[d] ...V. M. Buck ...was the secretary of such party primary, and that said certificate and the statements therein contained are true, to the bes[t] of his information and belief.

O. D. Daley
V. M. Buck

Severally subscribed and sworn to before me, this 6th day of Octr. 1917

Herbert Tucker
Justice of the ~~peace~~

I, Herbert Tucker, ~~a notary public~~ justice of the peace in and for the county of Dutchess ...before whom the above oath was taken, do hereby certify th[at] such oath has been administered by me.

Herbert Tucker
Justice of the [Peace]

LaGrange had become a "no license" town in 1868, meaning liquor could not legally be sold. In 1917, the Prohibition party filed this notice of elected officials, showing that the majority of residents were still in favor of keeping LaGrange dry. It remained so until the mid-1930s, after the repeal of the Prohibition laws.

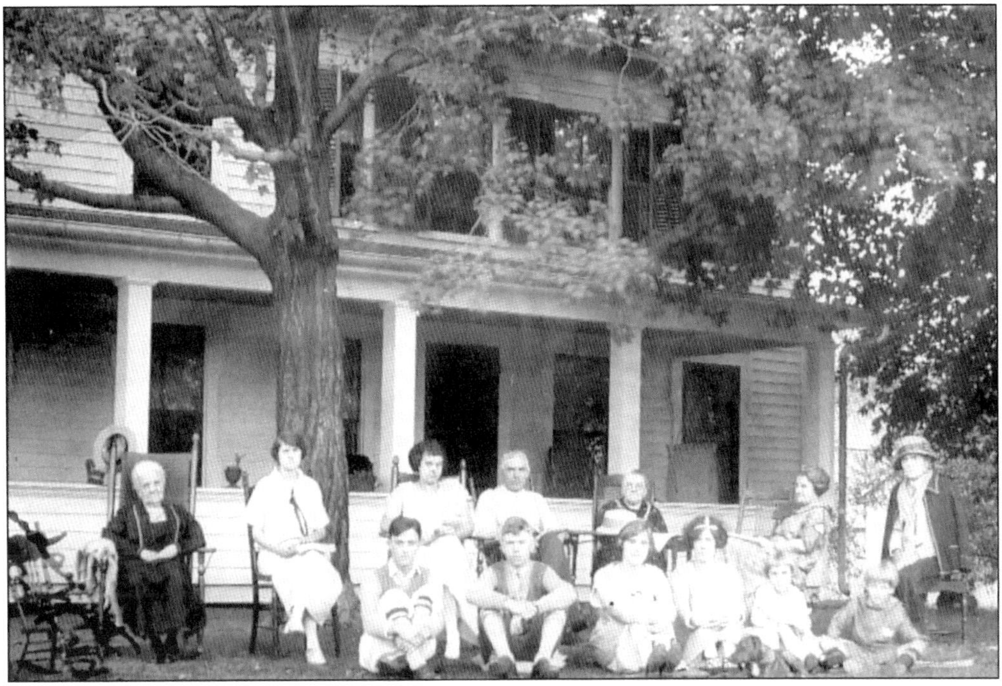

The Smith family is seen here in the early 1920s, enjoying a warm summer day. Daughter Margaret was visiting with her husband Monfort Wade (in the center). Grandmother, aunts, and cousins also gathered for the photograph. (GW.)

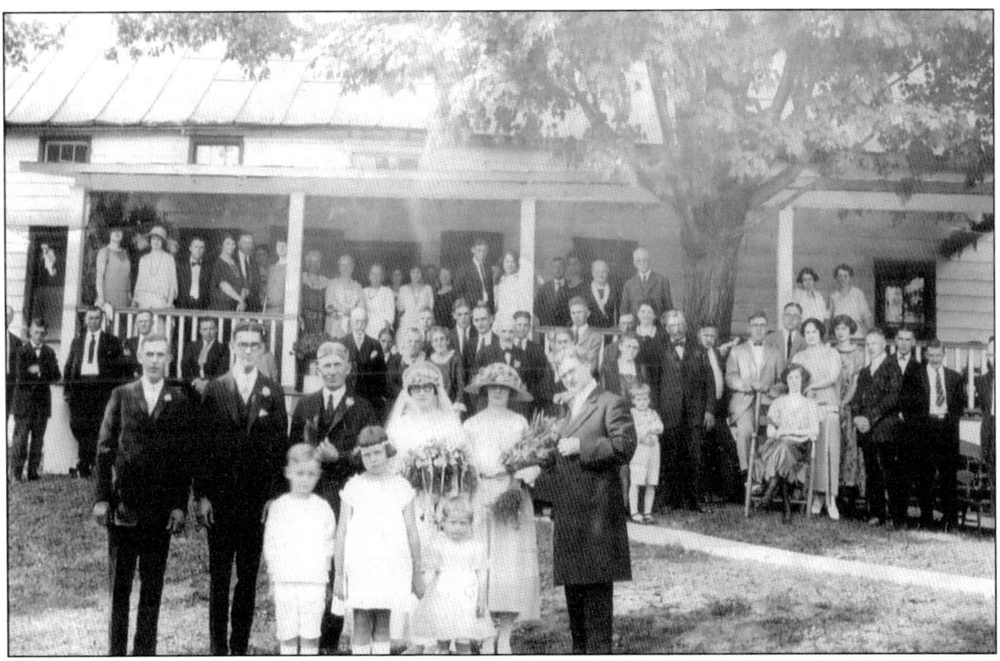

Here again is Pastor William Hanford Wilcox, officiating at a Smith family wedding around 1925. Rather solemn looks for such a happy occasion! Pastor Wilcox served at the church for many years and was well loved by the parishioners. (GW.)

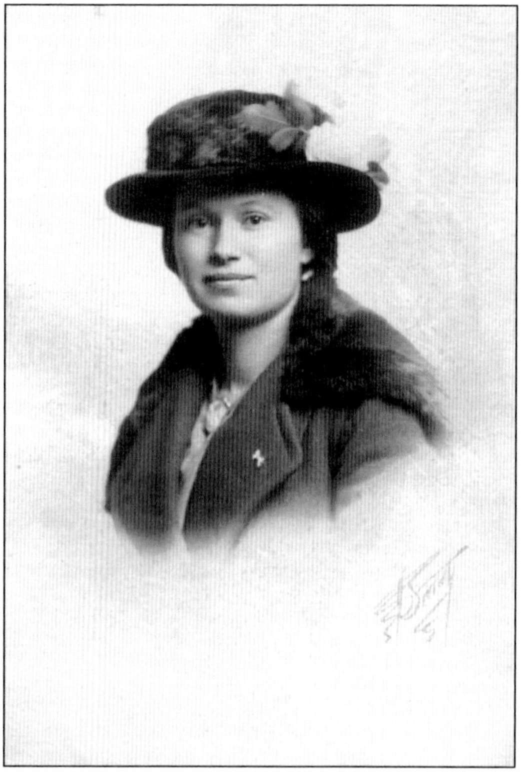

This stylish young lady in the flowered hat is Elma Moore. She and her sister Louella were daughters of Steven Moore and cousins of Susan. They were the sixth-generation descendants of the original Quakers who settled on Oswego Road.

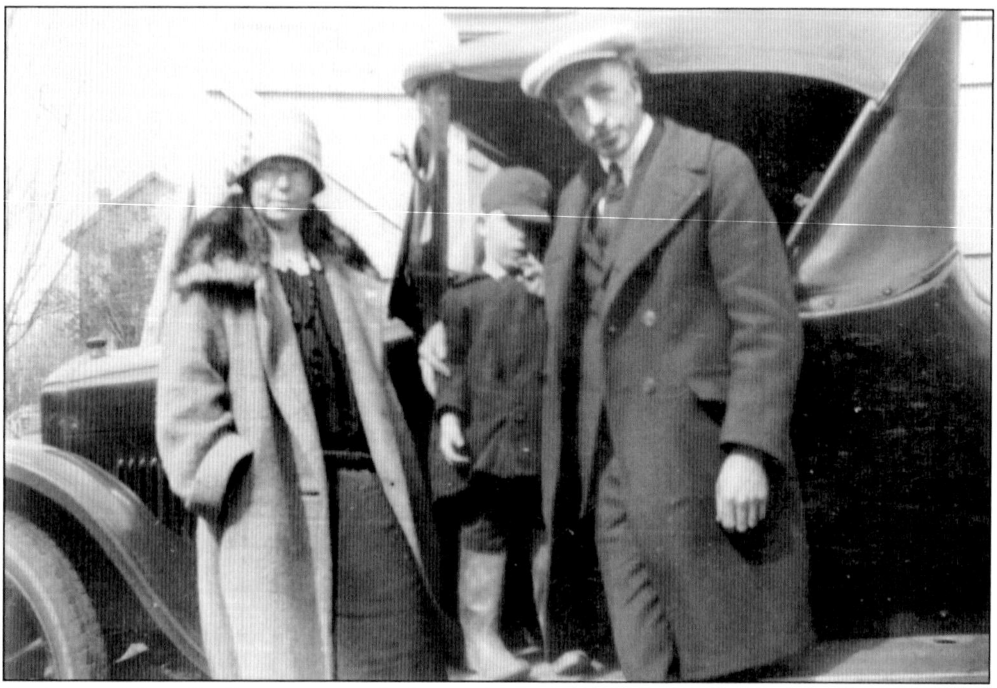

Andrew and Louella Brower are ready for a ride in their automobile in this 1920s photograph. They were paying a visit to the home of Sara Wells. The young boy, looking a little camera shy, is one of Sara's sons.

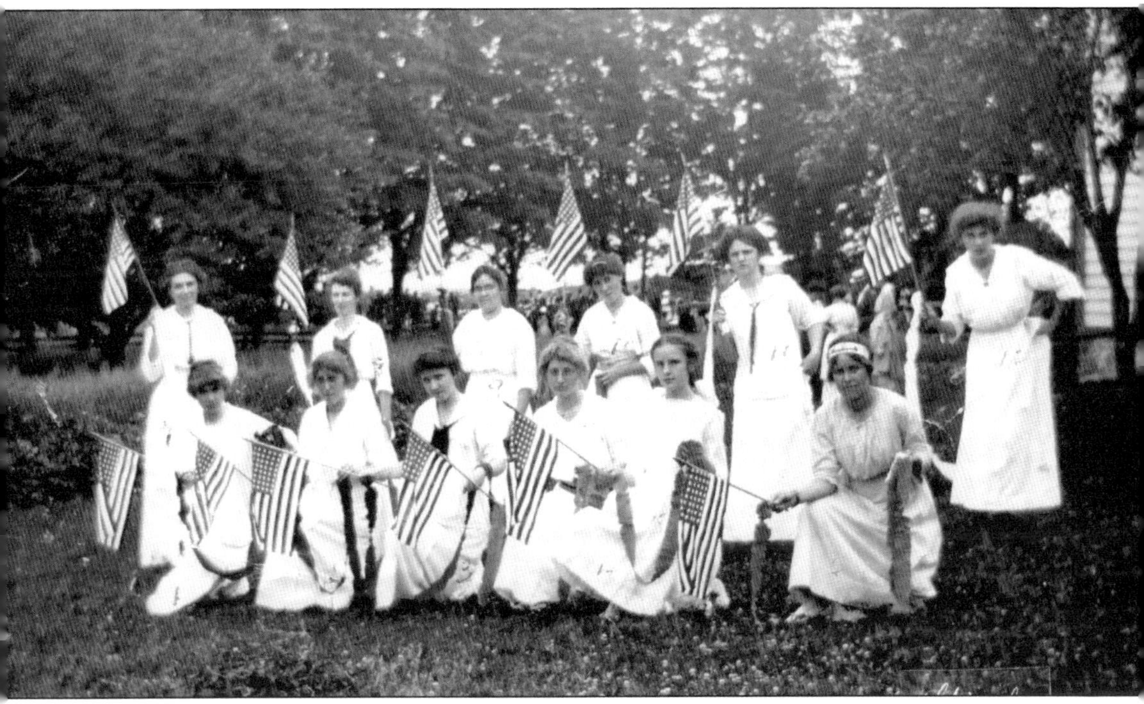

The Fourth of July celebration took place each year in Freedom Plains. Photographs of the event were taken by Mrs. Edward Stringham. Here some local young ladies show their patriotism with a display of flags on the lawn of the Wardell home. Included in the picture are sisters in the Berger, Hallock, Velie, and Tompkins families.

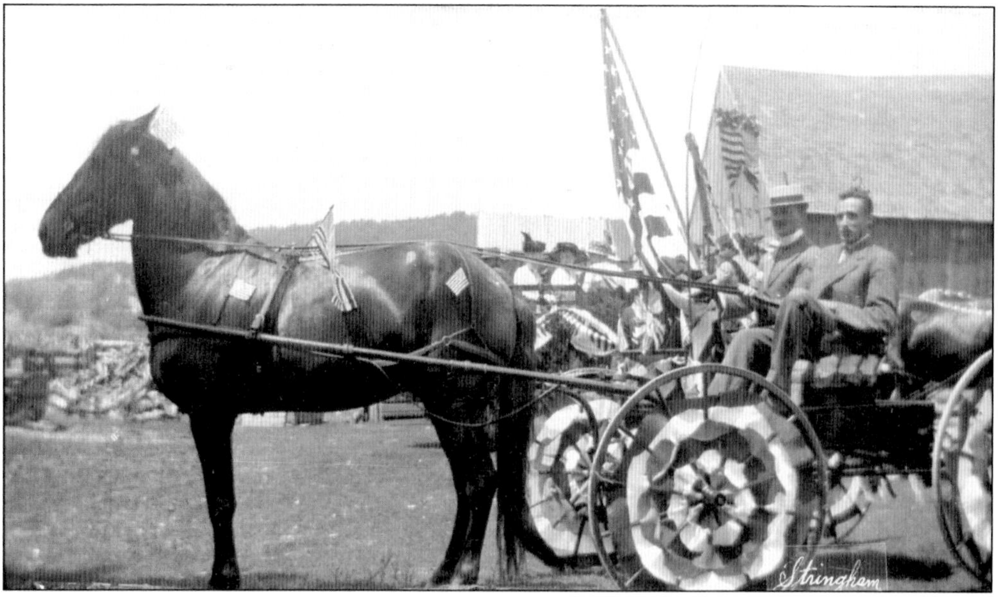

Rev. William Hanford Wilcox takes the reins, with Harold Taylor riding shotgun. The Phelps property and barns can be seen in the background. Taylor was the town clerk at the time of this photograph.

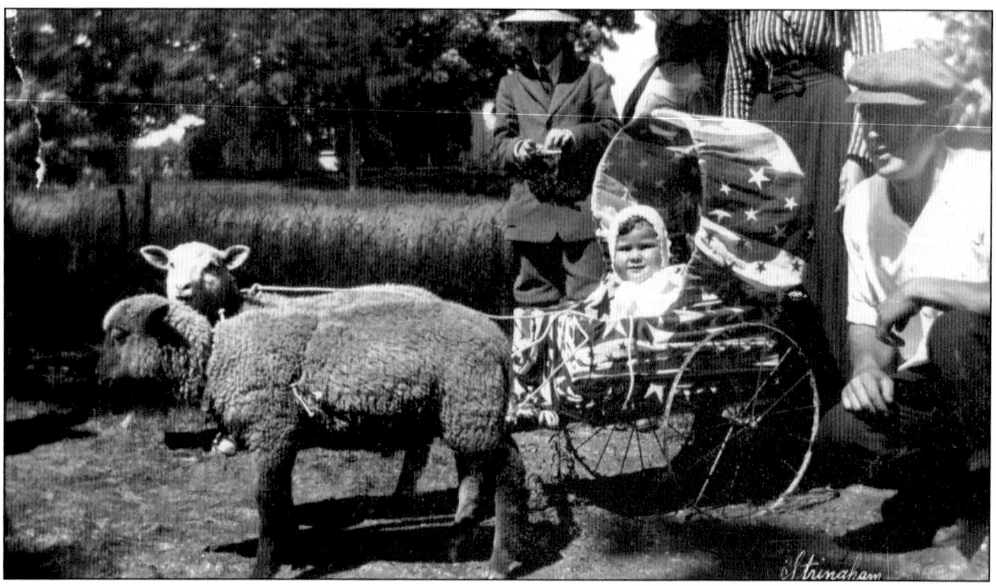

Adorable young Vivian Rooney, driving her team of lambs, also took part in the 1915 parade and stole the show. She was just two years old at the time. The gentleman kneeling beside her is probably her proud father, Cornelius Rooney.

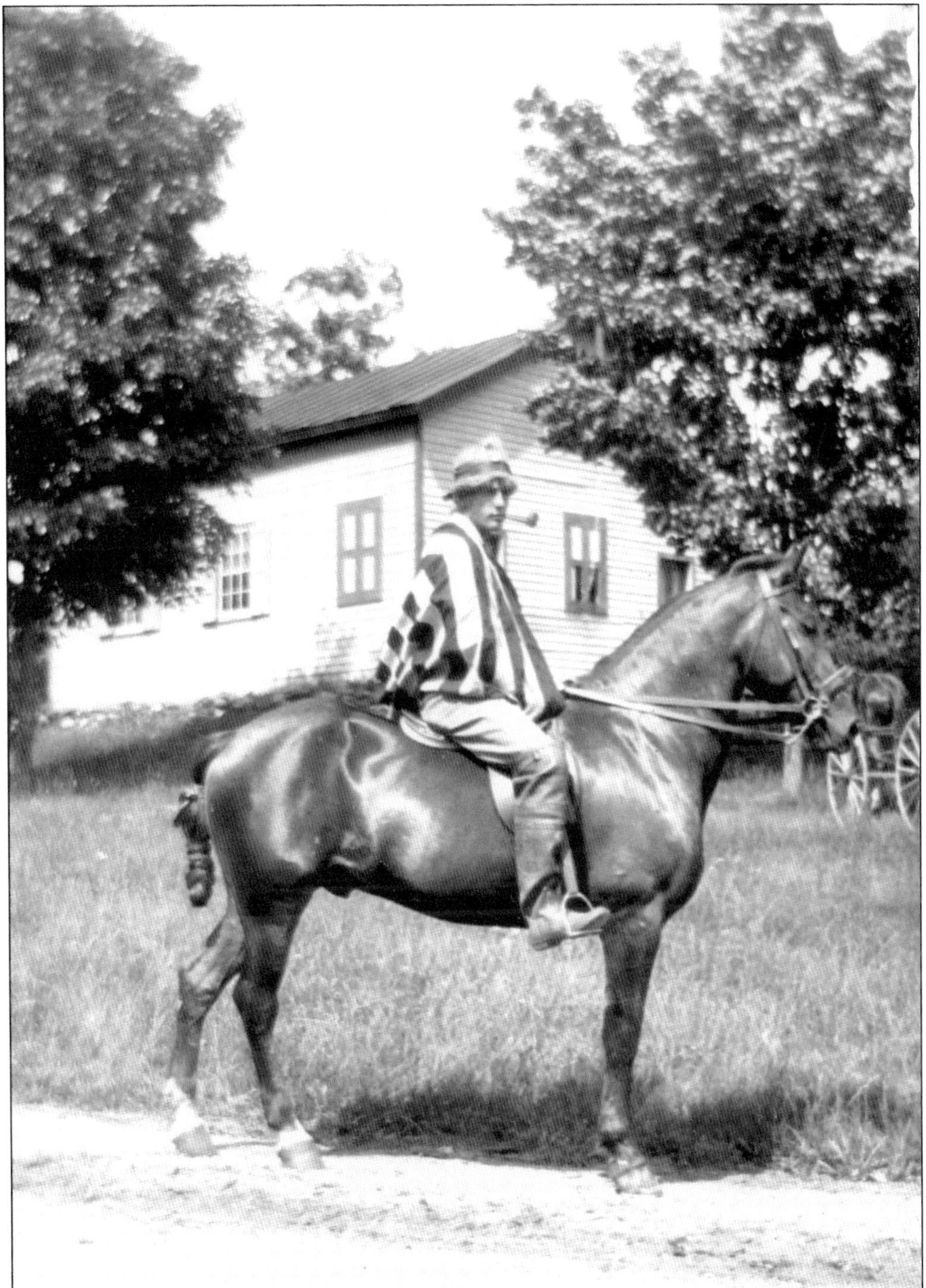

Another parade participant poses here on his horse along Freedom Road, still unpaved at that time. Seen in the background is the school, which was painted white until the 1960s. Following a New England tradition, it was spruced up with a barn red color, after which it became known as the Little Red Schoolhouse.

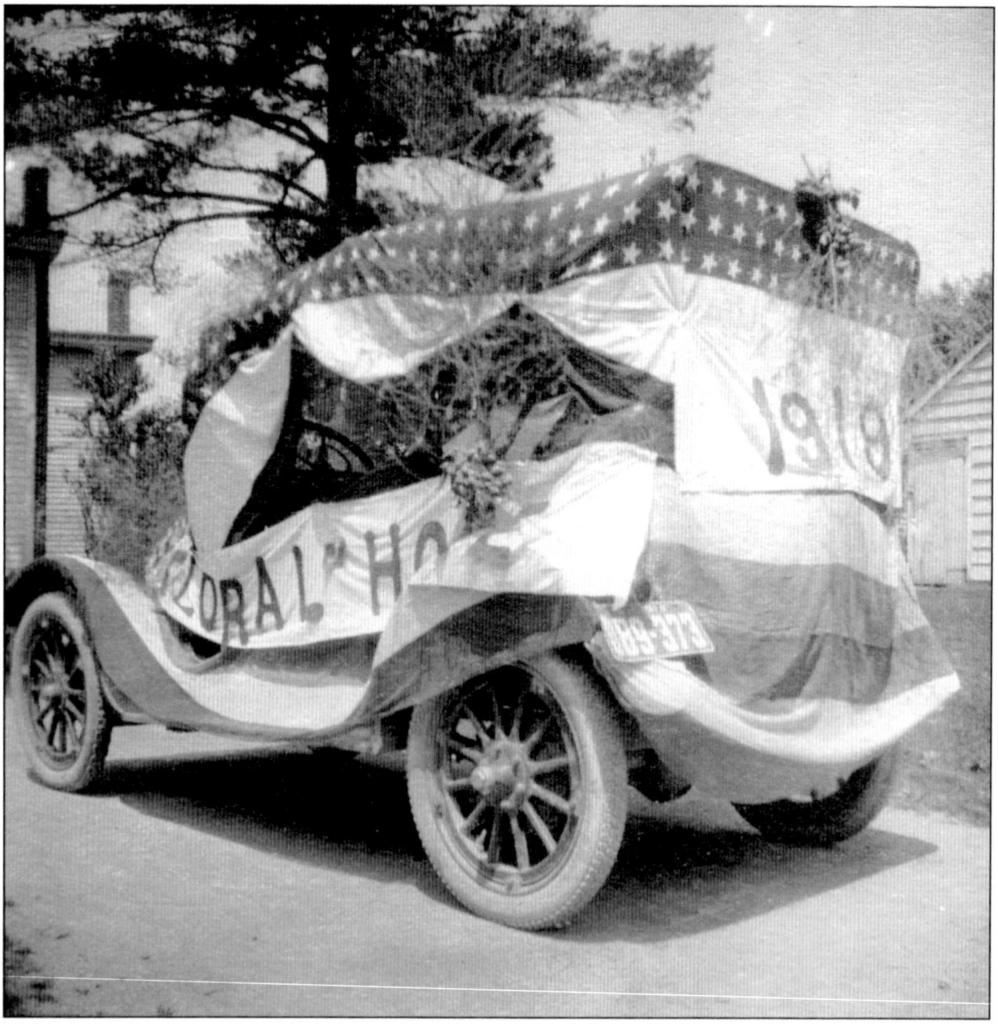

In 1919, the Junior Order of American Mechanics (JOAM) celebration was held in Moore's Mills. The group was a fraternal order, the term *mechanic* simply meaning builder of character. Members supported separation of church and state and free education through the public school system. The Floral Home participated in the day's festivities with a decorated Model T automobile.

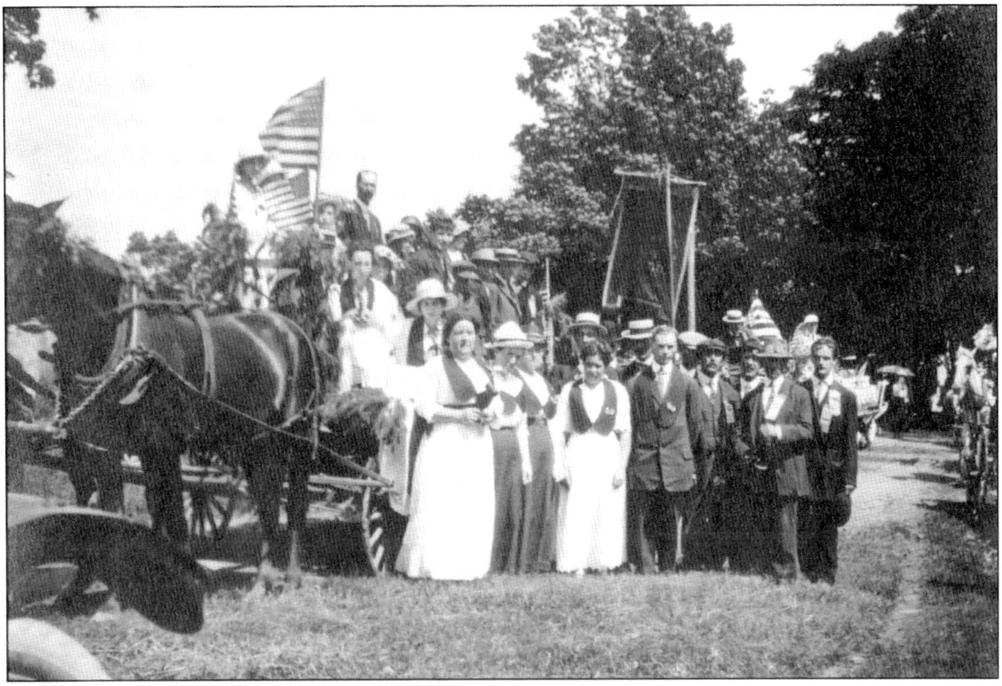

The JOAM was originally open to white males only but later allowed anyone to join. This group photograph shows some town residents posing in their patriotic finery. A few seem to be wearing ribbons, perhaps for prizes won in contests. Parades and other events were infrequent occasions in those days, so hardworking folks relished the chance for some frivolous fun.

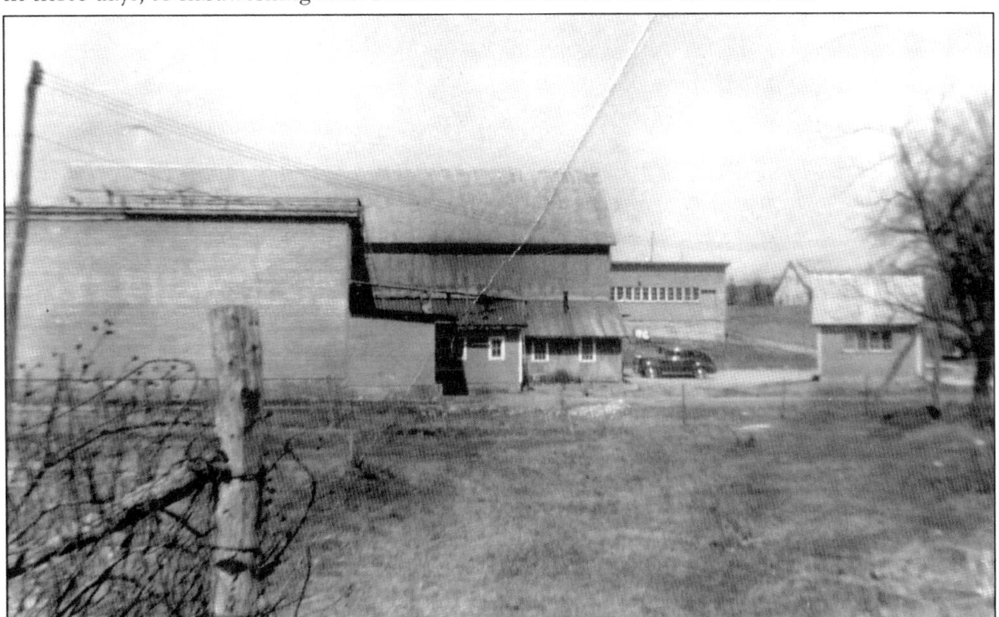

This cold storage building, built in 1927, was used for the apples from Cross Orchards. McIntoshes were the most popular, although several varieties were grown, including Delicious, Northern Spies, and Baldwins. The orchard was started in 1907 by Thomas E. Cross and was in business until 1995. The storage building burned a few years later. (TC.)

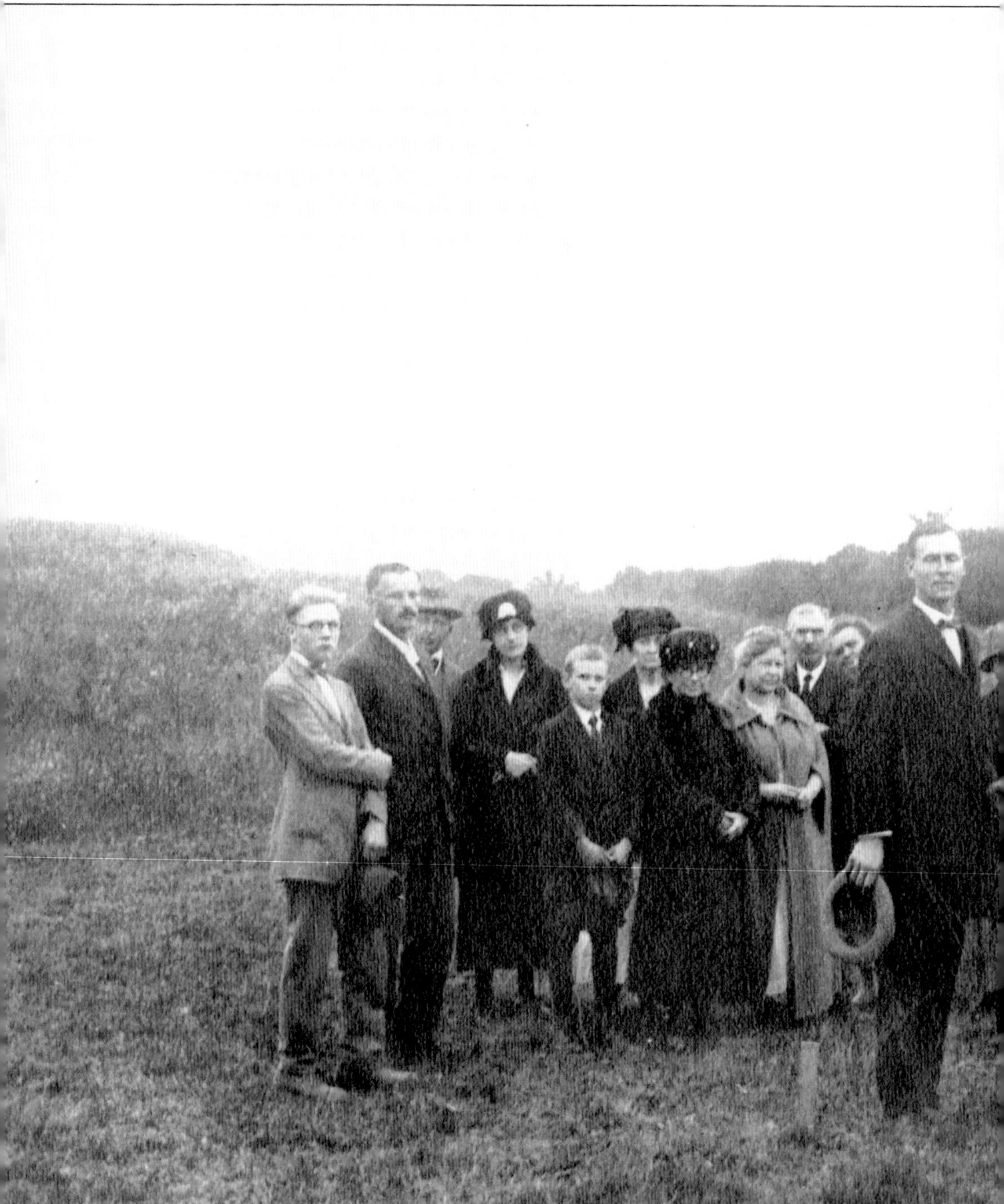

The Grange movement came about in response to the difficulties faced by farmers after the Civil War. The organization's goal was to provide leadership and education to those in agriculture, while gaining strength in numbers. The Freedom Plains Grange organized in 1898 with 18 charter members, with Edward Barmore as the first master. Meetings took place in members' homes until a hall could be built. The groundbreaking ceremony of the Grange hall

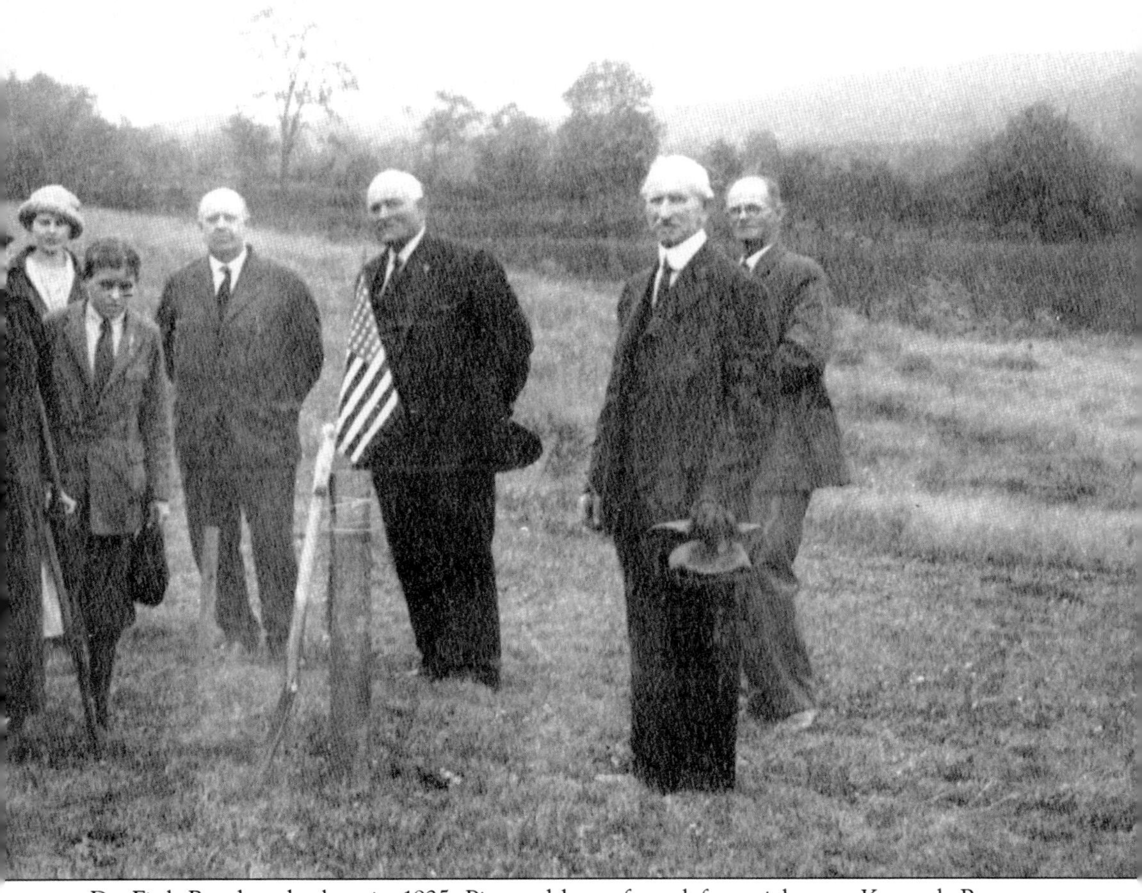

on Dr. Fink Road took place in 1925. Pictured here, from left to right, are Kenneth Burgess, George Eberhard, Fred Burgess and his wife, Howard Travis, Mrs. Clark Barmore, Mrs. George McConaghy, Mrs. S. A. Noon, George McConaghy, Mrs. Theo Heeg, Leonard Travis (master), Mrs. W. C. Crosby, Rosamond Wardell, Mrs. R. H. Smith, Ethel Hoos, Rev S. A. Noon, Harvey Lester, C. H. Wardell, and George Hoos Sr. (FPG.)

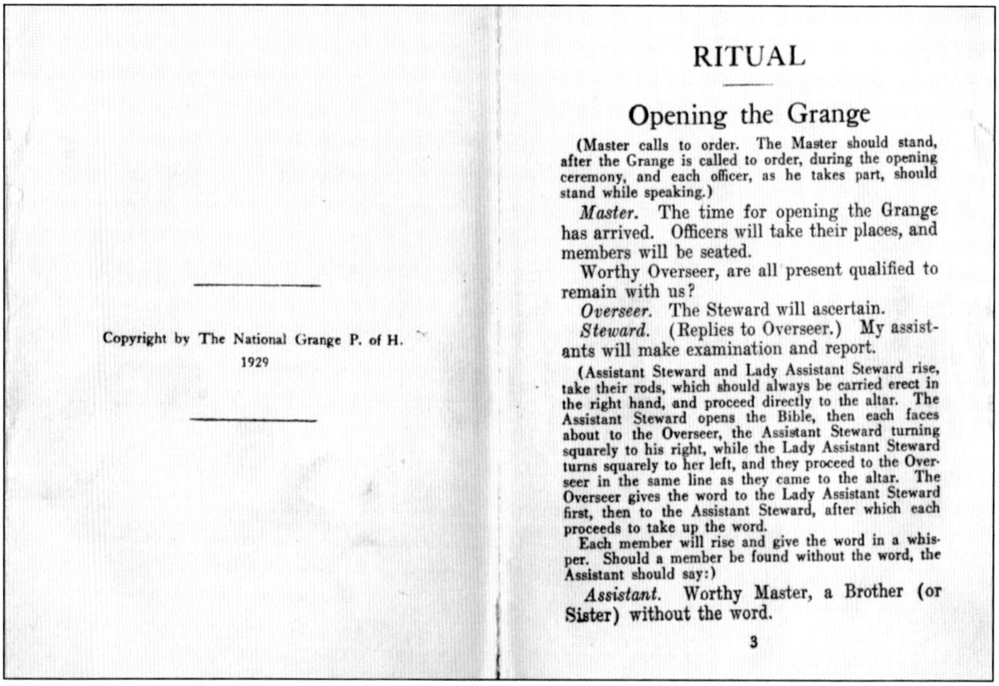

Copyright by The National Grange P. of H.
1929

RITUAL

Opening the Grange

(Master calls to order. The Master should stand, after the Grange is called to order, during the opening ceremony, and each officer, as he takes part, should stand while speaking.)

Master. The time for opening the Grange has arrived. Officers will take their places, and members will be seated.

Worthy Overseer, are all present qualified to remain with us?

Overseer. The Steward will ascertain.

Steward. (Replies to Overseer.) My assistants will make examination and report.

(Assistant Steward and Lady Assistant Steward rise, take their rods, which should always be carried erect in the right hand, and proceed directly to the altar. The Assistant Steward opens the Bible, then each faces about to the Overseer, the Assistant Steward turning squarely to his right, while the Lady Assistant Steward turns squarely to her left, and they proceed to the Overseer in the same line as they came to the altar. The Overseer gives the word to the Lady Assistant Steward first, then to the Assistant Steward, after which each proceeds to take up the word.

Each member will rise and give the word in a whisper. Should a member be found without the word, the Assistant should say:)

Assistant. Worthy Master, a Brother (or Sister) without the word.

3

Grange No. 857 also had a juvenile order; this manual instructs young people in the proper procedure of the ceremonies. Titles within the organization included Ceres, Pomona, and Flora, named after the goddesses of grain, fruit, and flowers—all of which were important symbols for this agriculture-based group. (FPG.)

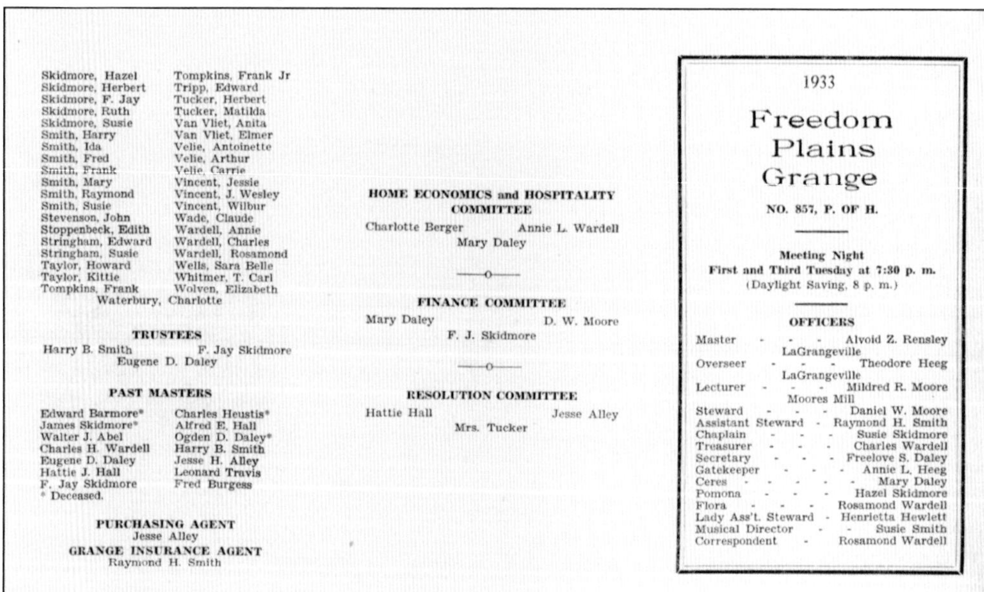

Skidmore, Hazel
Skidmore, Herbert
Skidmore, F. Jay
Skidmore, Ruth
Skidmore, Susie
Smith, Harry
Smith, Ida
Smith, Fred
Smith, Frank
Smith, Mary
Smith, Raymond
Smith, Susie
Stevenson, John
Stoppenbeck, Edith
Stringham, Edward
Stringham, Susie
Taylor, Howard
Taylor, Kittie
Tompkins, Frank
Tompkins, Frank Jr
Tripp, Edward
Tucker, Herbert
Tucker, Matilda
Van Vliet, Anita
Van Vliet, Elmer
Velie, Antoinette
Velie, Arthur
Velie, Carrie
Vincent, Jessie
Vincent, J. Wesley
Vincent, Wilbur
Wade, Claude
Wardell, Annie
Wardell, Charles
Wardell, Rosamond
Wells, Sara Belle
Whitmer, T. Carl
Wolven, Elizabeth
Waterbury, Charlotte

TRUSTEES

Harry B. Smith — F. Jay Skidmore — Eugene D. Daley

PAST MASTERS

Edward Barmore*
James Skidmore*
Walter J. Abel
Charles H. Wardell
Eugene D. Daley
Hattie J. Hall
F. Jay Skidmore
Charles Heustis*
Alfred E. Hall
Ogden D. Daley*
Harry B. Smith
Jesse H. Alley
Leonard Travis
Fred Burgess

* Deceased.

PURCHASING AGENT
Jesse Alley

GRANGE INSURANCE AGENT
Raymond H. Smith

HOME ECONOMICS and HOSPITALITY COMMITTEE

Charlotte Berger — Annie L. Wardell — Mary Daley

—o—

FINANCE COMMITTEE

Mary Daley — D. W. Moore — F. J. Skidmore

—o—

RESOLUTION COMMITTEE

Hattie Hall — Jesse Alley — Mrs. Tucker

1933

Freedom Plains Grange

NO. 857, P. OF H.

Meeting Night
First and Third Tuesday at 7:30 p. m.
(Daylight Saving, 8 p. m.)

OFFICERS

Master	Alvoid Z. Rensley, LaGrangeville
Overseer	Theodore Heeg, LaGrangeville
Lecturer	Mildred R. Moore, Moores Mill
Steward	Daniel W. Moore
Assistant Steward	Raymond H. Smith
Chaplain	Susie Skidmore
Treasurer	Charles Wardell
Secretary	Freelove S. Daley
Gatekeeper	Annie L. Heeg
Ceres	Mary Daley
Pomona	Hazel Skidmore
Flora	Rosamond Wardell
Lady Ass't. Steward	Henrietta Hewlett
Musical Director	Susie Smith
Correspondent	Rosamond Wardell

In the 1930s, there were still many farmers in the town, and virtually all of them were Grange members. Gatherings occurred throughout the year blending business with entertainment, including plays, debates, and humorous sketches. Members no doubt looked forward to these outings that the entire family could enjoy. (FPG.)

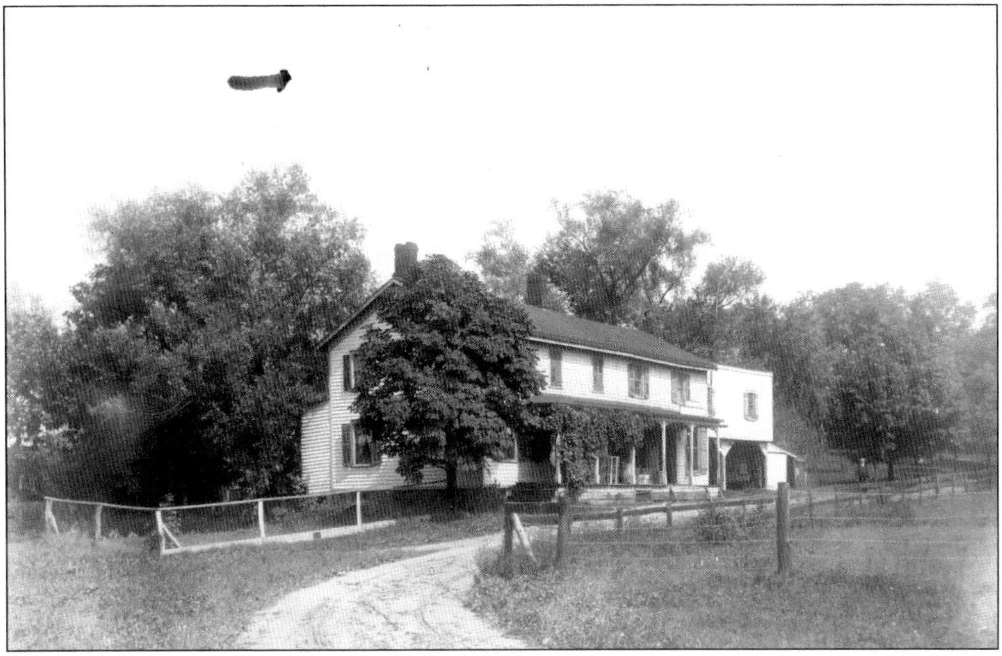

Shown here is Charlie Davis's store, a fixture in the Moore's Mills area for many years. Kids who grew up in the area remember the excitement of choosing which kind of candy or other treat to spend their pennies on, while their parents went about the business of buying groceries and other supplies. (BD.)

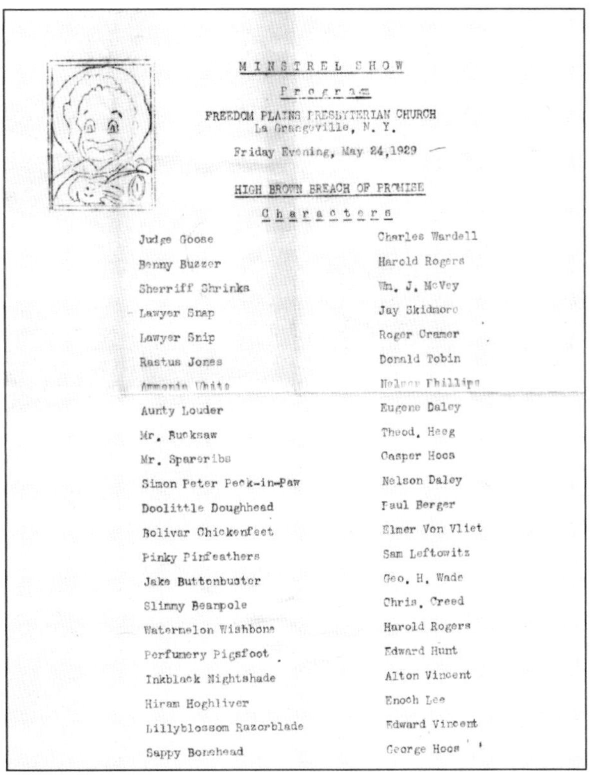

MINSTREL SHOW

Program

FREEDOM PLAINS PRESBYTERIAN CHURCH
La Grangeville, N. Y.

Friday Evening, May 24,1929

HIGH BROWN BREACH OF PROMISE

Characters

Judge Goose	Charles Wardell
Benny Buzzer	Harold Rogers
Sherriff Shrinks	Wm. J. McVey
Lawyer Snap	Jay Skidmore
Lawyer Snip	Roger Cramer
Rastus Jones	Donald Tobin
Ammonia White	Nelson Phillips
Aunty Louder	Eugene Daley
Mr. Bucksaw	Theod. Heeg
Mr. Spareribs	Casper Hoos
Simon Peter Peck-in-Paw	Nelson Daley
Doolittle Doughhead	Paul Berger
Bolivar Chickenfeet	Elmer Von Vliet
Pinky Pinfeathers	Sam Leftowitz
Jake Buttonbuster	Geo. H. Wade
Slimmy Beanpole	Chris. Creed
Watermelon Wishbone	Harold Rogers
Perfumery Pigsfoot	Edward Hunt
Inkblack Nightshade	Alton Vincent
Hiram Hoghliver	Enoch Lee
Lillyblossom Razorblade	Edward Vincent
Sappy Bonehead	George Hoos

A minstrel show was put on by the Presbyterian Church in 1928, an example of how society has changed over the years. Although now considered extremely racist, minstrel shows were an accepted form of entertainment at the time. All roles were played by members of the church. (FPC.)

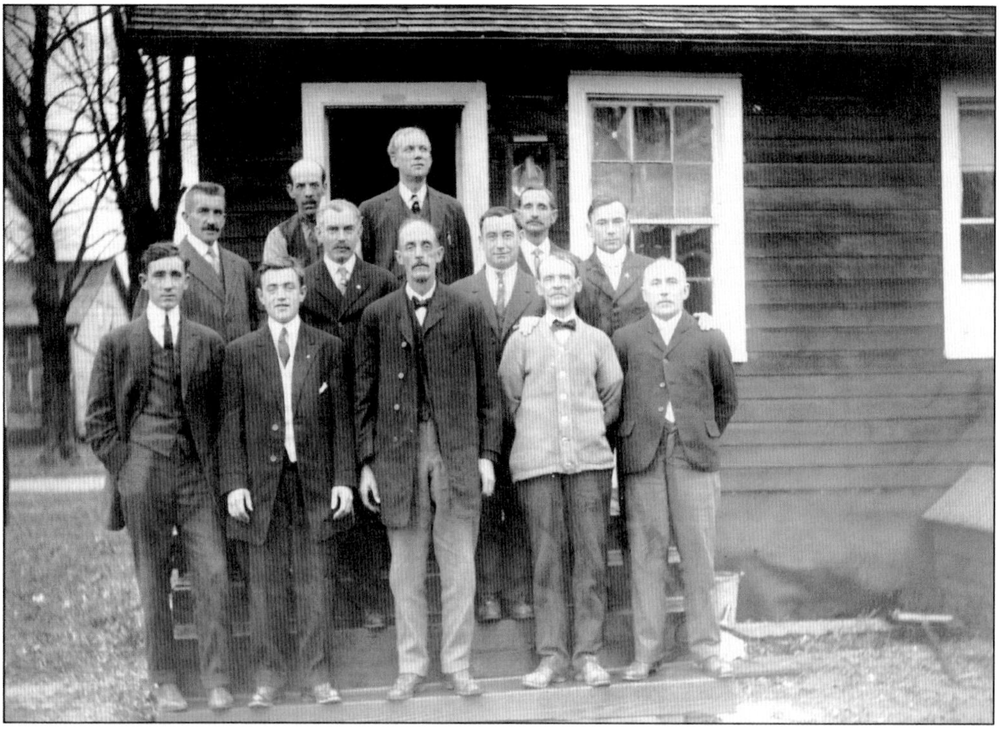

Monfort Wade (second row, second from left) and other gentlemen of the town are gathered in front of the schoolhouse on Dr. Fink Road. The occasion is unknown, presumably a committee meeting of some sort. The only other identified individual is Chet Phillips, on the right in the first row. (GW.)

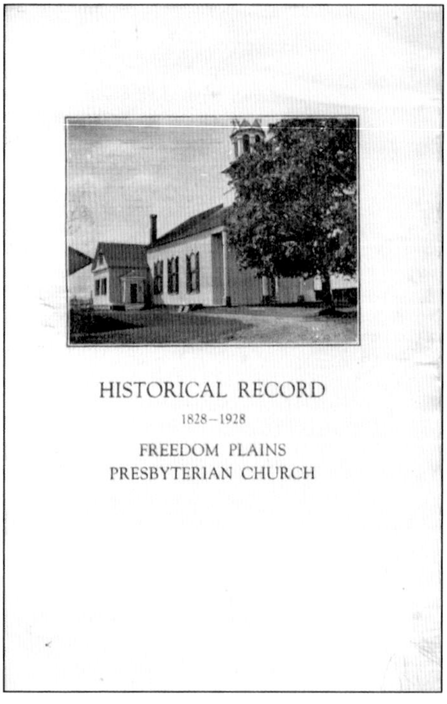

This booklet was produced by the Freedom Plains Church in 1928 to commemorate 100 years since its founding. The introduction was written by Carrie Moore and gives a wonderfully detailed accounting of the history of the congregation, including all the pastors who served the church over the years. Anniversary celebrations included a pageant, a basket lunch, and a communion supper. (GW.)

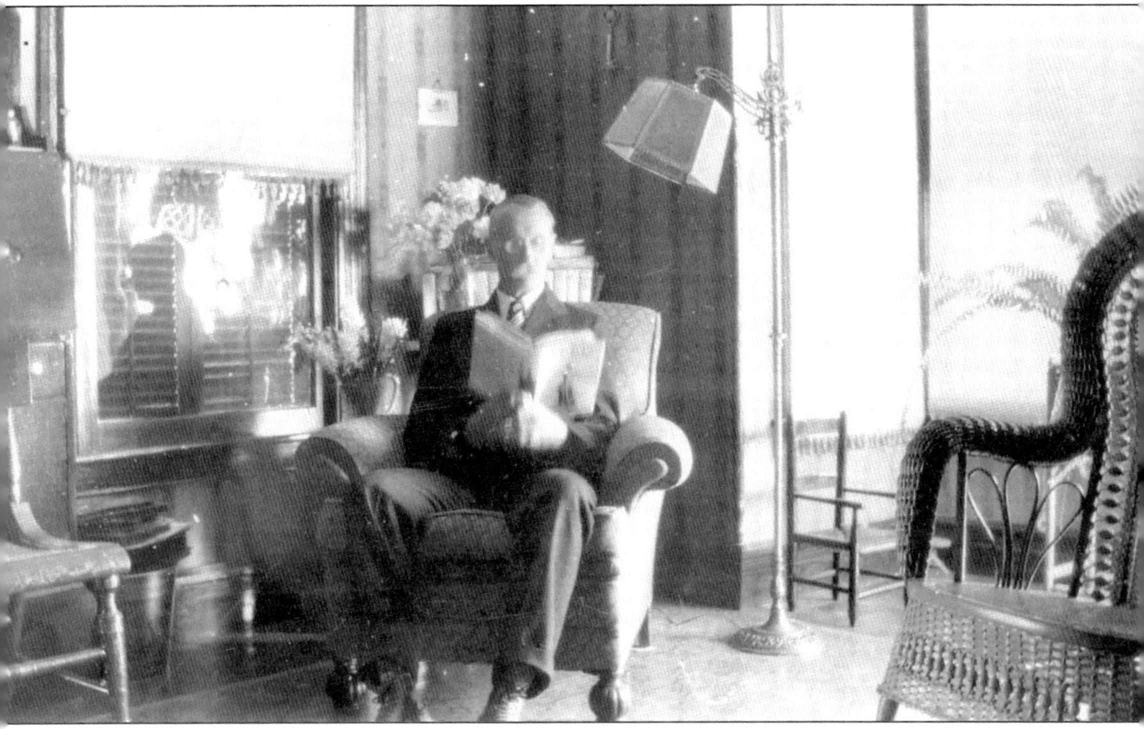

Delivery of mail was done first by horse and wagon (or sleigh during the winters) and later by the first cars. In 1914, the Schryver's General Store served as the post office. Alice Schryver was the postmistress at that time, and Alvoid Rensley was the mail carrier. This photograph shows Rensley in his home in 1931, on the occasion of his being honored by the town for his years of service. Rensley served on the town's Service and Hospitality Committee as well.

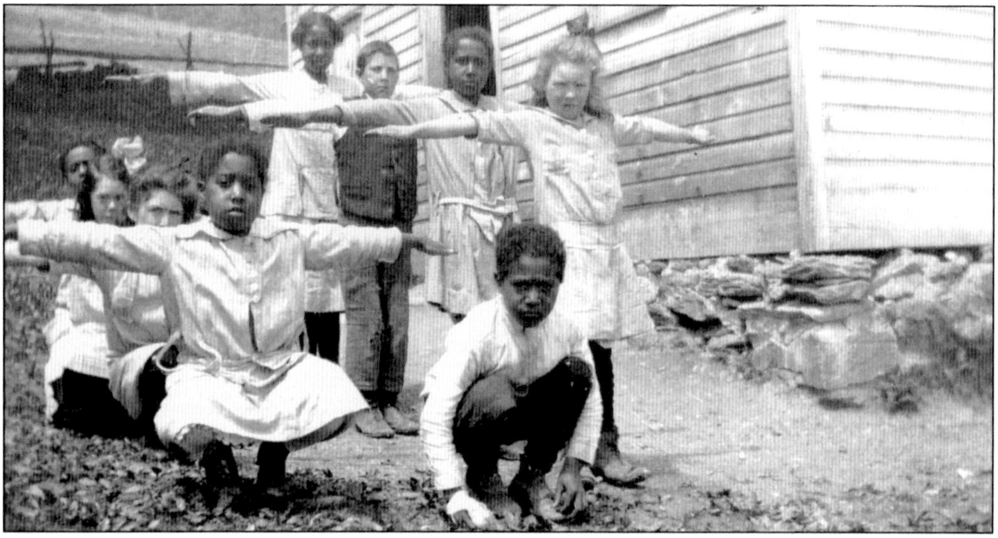

Some students at the one-room school on Skidmore Road seem to be doing calisthenics here. Hazel Skidmore taught at the school during the 1930s. Her cousin, Elizabeth Pierson, remembers that each Arbor Day, the teacher would take the students on a field trip up Mountain Road to see the "Indian caves" that were said to have once been used by local tribes.

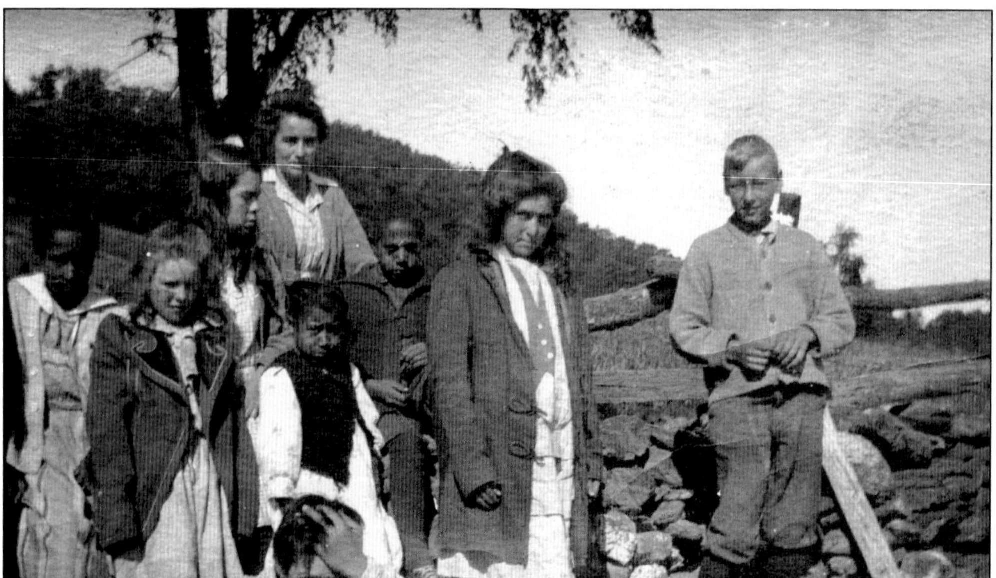

The students and an unidentified woman pose for this picture by the stone wall near the schoolhouse. Known as Hillside School, it stood on what is now the Pierson farm. Neil Pierson came from Sweden on a cattle boat during World War II, and his family purchased the farm shortly afterward. The house dates from the Civil War.

HEALTH CONTEST IN THE TOWN OF LA GRANGE 1930-1931

Schools receiving 100 points or nearest to that receive a worth while prize.
Judging to be done sometime in January.

I. Health Activities
- 1. Morning inspection — 10
- 2. Ventilation and temperature
  - a. Flushing the room three times — 3
  - b. Use of window ventilators (boards or cloth) in schools without ventilating system or use of ventilating system — 3
  - c. Temperature at about 68 - temperature recorded by a child 3 or 4 times daily on chart made at school — 3
- 3. Cleanliness
  - a. General appearance of school room — 5
  - b. Floor swept every day at the close of school (should not be swept during school hours or in the morning) — 3
  - c. Furniture dusted every day with oily cloth — 3
- 4. Drinking water kept under recommended sanitary conditions — 5
  - a. Closed container with faucet or pump
  - b. Paper cups
- 5. Washing hands after going to toilet — 5
- 6. Toilets
  - a. Clean and sanitary — 5
  - b. No defacements — 5

II. Noon Hour
- 1. Preparation for noon meal
  - a. Cleared desks — 1
  - b. Airing room — 2
  - c. Toilet — 5
  - d. Washing hands - approved method — 5
  - e. Covering desks or tables with lunch cloths (white oilcloth covers, white paper covers, or any other good substitute teacher may devise) — 5
- 2. Eating the noon meal
  - a. Sufficient time - at least twenty minutes — 10
  - b. Cheerful and mannerly at table — 5
  - c. Hot dish or drink served during winter months (see approved method of serving hot lunch) — 5

The health contest outlined here was initiated by Mrs. George Kuchler in an attempt to raise the standards of the remaining one-room schoolhouses in LaGrange. Unspecified prizes were an incentive for the students to participate. The suggestion for paper cups is an indication that many of the schools were still using the communal tin dippers and pails for the children's drinking water.

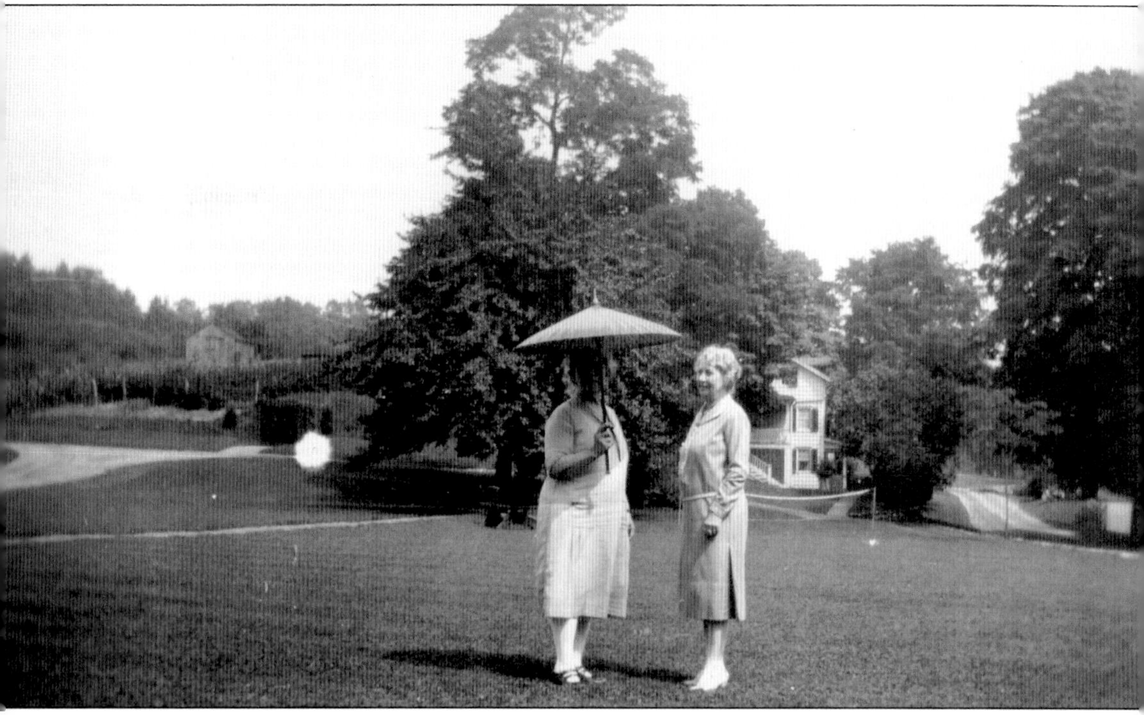

Two ladies enjoy a sunny day at the Watchhorn place in the early 1930s. Robert Watchorn, who served as immigration commissioner at Ellis Island, bought the former Floral Home from the Wells family and continued to keep it open to guests. Watchorn was known for having constructed the Lincoln Memorial Shrine in Redlands, California.

Four

MODERN DAYS

The war years arrived with rationing, victory gardens, and a renewed patriotism. Local families waited anxiously, praying for their servicemen to come home safely, as Dutchess County native Pres. Franklin D. Roosevelt led the country through the difficult times toward revitalization. The following baby boom contributed to the continuing growth of LaGrange, as it did everywhere.

The one-room schoolhouses gradually disappeared as the school districts became centralized, and buses now transported the children to their classes. Farms became more rare also, although orchards still thrived since the area was well known for its wonderful apples. From the 1950s on, local businesses continued to multiply. With IBM as an ever-greater presence as employer, new houses were built by the score, and the Taconic Parkway became the preferred way to commute to and from New York City.

The 1960s and 1970s were a time of change everywhere, and LaGrange was no exception. Some old businesses faded away while new ones appeared; the local schools enlarged both their space and their curriculums; and many familiar faces either moved to warmer climates or passed on. Unfortunately, some of the oldest and most historic buildings yielded to neglect or demolition.

Then the bicentennial of 1976 began a resurgence of interest in the past. Many of the town's early homes were lovingly preserved or restored by owners who appreciated their long history. Historic house tours allowed residents to become acquainted with the story of LaGrange in the old days. Local teachers and history buffs also helped to bring attention to the need to learn about and preserve the past.

But progress could not be halted, and more than ever the focus was on the future. Most of the oldest farms were eventually turned into communities of new homes, as were the orchards. LaGrange is no longer the rural community it was in the beginning, but it is now a highly desirable location to those seeking an alternative to Westchester and its congestion. It is hoped that the newcomers will seek to learn more about LaGrange's past, so that they may come to appreciate the history of their adopted town.

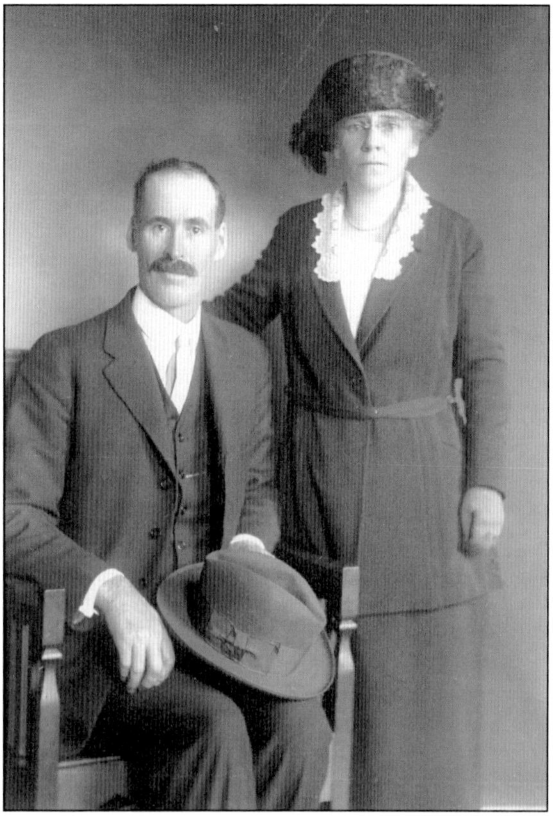

After many years of assisting at the Floral Home, Jennie Rhinehart left to set up housekeeping for herself when she married Henry Clinton Thibideau. They posed for this formal portrait at the time of their marriage.

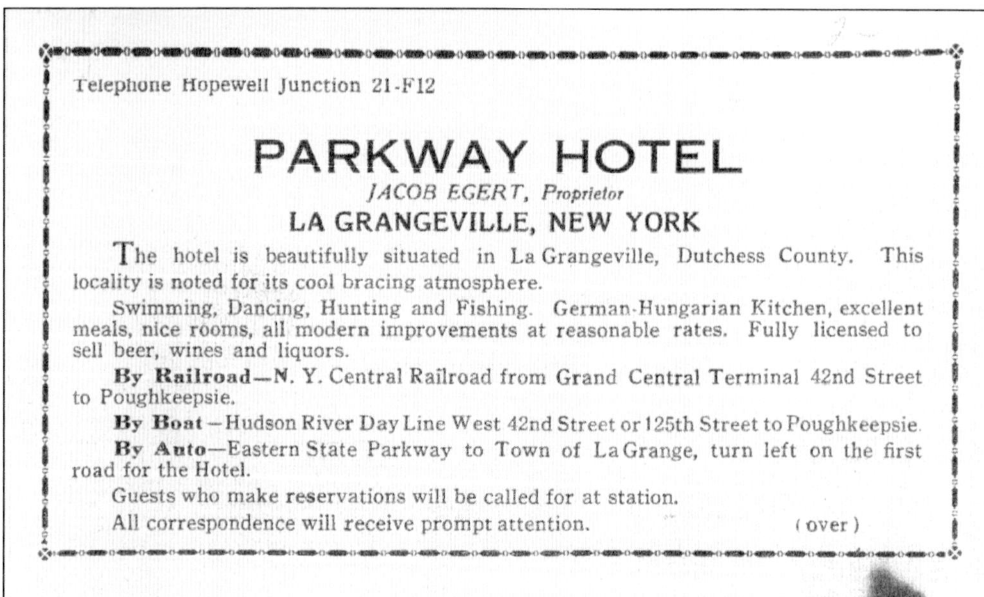

This advertisement for the Parkway Hotel promotes the scenic beauty of the town as an enticement to guests, as well as the convenience of being right off the Eastern State Parkway (as the Taconic was known then). This type of establishment found it hard to compete with the larger hotels in Poughkeepsie. (AC.)

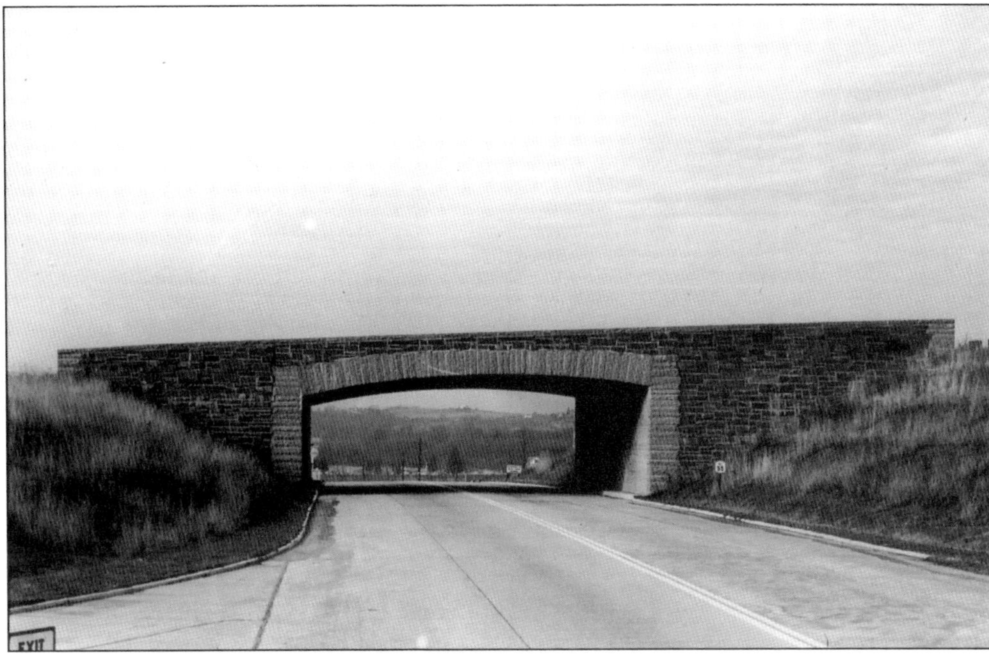

The Taconic State Parkway was extended through LaGrange in the mid-1940s. Shown is the bridge over Route 55, with the Presbyterian church visible in the far background, in 1949. The construction of the parkway was heavily promoted by Franklin Delano Roosevelt as a stimulus to tourism in the area, as well as a means to create jobs. (DOT.)

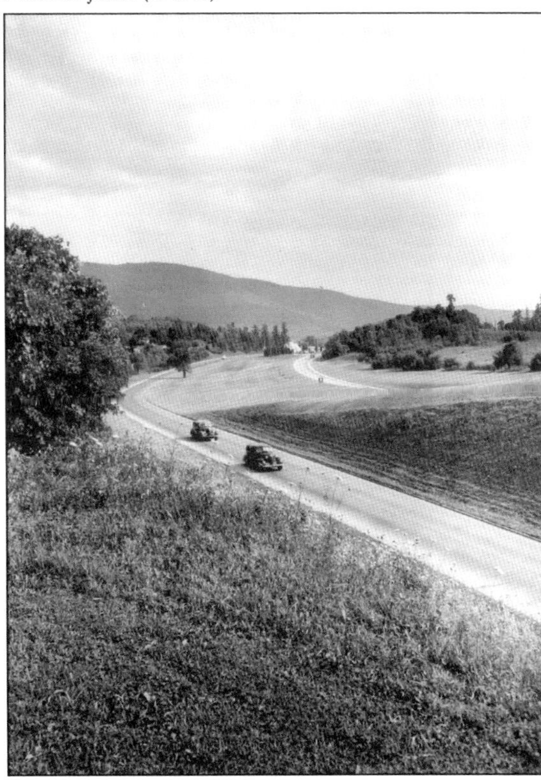

This was the view of the parkway near Todd Hill in 1948. Travelers were few and the pace was slow then, with motorists taking time to enjoy the lovely views in Dutchess County. Traffic increased greatly once New York City and Westchester residents began to move north and commute to their jobs. (DOT.)

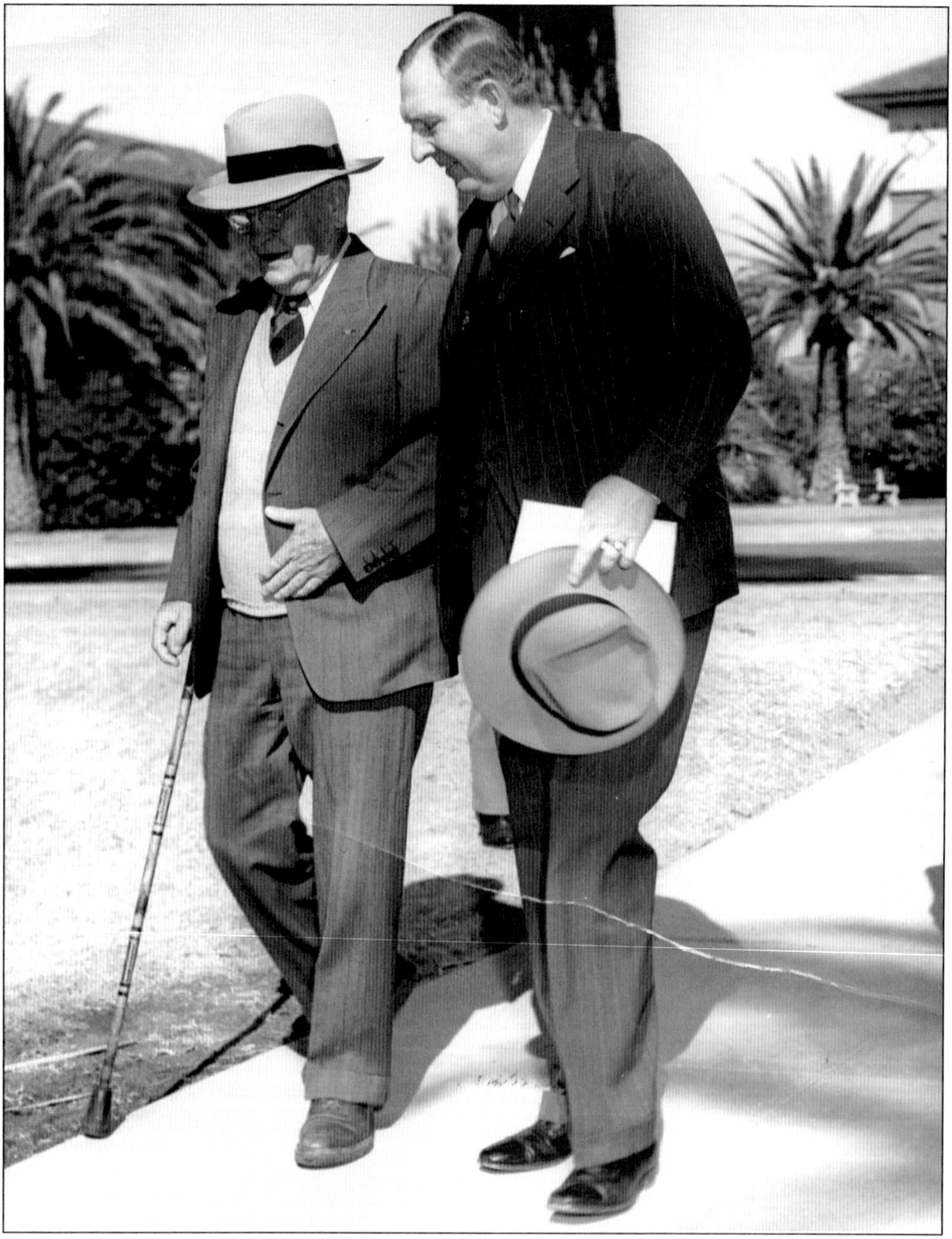

James Baird (on the left) donated a large tract of land to the state in 1939 for use as a recreation area. The property included a farm that dates back to the mid-1700s, with a succession of owners including the Beekman and Livingston families. Baird was a well-known engineer and president of the construction company that built the Lincoln Memorial in Washington, D.C. (OPRHP.)

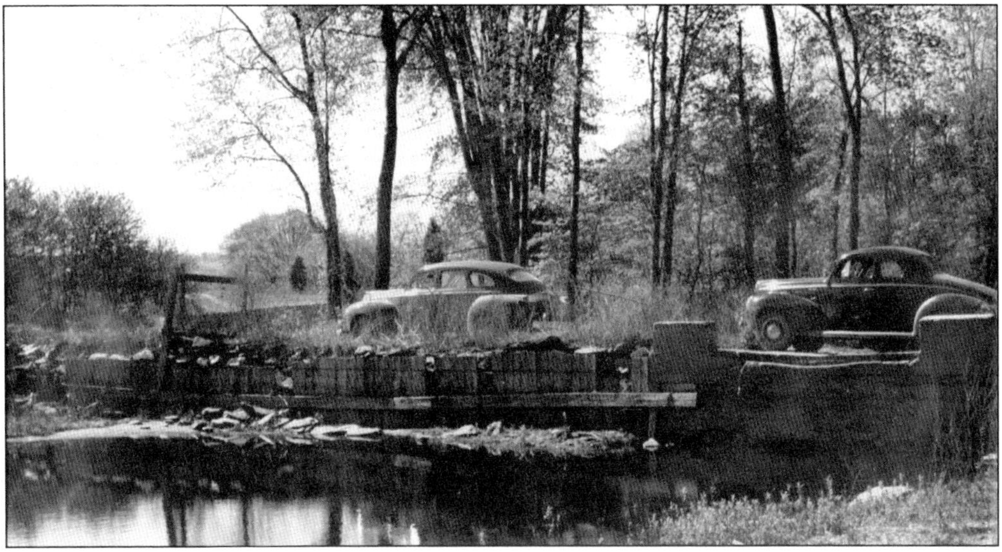

This photograph of the James Baird Park shows the old dam during construction in 1941. A Civilian Conservation Corps camp had been built on the site to house the laborers. This project, along with the completion of the parkway, brought some much-needed jobs to local men. (OPRHP.)

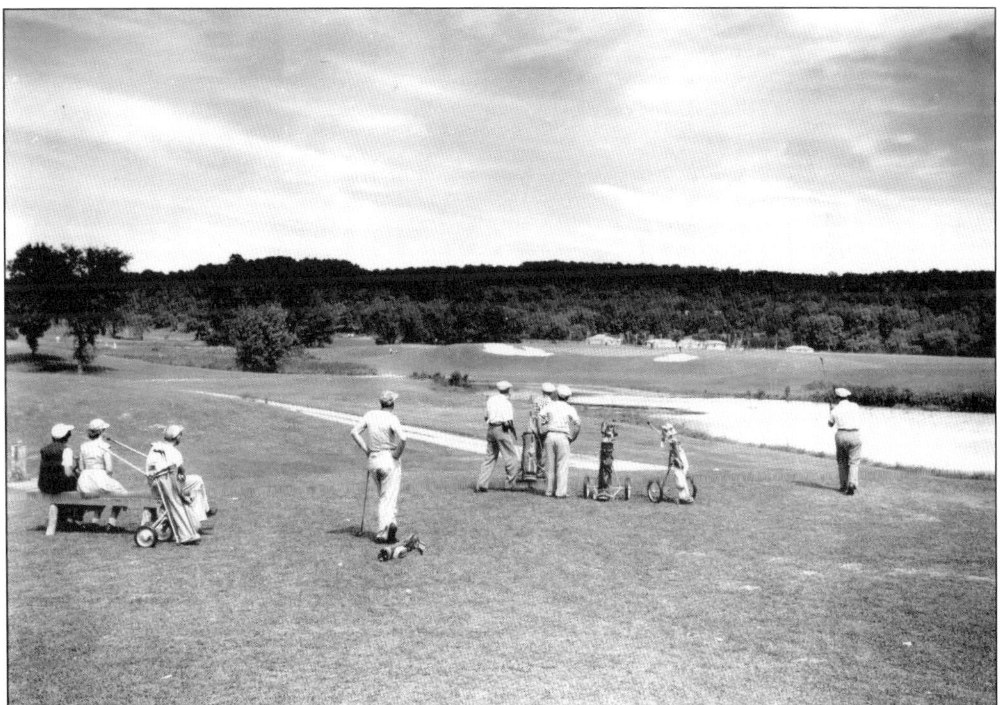

These 1950-era golfers on the 15th tee could see the pavilion and clubhouse in the far background. The 18-hole course at Baird was designed by Robert Trent Jones, notable in his field. The layout took advantage of the natural contours of the former farmland, including the pond. Nowadays the course is also used in the winter, attracting cross-country skiers and snowshoers. (OPRHP.)

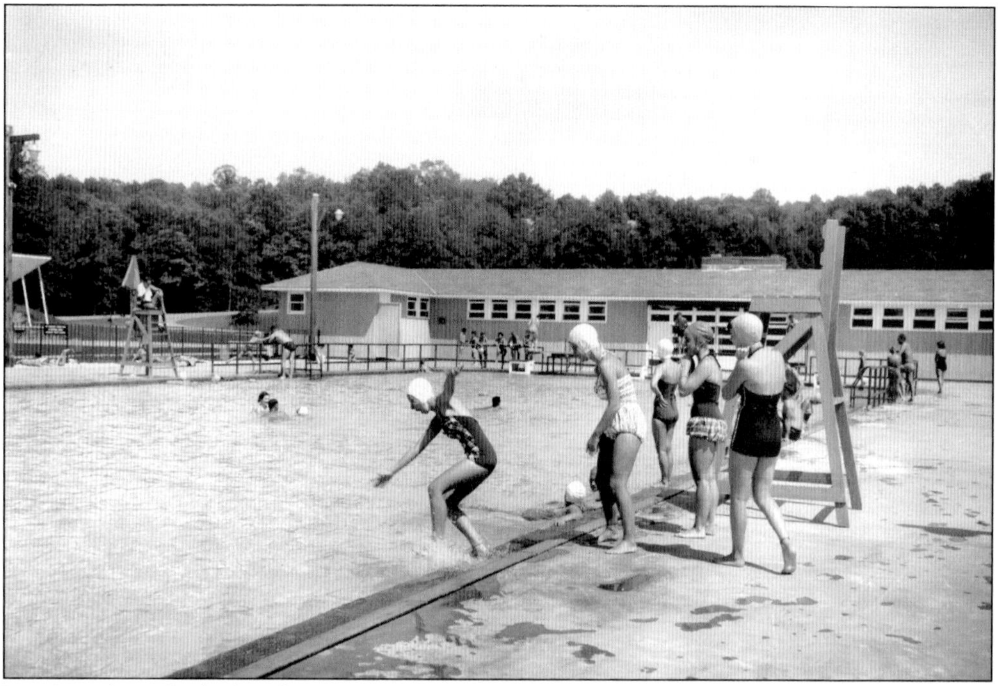

Local residents flocked to the swimming pool at Baird Park; it was full to capacity on every hot day. Bathing caps in place to protect their hairdos, these ladies wait their turn to enter the water. The first young woman appears to be unsure whether she wants to go in. (OPRHP.)

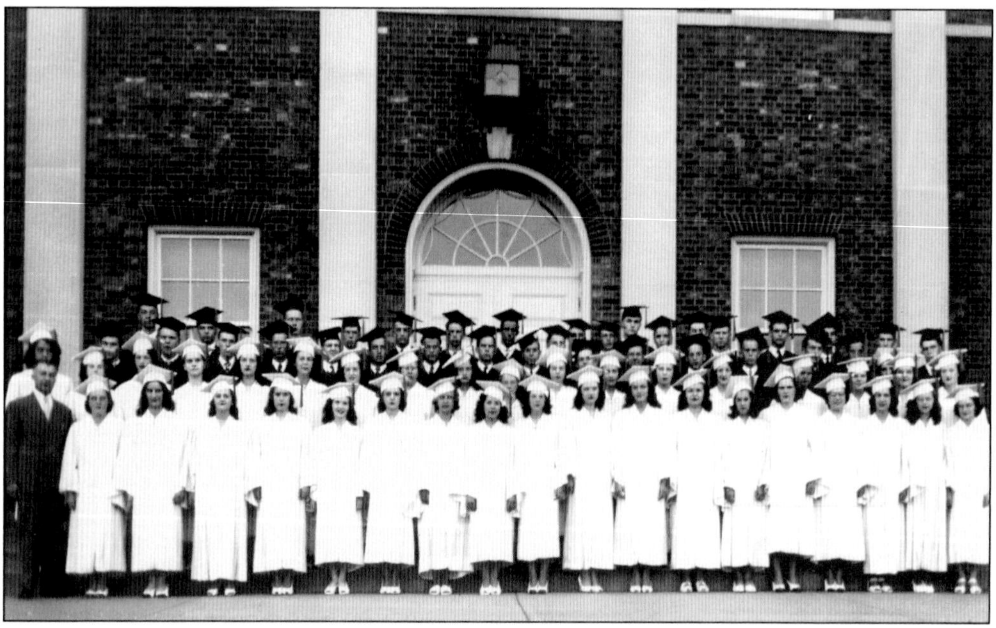

After the demise of the one-room schools in the 1940s, due to centralization, LaGrange teenagers attended either Millbrook High School or Arlington in Poughkeepsie. There were tuition costs, however, which some parents could not afford. Therefore the education of some young people—especially in farming families—ended in eighth grade. Seen here is Arlington's class of 1946, which included some LaGrange students. (ACSD.)

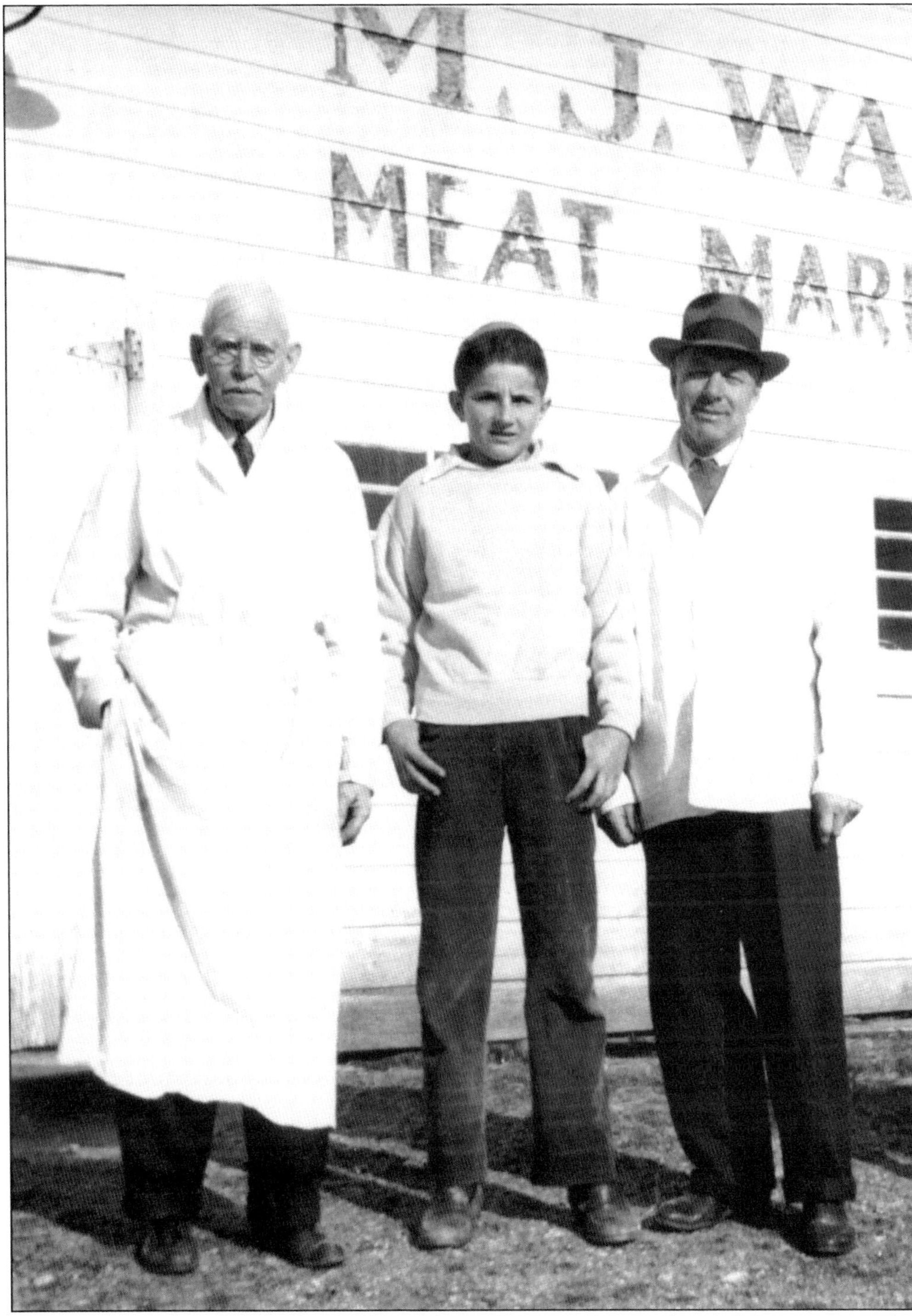

Three generations of the Wade family are shown here standing in front of their meat market on Cramer Road. Monfort Wade, with the snowy mustache, was named after his maternal grandfather, part of the Van Kleeck family that settled in the area in the early 1800s. Young George would later become town supervisor for several terms. (GW.)

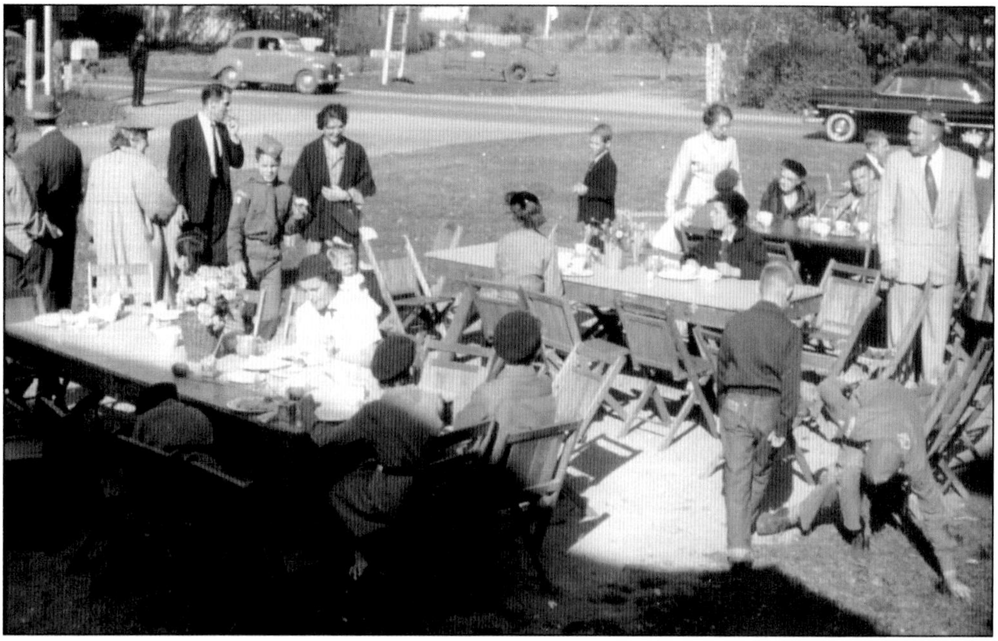

The local Scouts seem to be hosting this picnic at the Presbyterian church. A young man is escorting a lady (maybe his mother) to a seat at a table, where some girls are wearing the trademark Girl Scout berets. Scouting is still active in the town, with the local troops taking part in various events and volunteering their time. (FPC.)

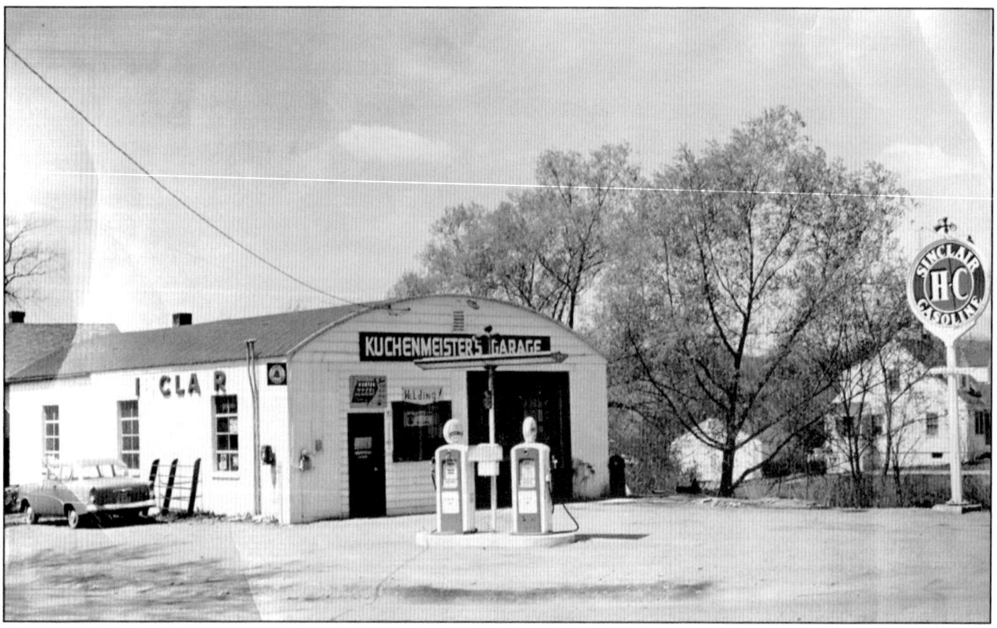

Kuchenmeister's Garage sat behind the current Knights of Columbus hall near the ball fields on Noxon Road. The building has had numerous occupants over its lifetime, having been the site of Pete Hulst's market during the Depression. It was later known as Chan's Superette in the late 1950s, then Angie's Store until about 1990.

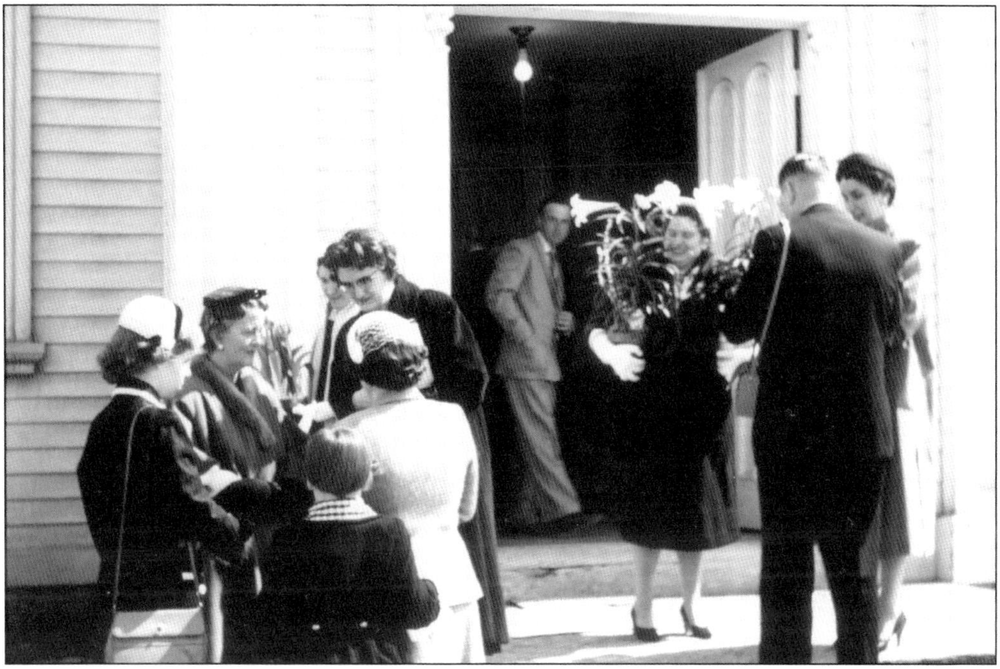

Members of the Cross, Kuchler, Knight, and Bronson families are seen here leaving the Methodist church on Cross Road in 1950. It appears to be Easter Sunday, judging from the lilies one of the ladies is carrying. The parish hall at the church was erected in 1954, with funds raised by members, and dedicated in 1958. (TUMC.)

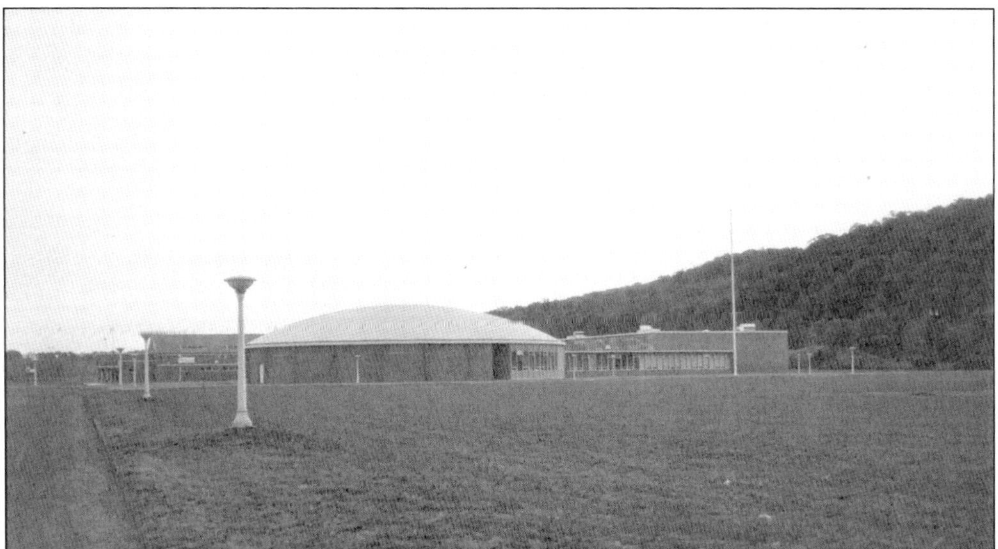

The construction of LaGrange's own high school in 1971 meant students could attend classes in town, instead of traveling to Poughkeepsie. The school has expanded twice since and is currently undergoing additional renovations to accommodate an ever-growing population. The enrollment in 2008 was 3,400. (IM.)

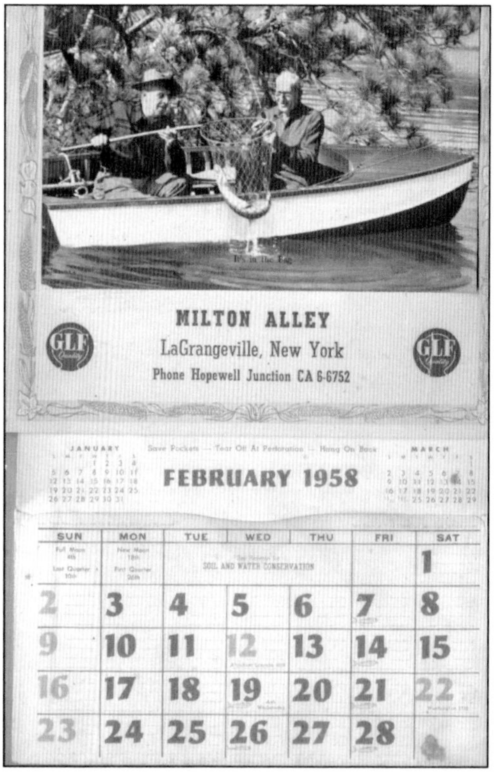

Customers at the Milton Alley Agway were given free calendars in the 1950s. Specifically for farmers, the back pages included articles on various agricultural practices, along with forms for recording expenses during the year. "Helpful Facts for Farmers" gave tips on such things as how to increase egg production and how to estimate the weight of heifers.

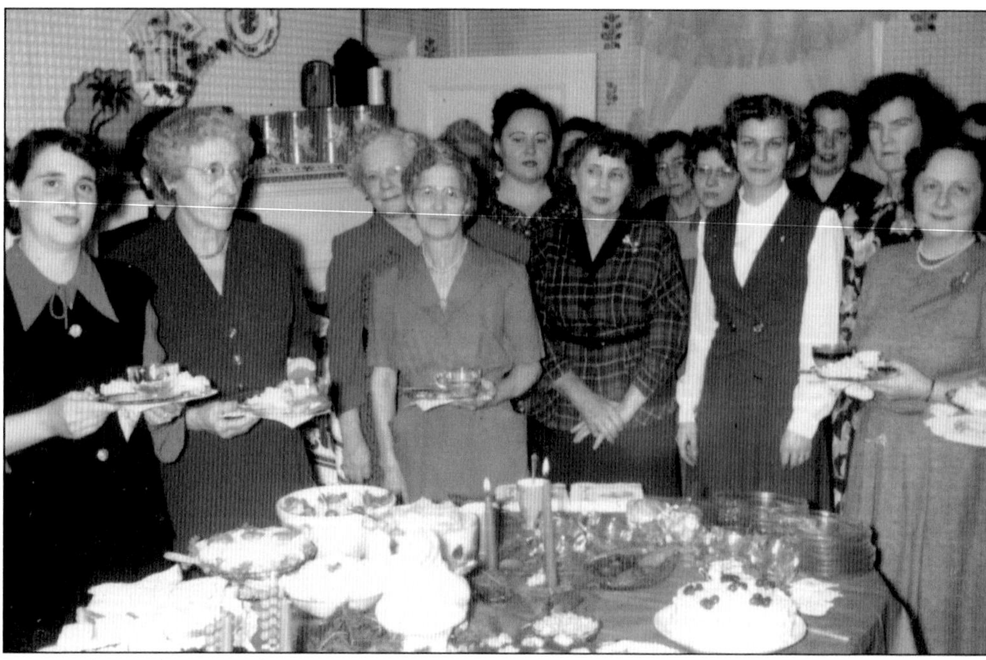

During the early 1950s, the Home Bureau was a popular organization that taught various home skills, such as sewing and cooking. In the Christmas season of 1951, Alice Tobin held a party at her home for some of the ladies of the group. A scrapbook made by the participants in is the collection of the historical society.

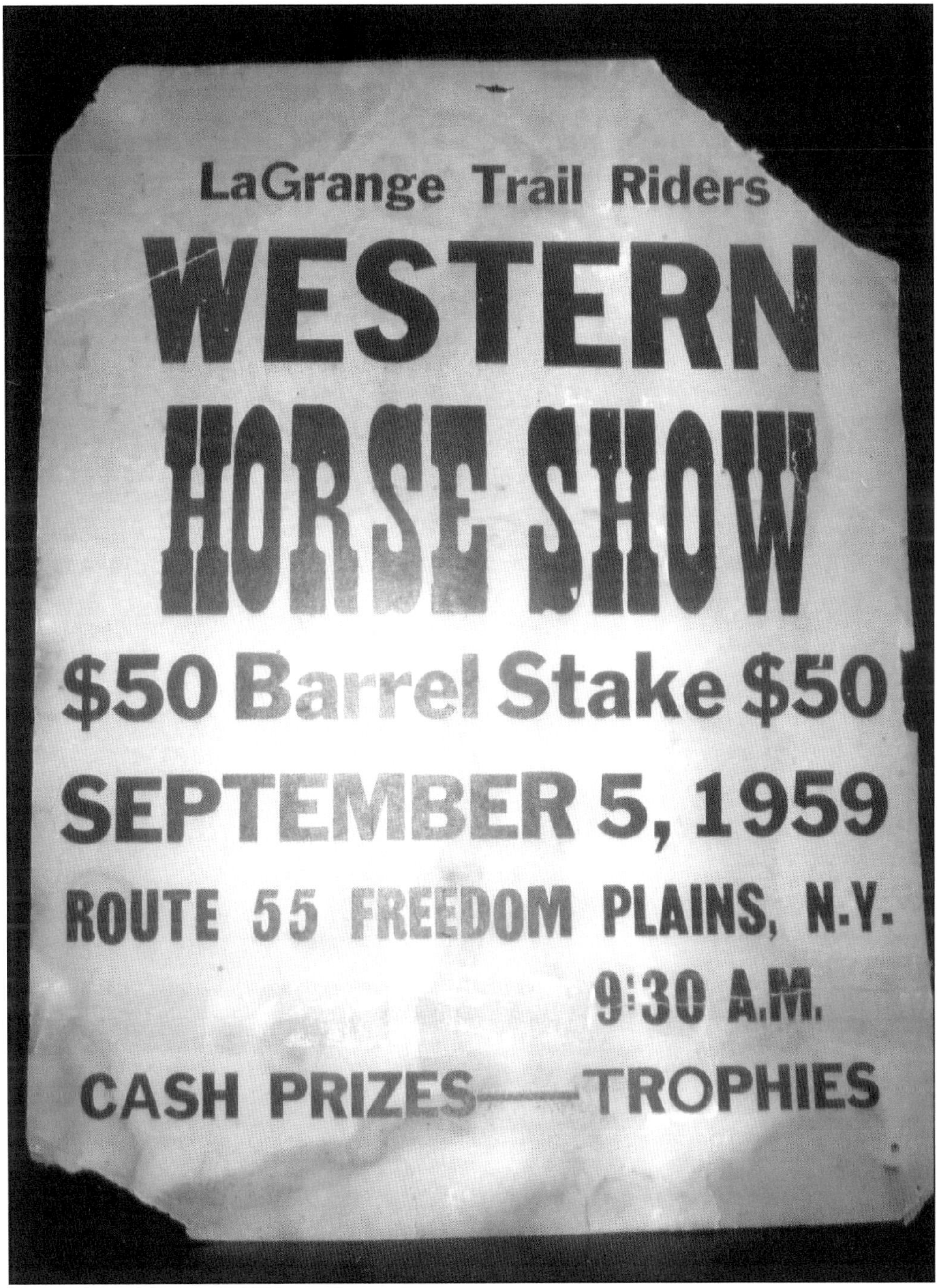

A horse show was a chance for riders to show their skills and maybe win some prize money as well. Elizabeth Jacobs, known to her family and friends as "Bubba," came from a family of avid horsemen who regularly took part in competitions. This poster is from her collection of riding memorabilia.

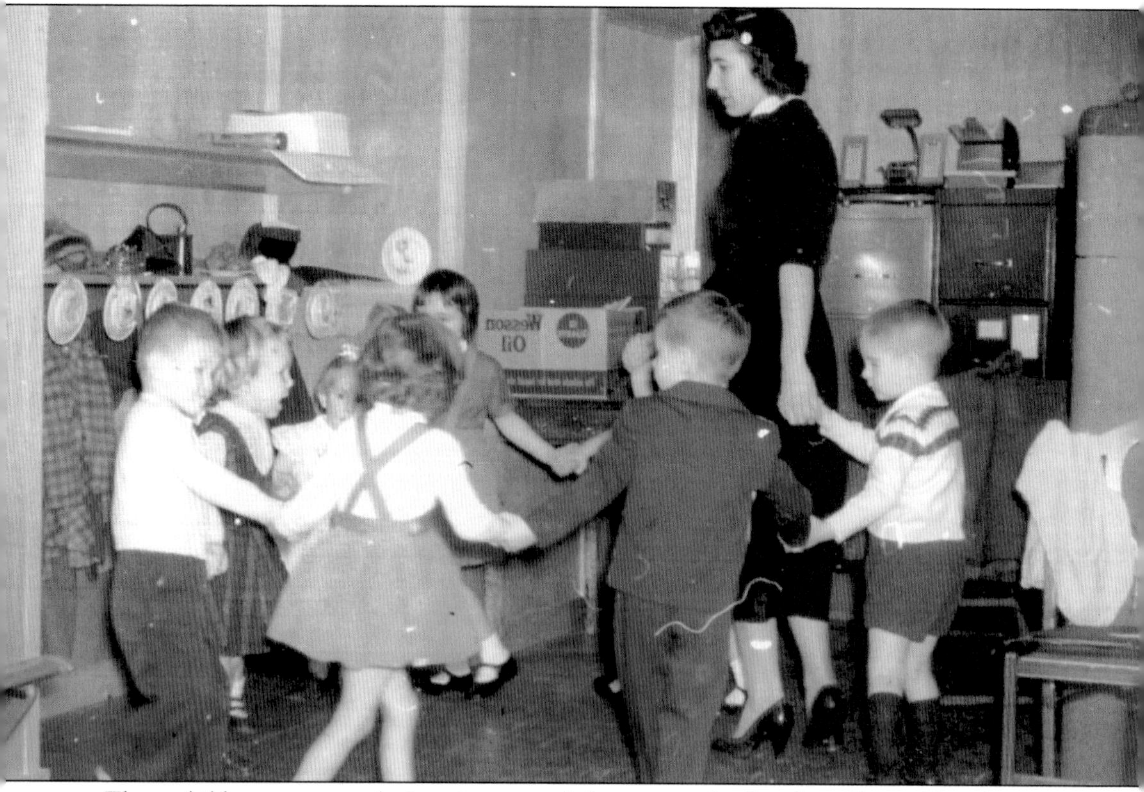

These children are seen playing ring-around-the-rosy at the Freedom Plains Church's nursery school in the 1950s. The teacher must have been glad to remove her high heels after a day of keeping up with the youngsters. The nursery school was initiated by Rev. William Eaton and has been an important part of the church since its inception. (FPPC.)

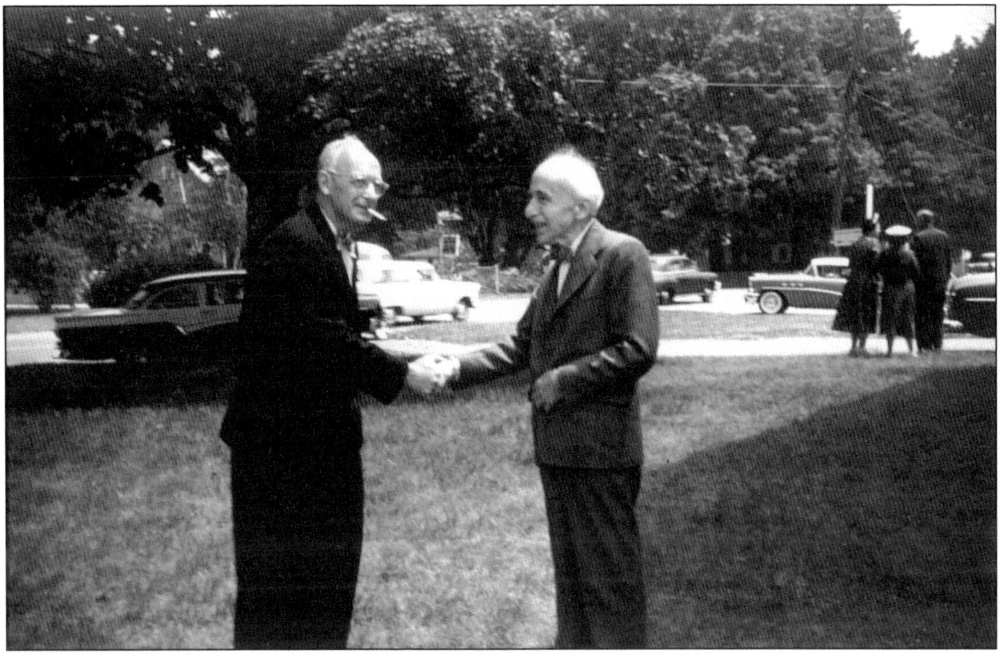

T. Carl Whitmer (on the right) was a well-known composer in the 1920s, when he and his wife, artist Helen Crosier, moved to LaGrange. They bought the property that later became known as Dramamount, where they hosted musical performances. They had plans for a theater on a much grander scale, but it was a bit too far out of the way to tempt artists from the city. (FPPC.)

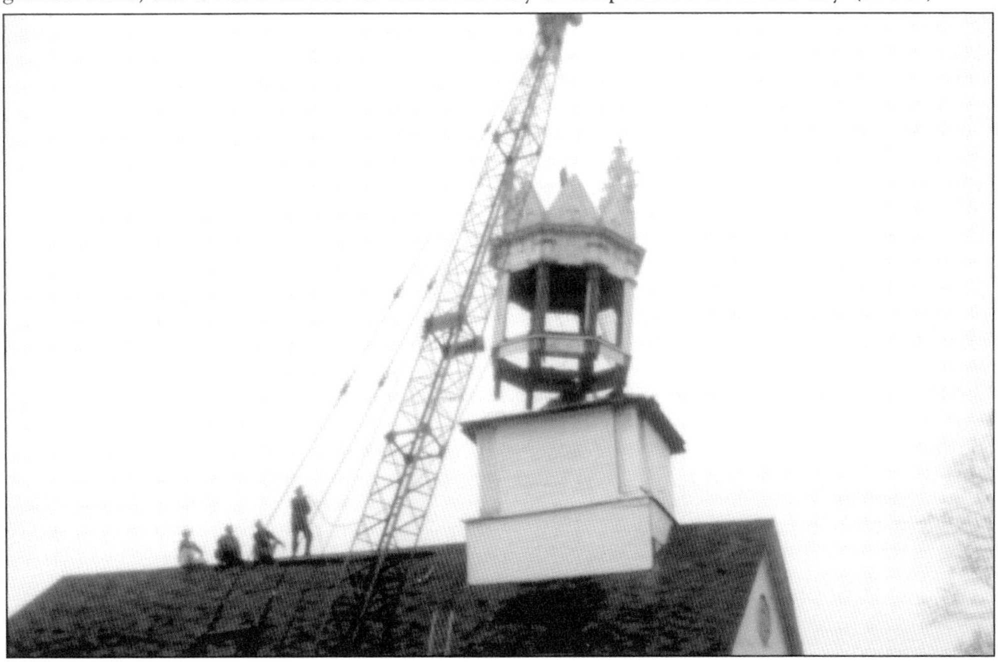

In 1967, the Presbyterian church's tower was struck by lightning, causing extensive damage. Funds were raised to replace the tower, and here a crane is taking down the old crown to be replaced by a new one. In 1978, church member Dorothy (Wardell) Boice wrote a poem, "The Church with a Crown," to commemorate the occasion of the church's 150th anniversary. (FPPC.)

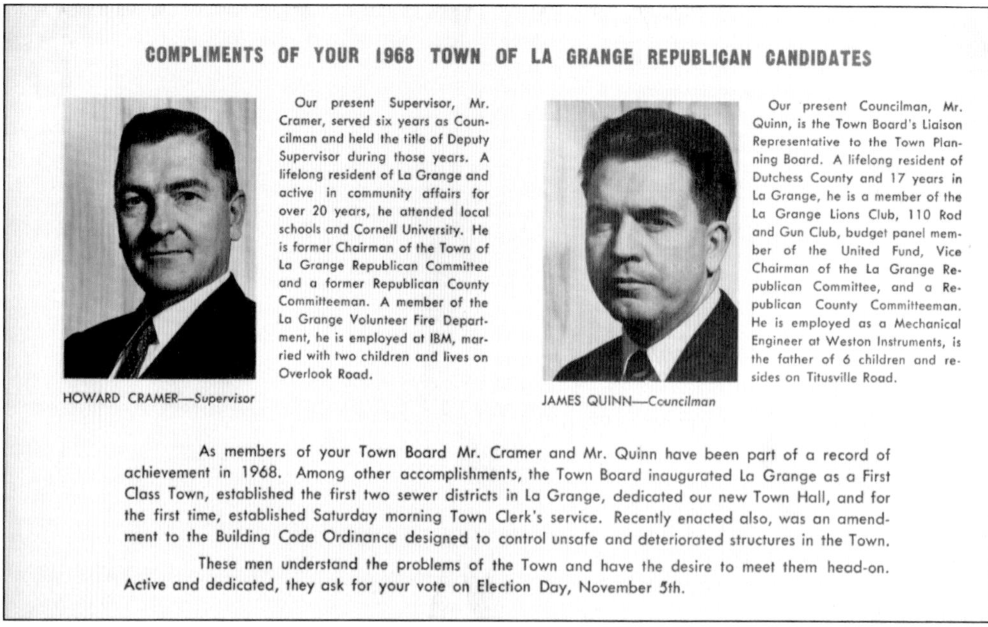

COMPLIMENTS OF YOUR 1968 TOWN OF LA GRANGE REPUBLICAN CANDIDATES

HOWARD CRAMER—*Supervisor*

Our present Supervisor, Mr. Cramer, served six years as Councilman and held the title of Deputy Supervisor during those years. A lifelong resident of La Grange and active in community affairs for over 20 years, he attended local schools and Cornell University. He is former Chairman of the Town of La Grange Republican Committee and a former Republican County Committeeman. A member of the La Grange Volunteer Fire Department, he is employed at IBM, married with two children and lives on Overlook Road.

JAMES QUINN—*Councilman*

Our present Councilman, Mr. Quinn, is the Town Board's Liaison Representative to the Town Planning Board. A lifelong resident of Dutchess County and 17 years in La Grange, he is a member of the La Grange Lions Club, 110 Rod and Gun Club, budget panel member of the United Fund, Vice Chairman of the La Grange Republican Committee, and a Republican County Committeeman. He is employed as a Mechanical Engineer at Weston Instruments, is the father of 6 children and resides on Titusville Road.

As members of your Town Board Mr. Cramer and Mr. Quinn have been part of a record of achievement in 1968. Among other accomplishments, the Town Board inaugurated La Grange as a First Class Town, established the first two sewer districts in La Grange, dedicated our new Town Hall, and for the first time, established Saturday morning Town Clerk's service. Recently enacted also, was an amendment to the Building Code Ordinance designed to control unsafe and deteriorated structures in the Town.

These men understand the problems of the Town and have the desire to meet them head-on. Active and dedicated, they ask for your vote on Election Day, November 5th.

In 1968, Howard Cramer and James Quinn sought election on the town board, in the Republican Party. Cramer would continue as town supervisor until 1971 and during that time also served as president of the historical society.

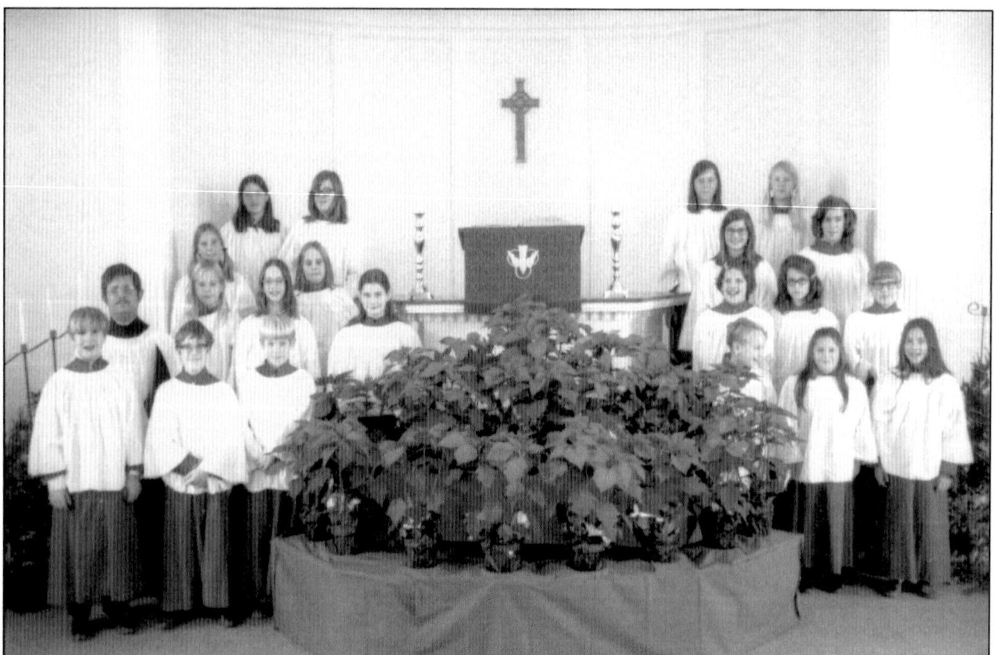

Since the late 1950s, the Freedom Plains Church has entertained parents and guests each year with a Christmas program, which always includes music performances by the youngsters. In this photograph from the 1970s, a few of the singers are trying not to giggle. (FPPC.)

Everett Clemett and Lois (Wade) Clemett celebrated their 25th wedding anniversary in 1971. Everett was a partner to the Wades in their meat market for over 40 years and served as treasurer of the historical society, while Lois was active in the Methodist Church. The couple now lives in Florida. (GW.)

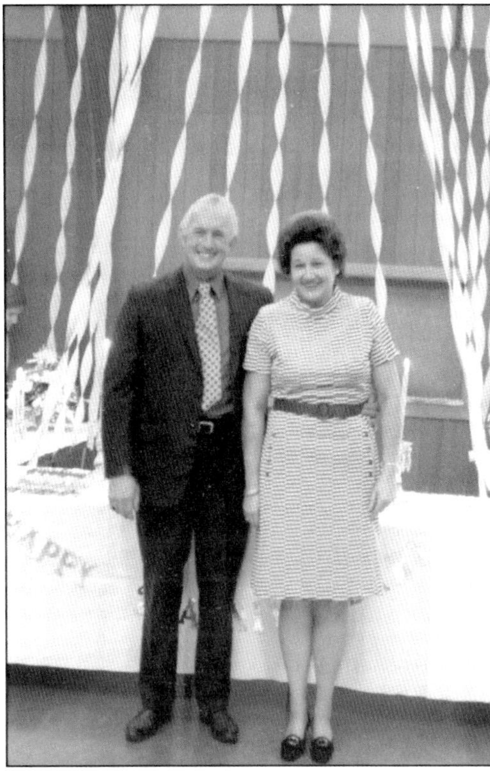

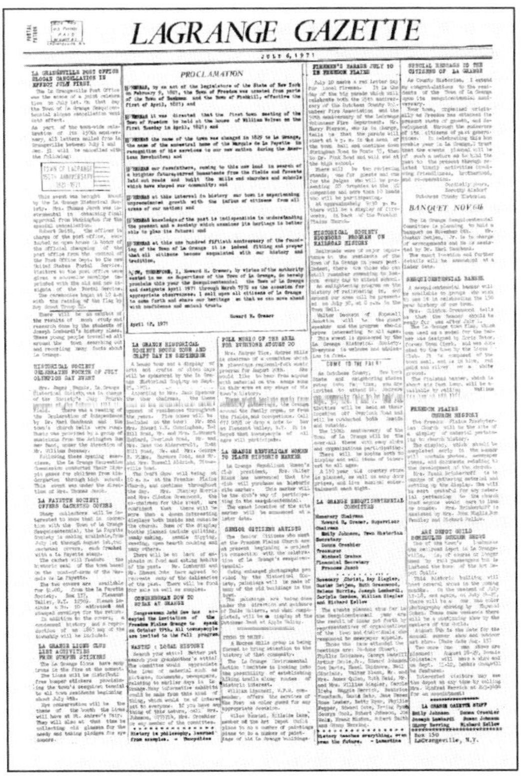

LAGRANGE GAZETTE

JULY 6, 1971

PROCLAMATION

BANQUET NOV 6th

In 1971, the town celebrated the 150th anniversary of its founding This *LaGrange Gazette* was published by the Sesquicentennial Committee, headed by chairman Emily Johnson, the town historian. A wonderful blend of history and current events, the paper demonstrates the pride and affection of the citizens for their hometown.

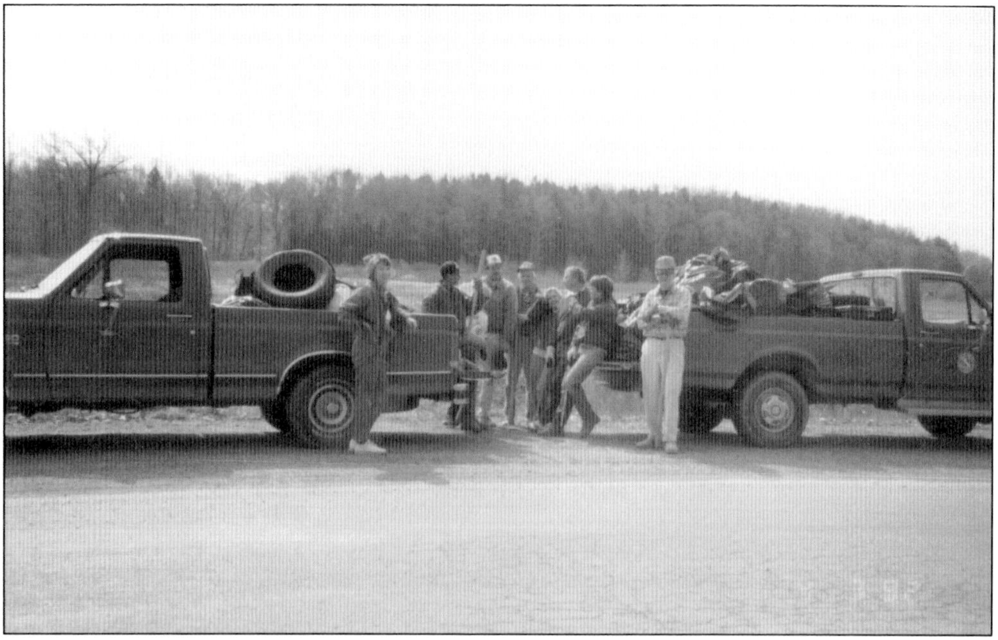

Trash Bash takes place each spring. Volunteers gather at the town hall for their assignments, then head out to pick up litter along the roadways. Afterward, refreshments are provided to the workers in appreciation for their efforts to keep LaGrange beautiful.

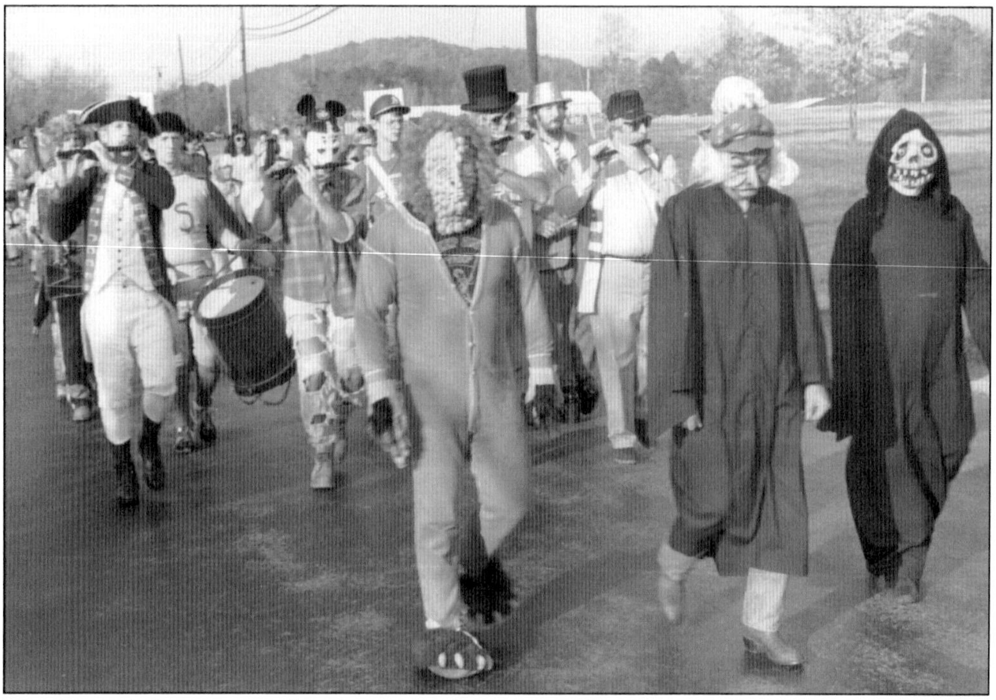

The fife and drum corps played the marching music for the Halloween parade, which was popular in the late 1990s. The procession started at the town hall and ended at the middle school, with refreshments provided by the Ladies Auxiliary. Some of the homemade costumes were quite inventive.

The annual goose dinner at the Presbyterian church was a November tradition started in the 1920s to raise funds. Ladies of the church continued to make the delicious meal with all the trimmings for an appreciative public for 50 years, right after Election Day. In the early days, it was customary for the losers to buy dinner for their winning opponents. (FPC.)

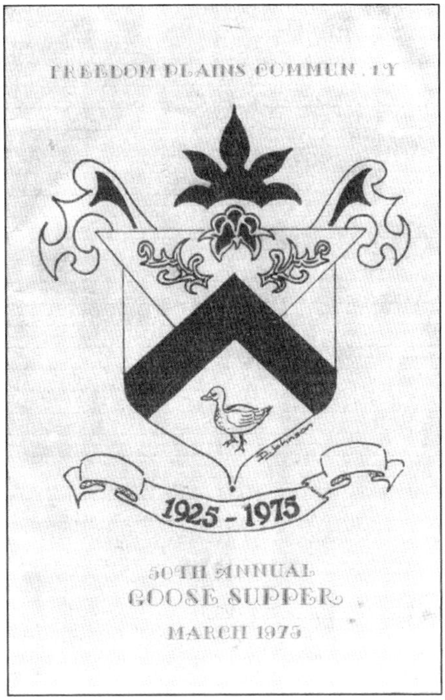

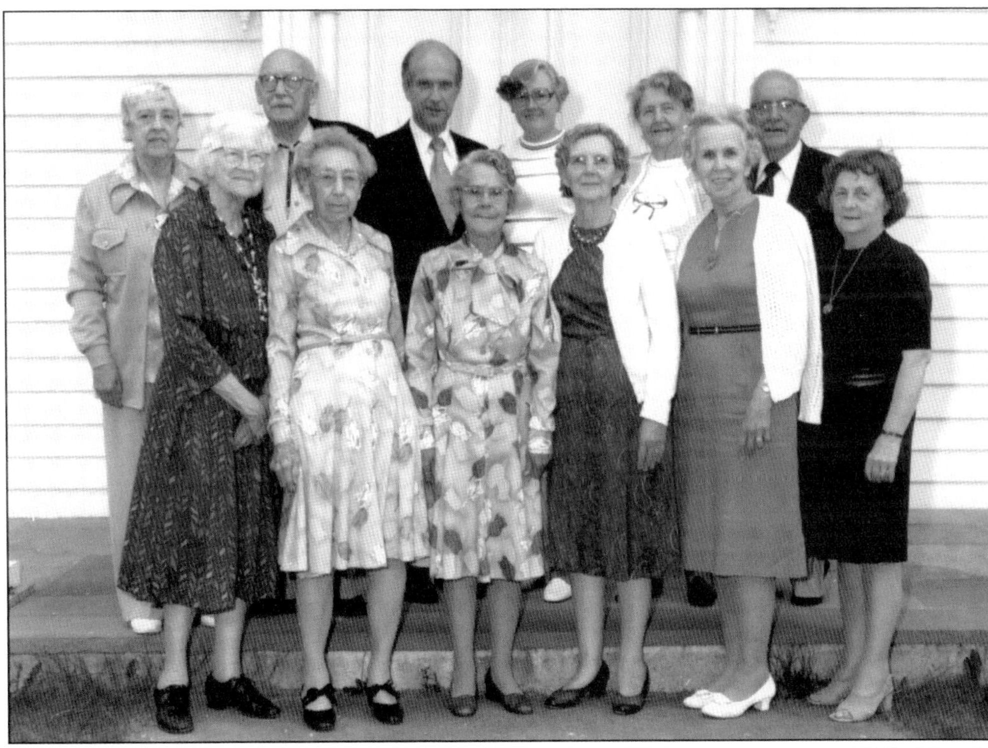

The Freedom Plains Presbyterian Church celebrated its 150th anniversary in 1978. Thanks to the efforts of the planning committee, many events were organized to help parishioners commemorate this special occasion. The ladies and gentlemen on the committee pose for this snapshot in front of the church.

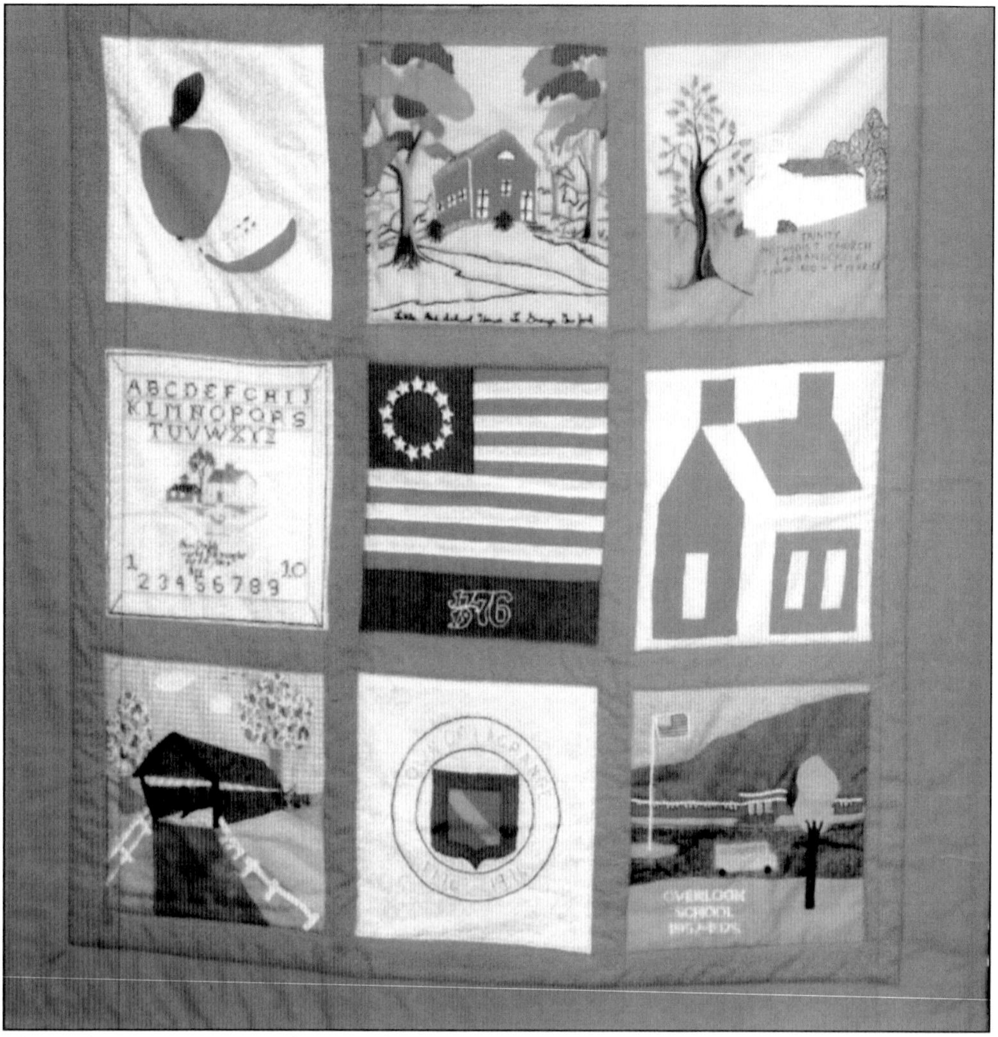

This quilt was a project involving students, parents, and teachers of the Overlook Road school. It was created during the bicentennial year of 1976 and presented to the historical society. Various town landmarks are represented, including the Manchester covered bridge. The quilt is now on display at the Little Red Schoolhouse during special events.

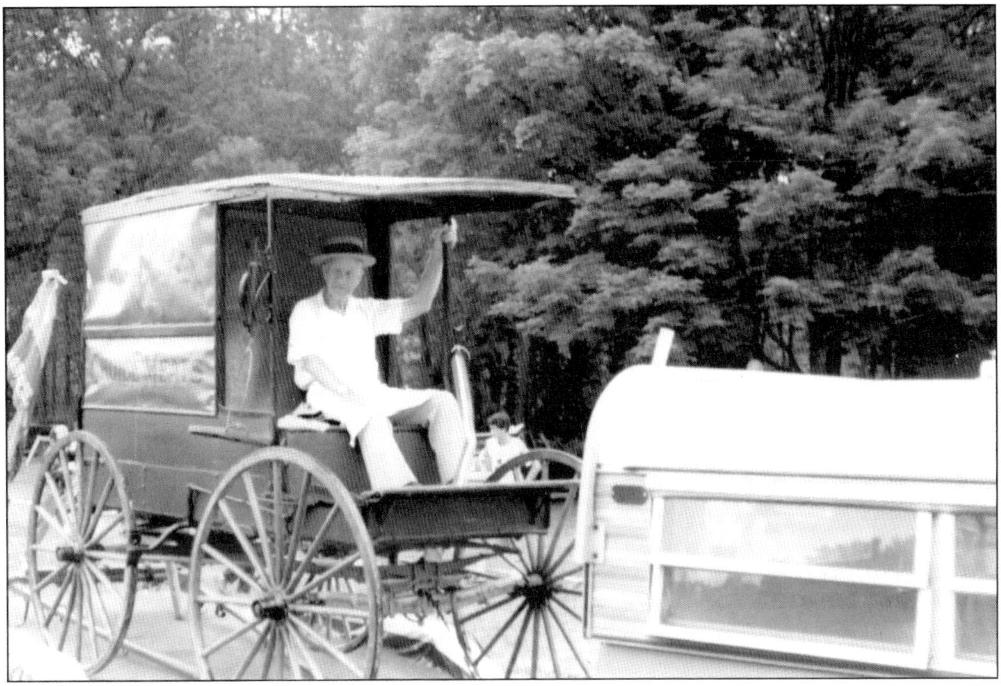

The Wade meat wagon was a feature in the town parade of 1981, with George Wade II at the reins. The wagon, used for countless trips over LaGrange roads, was later given a dignified retirement as an exhibit in the antiques barn at the Dutchess County fairgrounds. (GW).

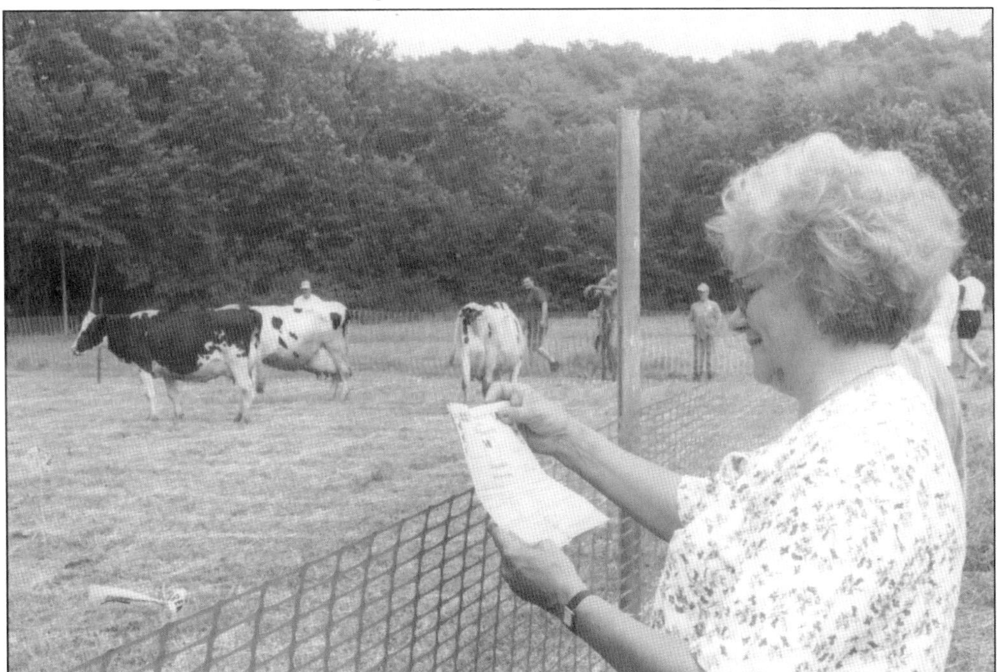

The cow plop contest was held at the ball fields in Freedom Park, with the assistance of some bovines. Players bought squares on the grid in the field and hoped that theirs would receive the most "fertilizer"—a humorous tribute to LaGrange's farming history.

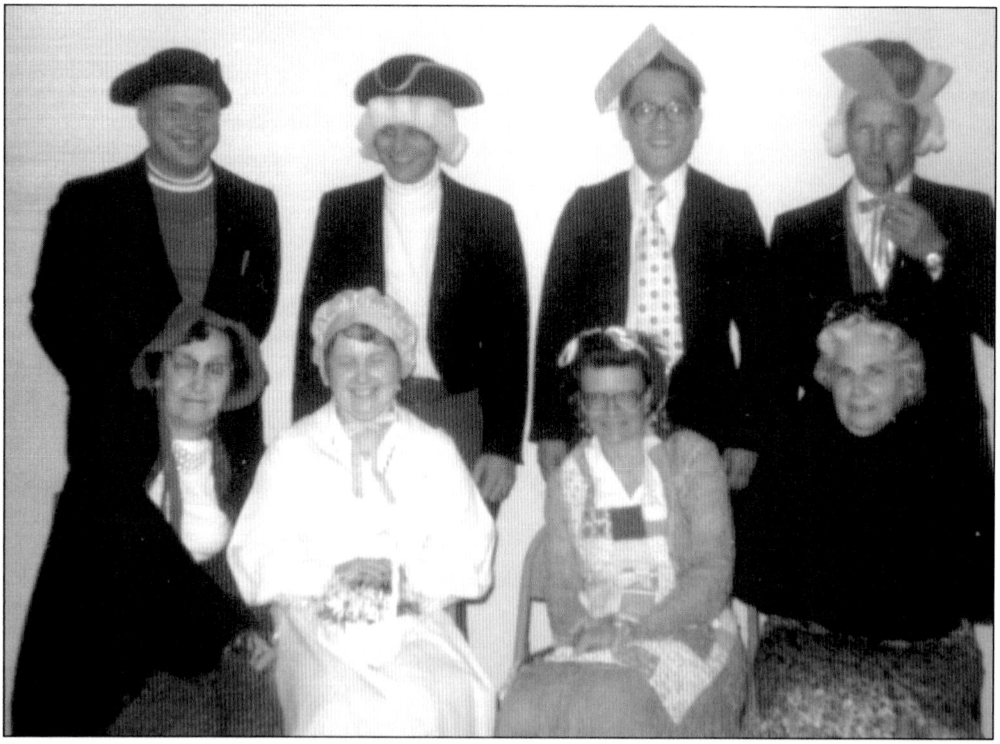

Some members of the Trinity United Methodist Church dressed in their best Colonial garb for the 1976 bicentennial. The program included reenactments of the founding of the nation by the pastor and parishioners, all of whom were good sports. (TUMC.)

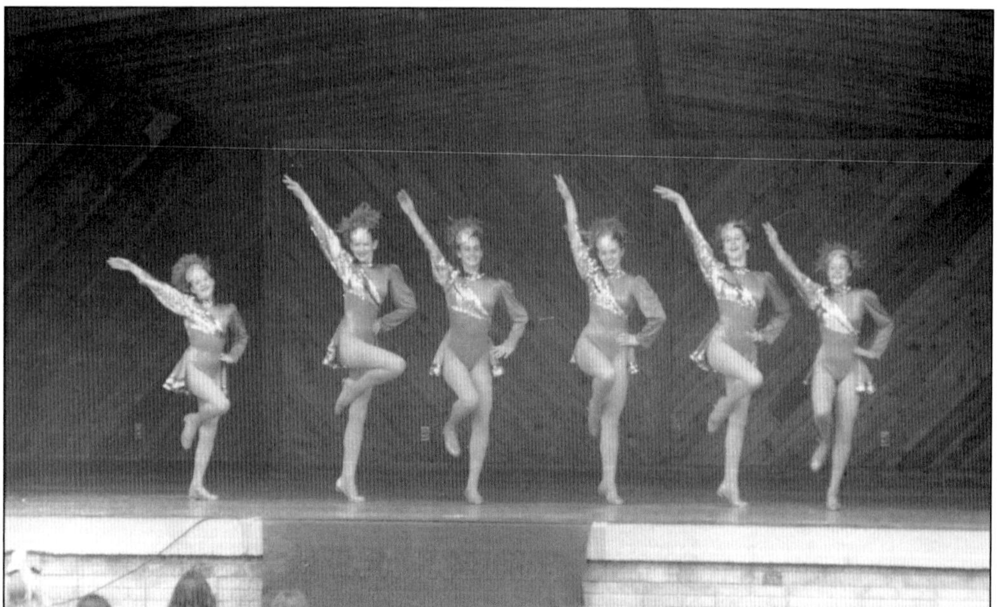

Some future Rockettes took the stage at Community Day in the 1990s. Music and dancing by local talent is one of the most popular features of the event. These talented young ladies were from Hammond's School of Dance.

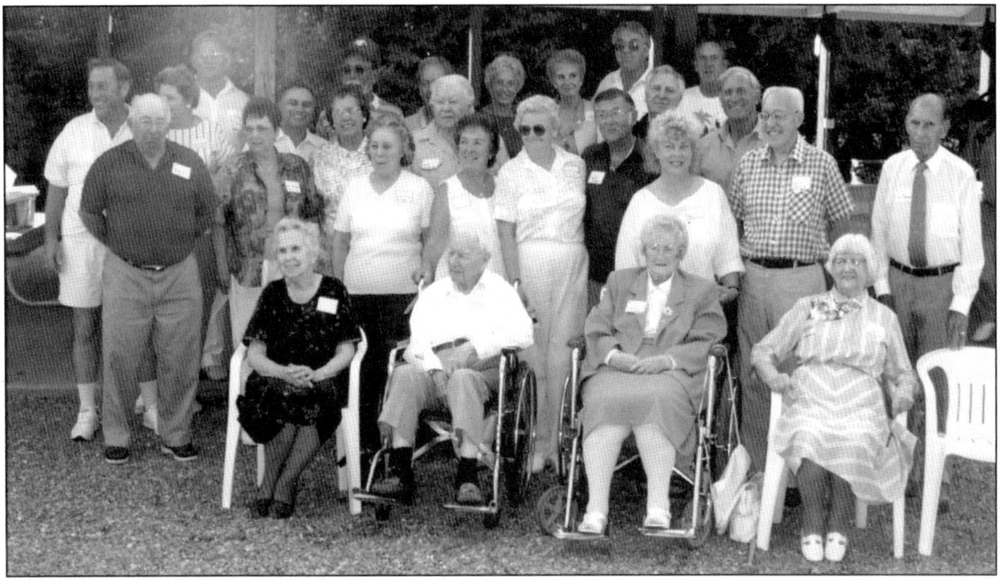

In 1990, some alumni of the Little Red Schoolhouse gathered for a reunion. Rosamund Fowler, on the left in the first row, later taught at the school in the 1940s. Catherine Seeberger, second from the right in the first row, went on to teach at another one-room school and later was instrumental in establishing Dutchess ARC, an organization for the developmentally disabled.

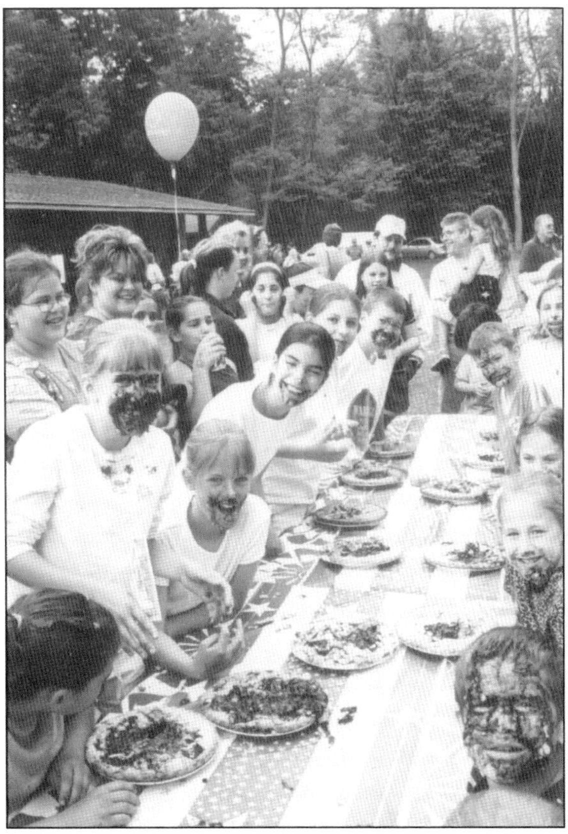

A pie-eating contest was the perfect excuse to forget table manners. These youngsters obviously delighted in the messiness, although their mothers probably did not. Some faces are barely recognizable under the blueberry stains. The contest has been a part of Community Day each year since it began.

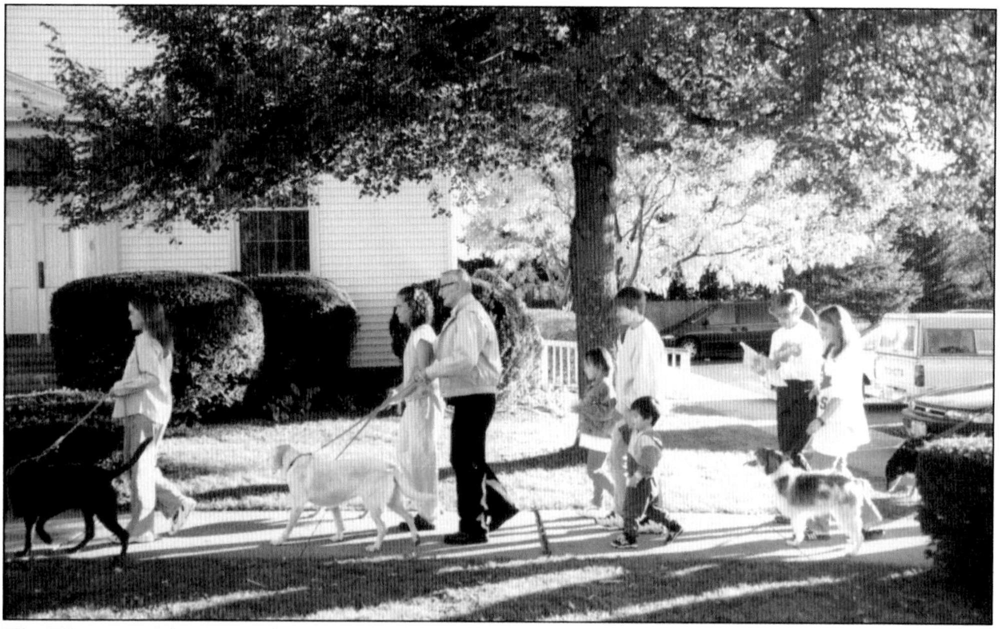

The Blessing of the Animals is a yearly event at the Presbyterian church. Residents are encouraged to bring family pets of all descriptions. This photograph from 1990 shows community members and their best friends coming to participate. Considering the proximity of cats and dogs, hopefully everyone was on their best behavior. (FPPC.)

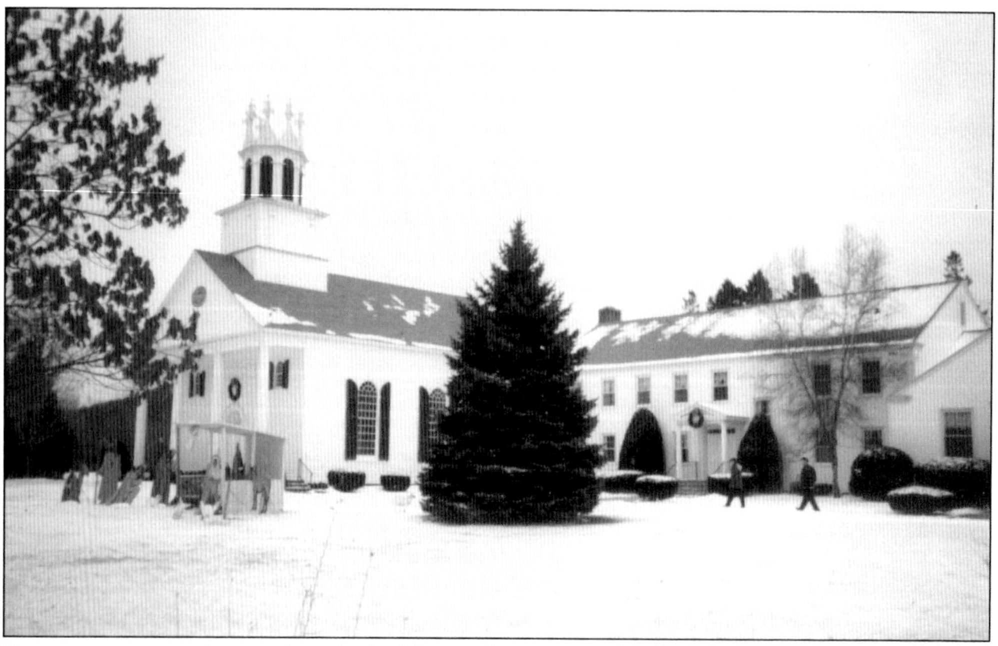

For years, community members looked forward to seeing the Christmas nativity scene appear each year as a signal that the holidays had arrived. The pieces were produced by church members Bob Hoffman, Dean Witham, and Neal and Nancy Townsend, with some other talented folks handling the painting. (FPPC.)

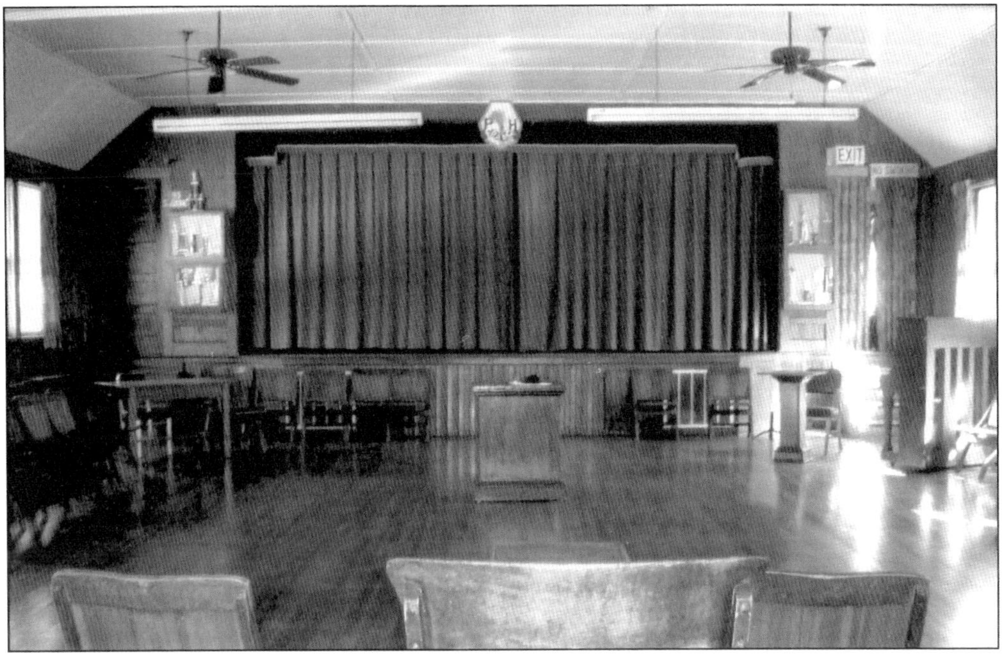

The upstairs of the Grange hall holds memories of the days of pageants, lectures, and other events. Although still used for monthly meetings, less activity at the building has made it a target of vandalism in recent years—an unfortunate chapter in the history of this respected organization.

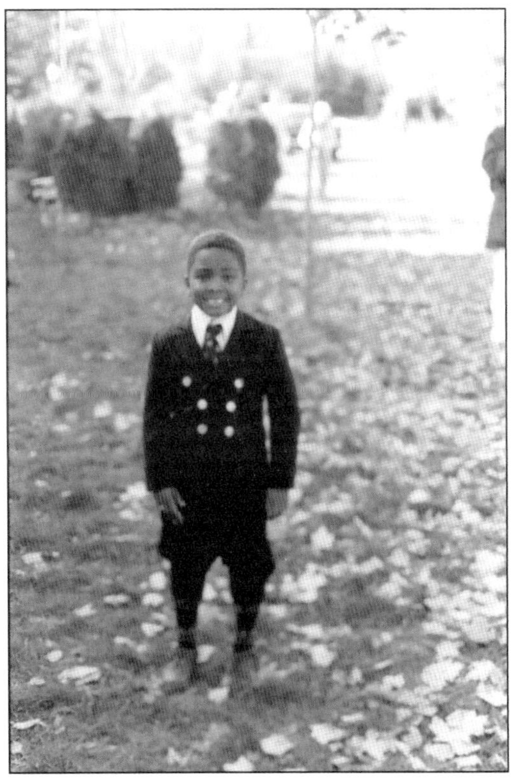

When a movie crew came to town in 1992 to shoot part of the film *Malcolm X* it caused a lot of excitement. The interior of the Grange hall on Dr. Fink Road was used for several scenes depicting the 1940s. This young man played the lead character as an eight-year-old. (FPG.)

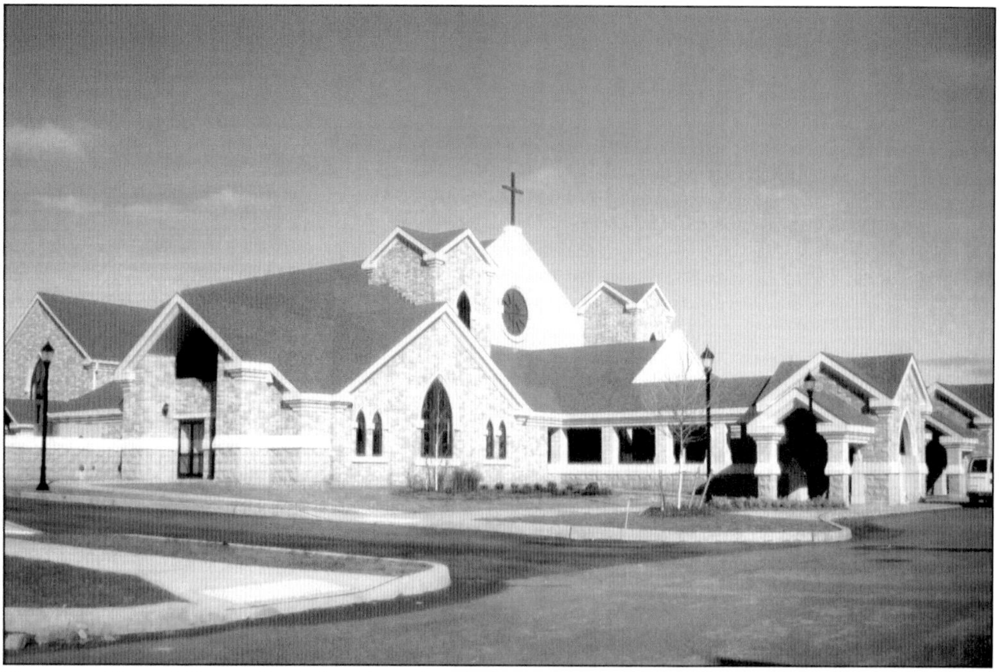

The new Blessed Kateri Catholic Church is an imposing structure being built along Route 82. Increases in attendance over the past few years necessitated the construction of a larger building. The stained-glass window soon to be installed came from a Harlem church, St. Thomas the Apostle.

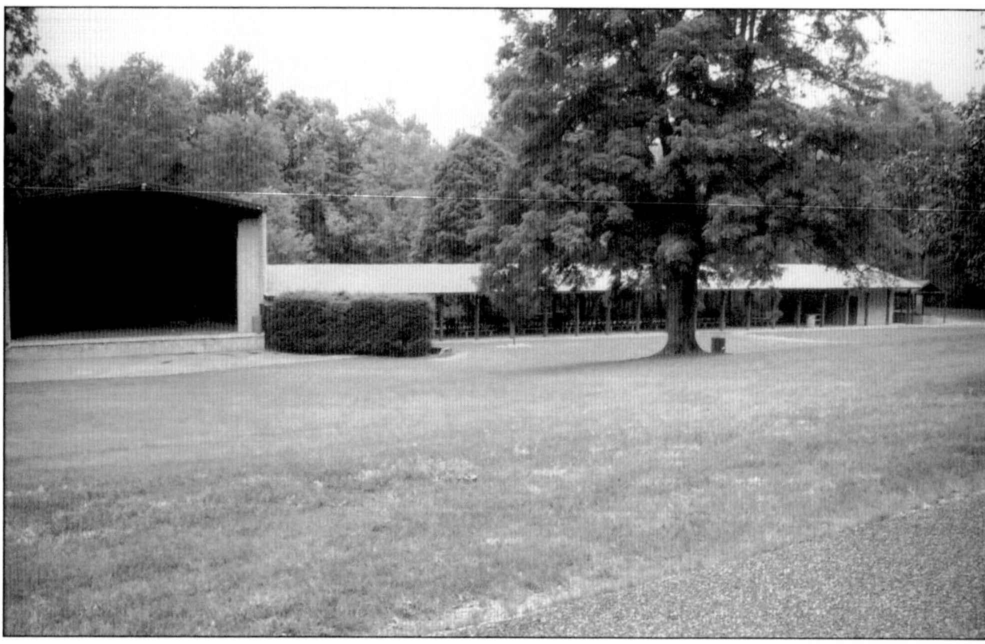

Freedom Park was created in the 1970s through the efforts of the Lion's Club and the Jaycees. They also financed the construction of the pavilion. Community Day has been held at the park for each year since, always drawing a large crowd. The lake is a great spot for cooling down in the summer or for taking swimming lessons.

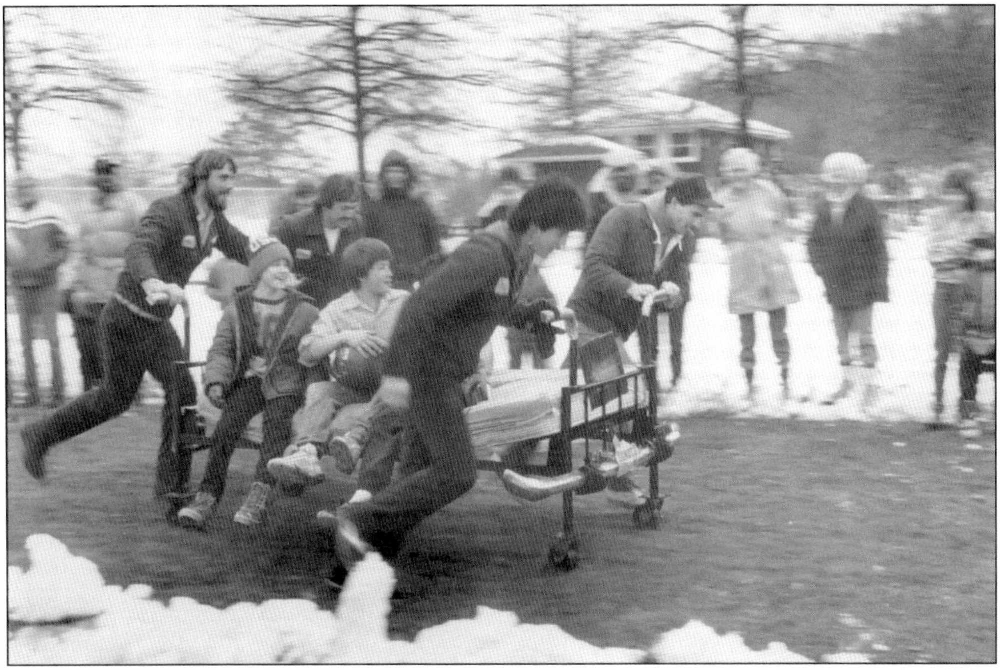

The winter carnival took place at Baird Park for several years. Fun and games included the popular bed race, shown here. A couple of young passengers hang on as their teammates run for the finish line, while amused spectators look on.

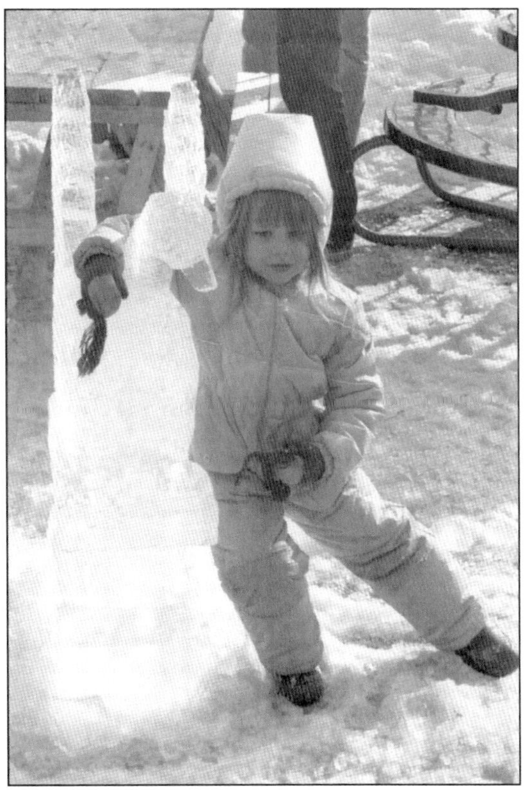

This little girl seems quite taken with the larger-than-life swan she is posing with. The winter carnival featured an ice sculpture competition, and here is one of the entries. Other events included sack races and softball games, all much more interesting when played in the snow.

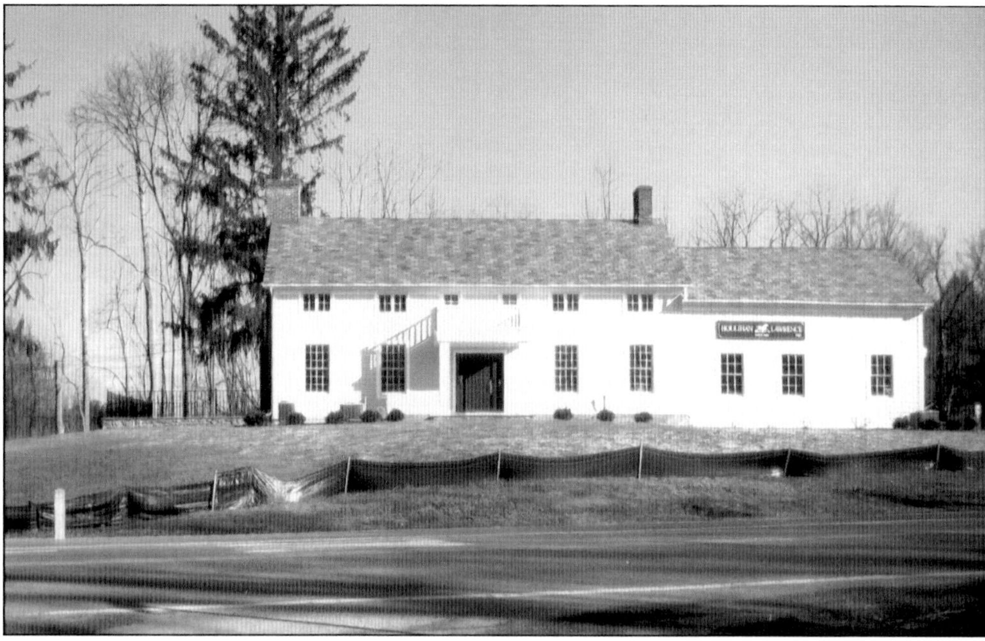

The newly renovated building at the intersection of Velie Road and Route 82 used to be known as Dramamount. T. Carl Whitmer and his wife Helen resided here during the 1920s through the 1950s, instructing students in music and other arts. The former home is now the office of Houlihan Lawrence real estate.

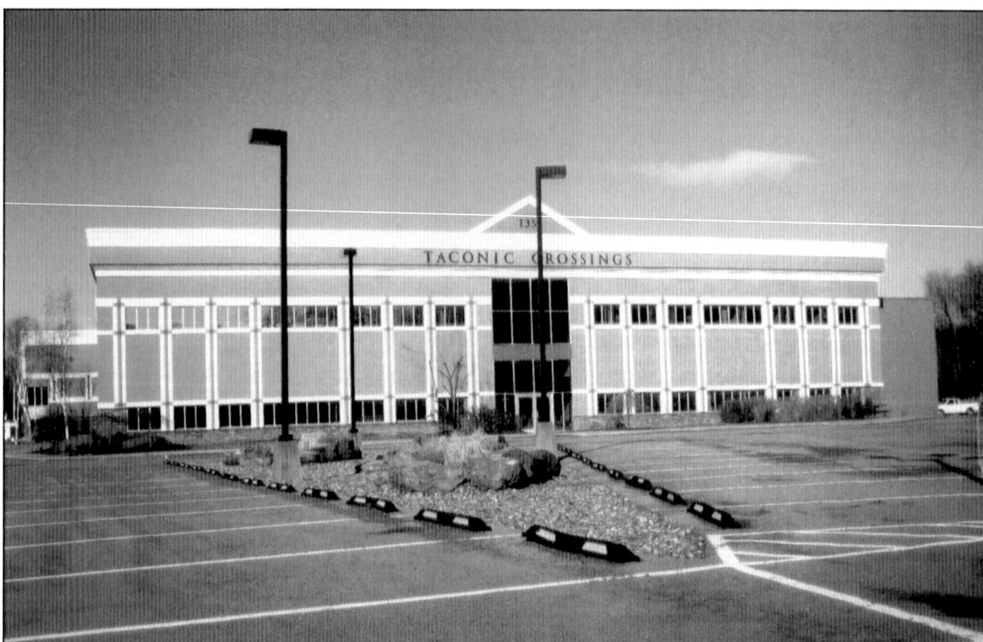

Formerly the site of CitiMortgage, and an IBM satellite building before that, the new Taconic Crossings will soon be home to the medical practice of DRA Imaging. The property, owned by the Page Corporation, has undergone extensive renovations both inside and out, in preparation for the new tenants.

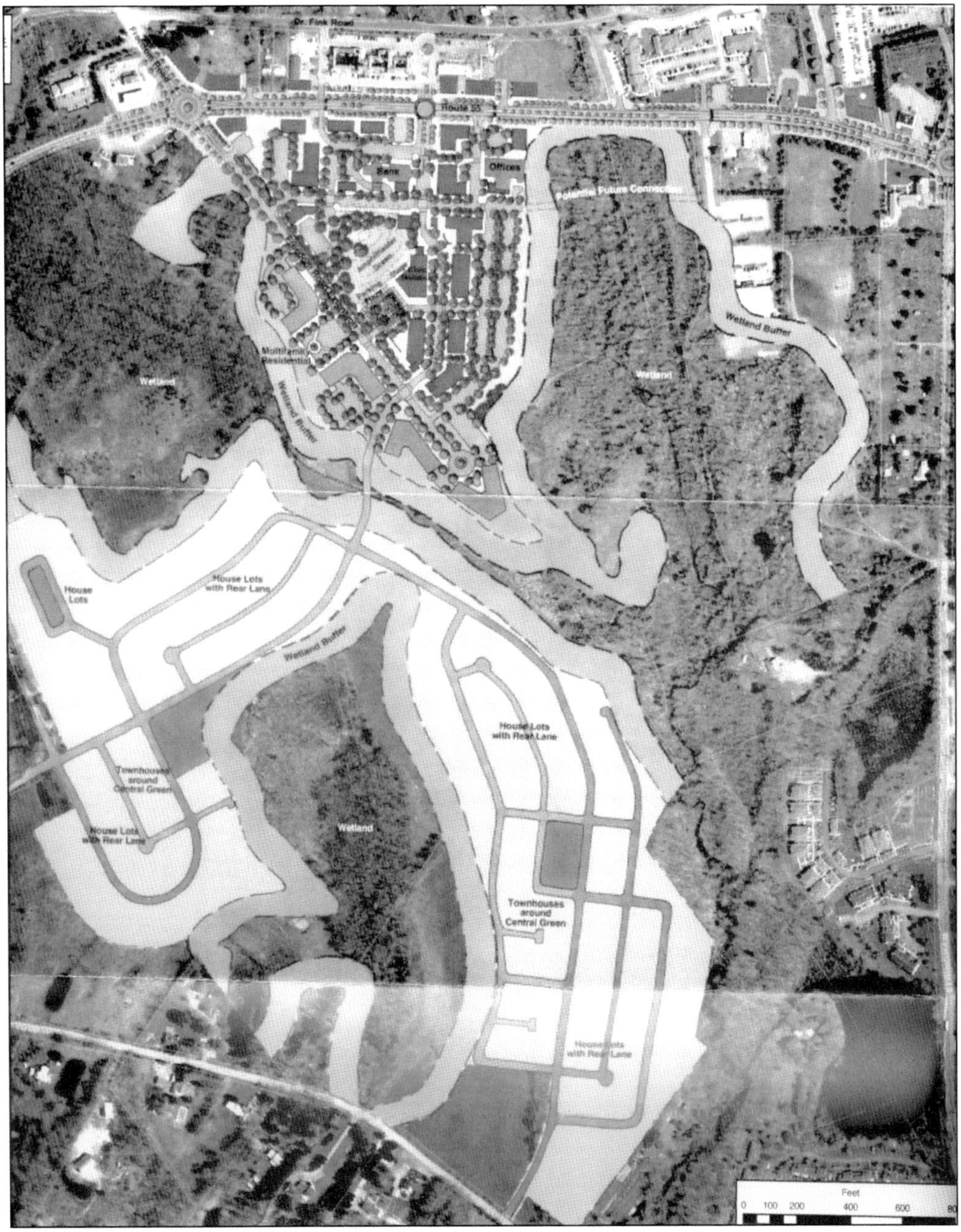

Much discussion is currently going on, both at town meetings and among residents, regarding the future of LaGrange. The subject of open space—protecting portions of the remaining farmland from development—is a matter of concern to many, along with the desire to re-create a small-town atmosphere. This rendering shows the proposed town center for LaGrange, parallel to Route 55. Plans include a village green, shops, and recreation areas, along with housing. The hope is that this will give LaGrange more of a community feeling, as well as provide a larger tax base. (LTH.)